G. Washington

THE

LIFE AND TIMES

OF

GEORGE WASHINGTON.

BY

SAMUEL M. SCHMUCKER, LL. D.,

Author of "Public and Private History of Napoleon III., "Life and Times of Alexander Hamilton," "Life and Times of Thomas Jefferson," "History of the Four Georges," etc.

PHILADELPHIA:

JOHN E. POTTER AND COMPANY,

617 SANSOM STREET.

PREFACE.

The life and achievements of George Washington have already been described by so many able and accomplished biographers, that it might be deemed superfluous in any other writer to attempt the same task, or to add to the large number of works now existing on the subject. It is true, indeed, that the records of Washington's career which have been published, have in a great measure exhausted the subject, so far as the discovery and accumulation of facts in reference to him are concerned; nor does the present writer presume to have made any researches which have brought to light details and incidents which were not previously known.

Nevertheless, it has been thought that the want still existed in our literature of a concise and condensed narrative of Washington's career, which would be suitable to the popular reader; for whose use the more aspiring style and ponderous bulk of other works on the same subject were not so well adapted. It was to supply this supposed necessity, that the present volume has been written. In preparing it the author has made a careful selection of the more important events connected with the public and private career of this illustrious man; and has narrated them in plain and simple language, as being best adapted to the purpose for which the volume was intended.

It had been useless on the part of the present writer, to have attempted an elaborate and extensive work upon a theme which has already been depicted by several of the master-minds of the age, with every charm of genius, and with every characteristic of ability. He has therefore contented himself with endeavoring to portray the subject in an unassuming, though, as he hopes, an accurate and reliable manner; at the same time making use of the most authentic and authoritative sources of information having reference to it. Whatever imperfections may exist in the work, will be amply atoned for by the superior interest and dignity of the subject; for the life and public services of Washington constitute one of those immortal themes, which no lapse of time or vicissitude of human affairs can deprive of their resistless hold upon the attention and admiration of mankind.

CONTENTS.

CHAPTER V.

CHAPTER VI.

CHAPTER VII.

CHAPTER VIII.

CHAPTER IX.

CHAPTER X.

CHAPTER XI.

CHAPTER XII.

CHAPTER XIII.

CHAPTER XIV.

CHAPTER XV.

CHAPTER XVI.

CHAPTER XVII.

CHAPTER XVIII.

CHAPTER XIX.

CHAPTER XX.

CHAPTER XXI.

CHAPTER XXII.

CHAPTER XXIII.

CHAPTER XXIV.

CHAPTER XXV.

CHAPTER XXVI.

CHAPTER XXVII.

CHAPTER XXVIII.

CHAPTER XXIX.

CHAPTER XXX.

APPENDIX.

I.

II.

III.

IV.

V.

GEORGE WASHINGTON.

CHAPTER I.

GENEALOGY OF THE WASHINGTON FAMILY — BIRTH OF GEORGE WASHINGTON—DEATH OF HIS FATHER — INFLUENCE OF HIS MOTHER—HIS EDUCATION—HIS EARLY PROMISE AND YOUTHFUL CHARACTERISTICS.

WHEN William the Conqueror devastated the territory of England north of the Humber, for the purpose of punishing the revolt of the Northumbrians, the estates of the vanquished became the spoils of his Norman followers, and the chief dignities in Church and State were conferred upon them. Durham, in which the bones of St. Cuthbert were entombed after their removal from the shrine of Holy Island, on Lindisfarne, became a city of great importance, and the see enjoyed privileges of an extraordinary character. The bishop appointed by the conqueror was invested with great power, as being more subservient to the purpose of William than were the proud and turbulent nobles of the period, and as creating a bulwark against the inroads of the Scots, whose incursions frequently assailed the border. The Bishop of Durham was created a Count Palatine, the see was erected into a palatinate, and temporal and spiritual authority was in a large degree conferred upon the bishops of this diocese. In those distant times, landed property was held by feudal tenure only; and abbots, bishops, lords, and barons, were obliged to furnish the king with military service. Whenever occasion rendered it necessary, and the banner of St. Cuthbert was unfurled, the feudatories of the prelate were required to take the field. William De Hertburn, whose surname was probably derived from the name of a village on the banks of Tees, called Hartburn, was one of the knights who held lands in the Palatinate of Durham. The first mention of this family occurs in 1183, at which period history declares that William De Hertburn exchanged Hertburn, his manor and village, for those of Wessyngton, and the family thenceforth took the name of De Wessyngton. Mention is made in 1264 of William Weshington, of Weshington, who assisted his sovereign in the unfortunate battle of Lewes; and in the reign of Edward III., the name of Sir Stephen De Wessyngton occurs in the list of gallant knights who tried their skill in arms in the tournament at Dunstable. Various members of this family were distinguished in the events which afterward transpired, and in many scenes of glory and chivalry in which the Douglasses and Percys were conspicuous. When Henry VIII. confiscated the monasteries, he conferred on Laurence Washington, who had been Mayor of Northampton, the manor of Sulgrave in 1538, which, with other lands, had belonged to the monastery of St. Andrews.

In 1646 Sir Henry Washington, a colonel in the royal army, displayed great gallantry in the defence of Worcester; and manifested a spirit of chivalry and heroic resistance which has transmitted his name with renown to posterity. The Sulgrave family had ever been the adherents of the Stuart dynasty. Among the emigrants to the New World who sought to escape the vengeance of Cromwell, which was excited against those who had attempted a general revolt, were John and Andrew Washington, great-grandsons of the grantee of Sulgrave, who landed in Virginia in 1657. The brothers purchased an extensive tract of land in Westmoreland County, between the rivers Potomac and Rappahannock. Near the place where Bridges Creek falls into the Potomac, John took up his abode, and married Miss Anne Pope. He became an extensive planter, a member of the House of Burgesses, and the leader of the Virginia forces against the Seneca Indians. His grandson Augustine was born in 1694, and was twice married. His first union was in 1715 to Jane Butler, of Westmoreland County, daughter of Caleb Butler. Four children were the fruit of this union, two of whom died in childhood. The survivors were Laurence and Augustine Washington, whose mother died in November, 1728. Augustine Washington married, in 1730, a beautiful young lady named Mary Ball. She bore him four sons and two daughters. The younger daughter, called Mildred, died in infancy; the other was named Elizabeth. The second son was called Samuel; his brothers were John Augustine, and Charles; and the eldest of the four was one whose name history loves to record, and which nations bless, — the father and founder of American freedom.

George Washington was born on Feb. 22d, 1732, on Bridges Creek, the old homestead of the family. His father, soon after his birth, removed to Stafford County. The house in which he resided was situated on an elevation; and a meadow near it, bordering on the Rappahannock, was the playground of the boy who was destined to bear such a conspicuous part in the history of his country.

Virginia, in those days, did not possess the advantages, in an educational point of view, which she afterward attained. The facilities for instruction were few, and the capabilities of teachers were of an humble character. To complete the education of their sons, the rich planters usually sent them to England; and this course was adopted frequently, in different parts of the land, till a much later date. While George was yet a child, Augustine Washington sent his eldest son Laurence to England to pursue his studies, considering him, at the age of fifteen, as the head of the family.

As soon as George was old enough, he was sent to the best school which the neighborhood afforded. It formed a striking contrast to the schools that have since grown up in the land; for it was of very little pretension, and presided over by one of his father's tenants, whose name was Hobby, who, to the dignity of preceptor, added that of parish sexton. Reading, writing, arithemetic, and such elementary branches, were doubtless the amount of what young Washington was then taught. At the same time, it should be remembered that he reaped the advantages of mental and moral instruction from his father at home;

and, as will afterward appear, from his excellent mother.

Laurence returned from England when George was seven or eight years of age. There existed a very strong attachment between the brothers. Laurence viewed George as a remarkable specimen of rectitude and truth, and the boy won his affections and a claim to his protection; while, on the other hand, George looked up to his brother, with his manly and cultivated mind, as a fit model for imitation, and thus, at an early age, these sentiments of affection and admiration impressed their influence on his future sentiments.

The military ardor of his ancestors had an effect on the mind of Laurence Washington, and he gratified his military taste by joining the expedition of Admiral Vernon, commander-in-chief in the West Indies; for which he embarked in 1740, in his twenty-second year. He received a captain's commission, and served with honor under Admiral Vernon and General Wentworth, in their joint expedition. He was present at the ineffectual attack on Carthagena; was distinguished there by his bravery; and was one of those who unflinchingly bore the enemy's fire, while his party retired with a loss of six hundred killed and wounded. This event gave his brother such a bias toward a military life, that his very recreations were afterward of a martial character. His playmates he turned into soldiers, and with reviews, parades, and sham-fights, he thus became, at a tender age, a commander and a hero.

George Washington, at the age of eleven, was left

after his father's death in 1743, with the other children of the second marriage, under the guardianship of his mother, whose good sense, conscientiousness, and excellent qualities, exacted deference while inspiring affection, formed the mind and stamped indelibly the moral character of her son. Both by precept and by example she inculcated the lessons by which a warm temper, inherited from herself, was governed and directed; and by her the principles of his future conduct were founded on the most rigid justice and equity. It was her wont to call her children around her, and read from some favorite work of morality and religion. Then flowed from her lips the instructions which guided the future man, and which will affect the race for good till the latest posterity. Those who desire to know the basis of the moral character of Washington, will discover it by perusing Sir Matthew Hale's "Contemplations, Moral and Divine," the favorite manual of his mother; in which volume her name was written with her own hand, preserved by her son with religious care, and still deposited in the archives of Mount Vernon. Mary Washington inculcated those principles, and inspired those sentiments, by which her son was guided throughout life; which rendered him one of the best, as well as one of the greatest, of men.

Washington's father being deceased, and Hobby's course of learning no longer suited to his wants, George was sent to the school of Mr. Williams, at Bridges Creek, and resided with Augustine. His own purpose, and the object of his friends, were, to fit him for ordinary business life; he never made any attempt to acquire a knowledge of the classics; nor does he seem to have had any inclination for such studies as the learned languages, rhetoric, or the belles lettres; though, at a more recent period, he gave some attention to the French. His education was plain and eminently practical; and his manuscript school books which are yet preserved, display great neatness and correctness. In a book of arithmetic still remaining at Mount Vernon, is an attempt to portray forms and faces, probably those of his school-mates; but in other respects it presents a business-like appearance. One thing of infinite service to him in after-life, both in the management of his estate and at the head of armies, was his practical and lawyer-like acquaintance with business forms. All sorts of mercantile and legal papers, bills of exchange, bonds, notes of hand, and deeds, gave him skill in keeping accounts; and monuments of his diligence are yet to be seen in financial affairs posted up in books, with his own hand, and relating to all the transactions of his property, dealings with persons at home or abroad, and accounts with Government. He had the good sense to appreciate physical education, which, by means of the athletic exercises of running, wrestling, pitching bars and quoits, exerts more influence on the mind than is generally supposed, and tends greatly to produce the *mens sana in sano corpore*. In these exercises Washington took the lead among his young associates; and the muscles of his large and powerful frame had attained such development, at this early period, that tradition points out the place where, when still a boy, he cast a stone across the Rappahannock; and anecdotes yet attest his achievements as a horseman, in which he excelled, so as to be able to mount and manage the most ungovernable steed. These accomplishments, and the rigid principles of justice and impartial probity on which his conduct was regulated, in the most minute particulars, rendered him an umpire among his young associates, from whose decisions there was no appeal; and the type of the future man was visible in the fact that, as he was their chosen military chief at an earlier age, he had now became their young legislator. One thing in particular, at every period of his career, prominently characterized him; and that was his reverence for the Supreme Being, the acknowledgment of his control of human affairs, and of the superintending Providence that directs all sublunary events.

CHAPTER II.

LAURENCE WASHINGTON — THE FAIRFAX FAMILY — GEORGE WASHINGTON'S DESIRE FOR A MILITARY LIFE — HIS MOTHER WITHDRAWS HER CONSENT TO HIS ENTERING THE NAVY — RETURN TO SCHOOL, AND APPLICATION TO MATHEMATICS — HIS PROFICIENCY IN SURVEYING — FALLS IN LOVE, AND GROWS MELANCHOLY — HIS ASSOCIATION WITH THE FAIRFAX FAMILY, AND ITS BENEFICIAL EFFECTS — HUNTING COMPLETES THE CURE — HIS SURVEY OF LORD FAIRFAX'S DOMAINS — HIS APPOINTMENT AS PUBLIC SURVEYOR — THE PERILS OF THE WILDERNESS — THE BRACING EFFECTS OF HIS DUTIES, PHYSICALLY AND MENTALLY — GREENWAY COURT — INFLUENCE OF HARDY TOIL AND GOOD SOCIETY COMBINED.

THE affection of Laurence Washington for his brother was greatly augmented after the death of their father. Laurence had now become an important man in Virginia, a member of the House of Burgesses, and adjutant-general of the district. Through him, George became intimate with the family of William Fairfax, whose princely seat of Belvoir was situated near Mount Vernon, on the Potomac. William Fairfax was a liberally educated man of the world, and combined experience with abstract learning, having served with honor both in the East and West Indies, and aided in freeing New Providence, of which he was governor, from pirates. He had charge of the Virginia estates of his cousin, Lord Fairfax, during some years, and Belvoir was the place of his residence. Here, in the management of the large interests of Lord Fairfax, he lived in considerable style; and a family of sons and daughters of refined tastes and cultivated minds, rendered his residence yet more delightful. Intimacy with a family like this, who combined the refinement of European with the rural simplicity of colonial life, was of the utmost service to George Washington at this period; and to his pleasant intercourse with them, is due, in a great measure, that polish and perfect good-breeding which formed one of his prominent characteristics. A manuscript still remains, in his hand-writing, which evinces the desire generated in his mind at this period, to behave with propriety in their society; and shows clearly the superior degree of self-control to which he rendered himself subject. The code in question was called "rules for behavior in company and conversation;" and though containing some things of a trivial nature, is, on the whole, such as any youth might use and imitate with profit.

During the visits of George at Mount Vernon, the desire for a military life was enkindled in his mind by various circumstances; among which were his intercourse with his brother, who was then adjutant-general, and retained pleasing reminiscences of his old cruises, and the society of William Fairfax, a soldier who had witnessed many scenes of trial. Some of the companions-in-arms of Laurence were visitors at Mount Vernon, and their conversation frequently turned on military matters by sea and land. Occasionally, too, one of Vernon's old ships anchored in the Potomac; and all these circumstances combined together made George desirous of entering the navy, to which he was encouraged by his brother and Mr. Fairfax. The navy then seemed the surest path of fame; but the difficulty was with Mrs. Washington. Her reluctant consent was at length obtained; a midshipman's warrant was procured, and George was about to enter the service at the age of fourteen. It is said his luggage was already on board a man-of-war then at anchor below Mount Vernon; but his mother's heart at last failed her, and, resolute as was her mind, she could not give up her son, the probable support of herself and the other children, to the perils of a seafaring life. Thus the scheme was abandoned. Instead of the sea, George returned to school, and during two years more applied himself to the study of mathematics, in those departments which are useful in a civil or military career. Land surveying was a branch in which he became an adept, and for which, by the most rigid application, he qualified himself in the highest degree. He kept regular field-books; surveyed the neighborhood; made accurate diagrams, and entered with the greatest precision the measurement of boundaries. He did everything in the most masterly manner; and he formed those habits of mind by which he was prepared for every emergency, and which rendered him equal to the most complicated difficulties and perilous undertakings. Amid documents which evince such close and rigid application, one in his own hand-writing was afterward found, which shows that at the age of fifteen he was not proof against the arrows of Cupid, but actually became smitten with the charms of some unknown beauty. This circumstance rendered him unhappy, perhaps for the reason that he was toc diffident to push his suit—a characteristic which he displayed in later years in female society. An old lady whom he used to visit when they were both young, said: "He was a bashful young man; I used often to wish he would talk more." Washington left school in the autumn of 1747, and went to Mount Vernon, where the image of the fair one still followed him; and, in his mathematical studies and surveying exercises, his spirits were yet affected with tender recollections. His sorrows were at last poured forth in verse, in which he mournfully speaks of his "poor restless heart, wounded by Cupid's dart."

Washington was a favorite of William Fairfax, the cousin of Lord Thomas Fairfax, for whose estates he was agent. This nobleman was a great friend of George, and, in a measure, the founder of his future fortunes. At this period he was sixty years of age, had been educated at the University of Oxford, and was there distinguished. He had made a figure in London society; had held a commission in the Blues; and had gained additional credit to his connections and title by contributing some papers to Addison's Spectator. He then launched into fashionable life; loved a beautiful young lady, who accepted his addresses; and, after purchasing her wedding dresses, broke her engagement and married a duke. Lord Fairfax, stung with mortified pride and wounded affection, avoided the sex ever afterward, except such as were connected with him; and visited his estates in Virginia in 1739. These had descended to him from his mother, daughter of Thomas, Lord Culpepper, who obtained a grant of them from Charles II., which included the lands between the Rappahannock and Potomac rivers. Finding the Potomac had its source in the Allegheny Mountains, his lordship claimed a commensurate enlargement of his grant; and matters being compromised, his domains extended into the Allegheny Mountains, and included a large portion of the Shenandoah Valley. The mildness of the climate and the noble forest scenery, the abundance of the game, and the frank cordiality of the Virginians, won upon Lord Fairfax, who made his abode with them; and, though eccentric, he was amiable in character and generous in temper. George William Fairfax, son of his lordship, educated in England, and afterward married to a daughter of Colonel Carey, on James River, was now, in his twenty-second year, on a visit to Belvoir, with his bride and her sister.

In such a scene Washington felt that female society produced a soothing effect upon his melancholy; and the charms of Miss Carey made an impression on his heart, which yet preserved the traces of his original passion for the "lowland beauty." He was then, at the age of sixteen, tall, athletic, and well calculated to inspire regard; and all this was enhanced by the soft melancholy depicted in his countenance. The confession made by him at the time to several confidants, prove that the sorrow and gloom of his former passion had been almost charmed away by the graces of the sister-in-law of Fairfax. The object of his first love is not certainly known. She is said to have been a Miss Grimes, of Westmoreland County, afterwards Mrs. Lee, mother of General Henry Lee, who became a favorite of Washington, as is supposed, from the tenderness once entertained for his mother. That which chiefly contributed to heal the wounds of disappointed affection in the breast of Washington, was the fox-hunting Lord Fairfax; whose society and influence, resulting from his having chosen him as the companion of his hunting excursions, gradually engrossed his attention and divided his thoughts. He took Washington into special favor. They rode together; and, under the tuition of his lordship, the youth acquired that zest for the chase for which he afterward became remarkable. His lordship had a fine stud of horses, and excellent hounds. An important result of the fox-hunting was the discovery by his lordship of the excellent qualities of Washington, his courage and capacity for enduring fatigue, as well as the modest self-restraint by which he was characterized. He had seen the accuracy and neatness with which his surveys were executed at Mount Vernon. Lord Fairfax now required a surveyor of his domains beyond the Blue Ridge, which squatters had taken possession of, and of which a regular survey had never been made. It was his earnest desire to have these lands examined, and apportioned into lots by a systematic measurement, in order to effect the ejectment of the squatters, or reduce them to terms of moderation. He made, therefore, an offer to Washington to undertake this important task, and the proposal was accepted. It was just what he desired; and after a few simple preparations were made, a short time was sufficient to fit the active youth for his first expedition amid the perils of the wilderness.

While the rigors of winter still prevailed in the mountains, and the lower parts of the landscape were becoming enlivened by the milder influence of spring, in the month of March, 1748, having completed his sixteenth year, Washington, accompanied by George William Fairfax, set out on his expedition. Their road lay by Ashley's Gap, a path through the Blue Ridge. At a place where it is about twenty-five miles wide, they entered the valley of the Shenandoah, bounded on the one side by the Blue Ridge, and on the other by the North Mountain, a branch of the Alleghenies. A beautiful and copious river, bearing the same name as the valley, flows through it, appropriately called by the Indians "the daughter of the stars." The travellers first halted at what Washington calls his "lordship's quarters," a lodge in the wilderness, near the present town of Winchester, and in a region of great beauty, crowned with stately trees and a noble maple grove, on the banks of the Shenandoah. He viewed the spot not with a poetical, but a business eye; the realities of life had started up in his path, and romance had forever vanished.

Washington describes in his journal the qualities of the soil, and makes a faithful record of the different localities as presented to his view, and their relative value. The habits of observation which he had so sedulously cultivated were now of the utmost importance to him, and he had become an adept in his art. Where the town of Winchester now stands, they lodged for a night. Civilization had scarcely reached this place at that early day. The company lay before the fire after supper, but Washington was shown to a bedroom. Having retired, he soon missed the clean sheets of Mount Vernon; and on a straw-matted couch he was so annoyed by insects beneath the threadbare blanket, that he was glad to dress again, and join the company at the fire. The survey began near the confluence of the Shenandoah with the Potomac, and was continued for a distance along the banks of the former, where the hand of industry had made some clearings, and had produced crops of grain, hemp, and tobacco. The Potomac was then swollen with rains, and could not be passed. Having to remain a few days until the waters should subside, they meanwhile made a visit to a mountain spring, since known as "Sulphur Springs." The location of their star-lit camp was what is now called Bath, one of the favorite watering-places of Virginia. Lord Fairfax, at a later date, used the waters of one of these, which still goes by his name. Soon afterward they crossed the river, in a canoe, to the Maryland side, their horses swimming over; and after a ride of forty miles over an execrable path, they halted at the house of Colonel Cresap, and remained for the night. Inclement weather yet detained them. A party of thirty Indians, carrying a scalp, appeared. They had a war-dance; a fire was made in a space in the centre of the circle; an orator delivered an exciting speech, and several Indian scenes were acted amid yells, whoops, and grotesque grimaces. Washington made notes of this strange exhibition, and his keen observation enabled him to form a just estimate of savage character, which rendered him capable of dealing with the wild natives of the forest. The next encampment was made after recrossing the river, at the mouth of Patterson's Creek, which was effected as before. They had now spent two weeks in Frederick County, in the wild mountains on the south of the Potomac, where lands were surveyed and laid out, and wild turkeys and game furnished their whole subsistence. The wind blew down their tent at one time; the smoke expelled them from it at another; and while each one was his own cook, and their dishes were of the most primitive description, they were often drenched with rain; and a companion once saved Washington from the fire which was burning the straw on which he was reposing.

As the survey progressed, many squatters were anxious to obtain a cheap title to the land upon which they had settled. Many Germans who had emigrated thither with their wives and families, and could not understand English, followed them; and at the house of Solomon Hodge, a justice of the peace, they had an amusing diversion from the camp life to which they had become accustomed. At his table they had only such knives as the guests brought with them. Washington describes himself as having been out all day, and laying on the straw or a bearskin before the fire, "with man, wife, and children, like dogs and cats; and happy is he who gets the berth nearest the fire."

The survey being completed, he returned to Mount Vernon on the 12th of April, from the southern branch of the Potomac, crossed the mountains, the Shenandoah Valley, and the Blue Ridge, and received for his services, when actively employed, a doubloon a day. Lord Fairfax was well satisfied with the manner in which Washington executed this important undertaking; and soon afterward laid out a manor of ten thousand acres in the spot on the other side of the Blue Ridge, called his "quarters." This place, which he named Greenway Court, included within its limits arable land, noble forests, and fertile meadows.

It is probable that the influence of Lord Fairfax obtained for Washington the post of public surveyor, which gave his labors superior authority, so as to entitle them to be recorded in the county offices. This occupation was lucrative, for at that time the number of public surveyors was very few; and the knowledge acquired in this occupation for a term of three years, enabled Washington to make advantageous purchases in future.

During his employment as public surveyor, Washington was a frequent guest at Greenway Court. The projected manor never was erected; but a one-storied building, with dormer windows, two wooden belfries, and a sloping roof in the antique Virginia fashion, with a verandah which extended the whole length of the house, was constructed on a green knoll embowered in trees. The noble proprietor never slept in the main building, but in a wooden house about twelve feet square. In a small structure he had his offices, and there all his business was transacted. A long train of black and white servants, stables for horses, and kennels for hounds, and a plentiful table in the English style, proclaimed the opulence of the owner; while a crowd of Indians, half-breeds, and loiterers, who freely partook of the good things the kitchen afforded, was an excellent comment on the hospitality and abundance of Lord Fairfax's establishment.

Greenway Court has fallen to decay, and in a magnificent county of great beauty, it is crumbling to the earth; but in those days Washington perused in its library the "History of England" and the pages of "The Spectator." His expanding mind reaped instruction from the man of literary talents and cultivated tastes, while his fondness for the chase was gratified, in the proper seasons, with his congenial friend and patron, Lord Fairfax. Washington had now spent three or four years beyond the Blue Ridge, occasionally visiting his brother at Mount Vernon. The toil and privations to which he had been exposed, his expeditions amid the rude inhabitants of the wilderness, and his occasional intercourse with his brother and the Fairfax family, had the effect of accustoming his mind to endurance, and softening his manners to courtliness, by which he attained the rare faculty of blending together the graceful suavity of the gentleman, with the martial powers of a hero.

CHAPTER III.

FRENCH AND ENGLISH DISPUTES RESPECTING THE VALLEY OF THE OHIO — GROUNDS OF THEIR SEVERAL CLAIMS — THE OHIO COMPANY — LAURENCE WASHINGTON — HIS LIBERAL POLICY — FRENCH COMPETITION — DE BIENVILLE — HIS PLANS — CHRISTOPHER GIST, THE PIONEER — HIS EXPEDITION TO THE FRONTIER, AND OPERATIONS WITH THE INDIAN TRIBES — HIS NEGOTIATIONS, AND THEIR SUCCESS — HIS RETURN — THE ATTEMPT OF IONCAIRE — HIS ILL SUCCESS AT LOG-TOWN, AND LETTER TO THE GOVERNOR OF PENNSYLVANIA — THE INDIAN TERRITORIES.

WHILE Washington was surveying in the wilderness, and acquiring mental strength and ampler experience, those events were in course of preparation which exerted a powerful influence on his subsequent destiny; and the secret counsels were elaborated in the workshops of diplomacy, which ultimately produced important results. To understand this assertion, it is necessary to remember that the peace of Aix-la-Chapelle, by which the general war in Europe was terminated, left the boundaries between the British and French possessions in America undefined; and, as a natural consequence, both nations laid claim to the same immense tracts of territory, and each hastened to anticipate the other in obtaining possession of them.

The Ohio Valley, west of the Allegheny Mountains, was remarkable for its fertility, its fine hunting and fishing grounds, its healthful climate, and its great resources and facilities for inland commerce; and it became the chief bone of contention. The French claimed that they had a right to the territory in consequence of its discovery by Padre Marquette and his comrade, Joliet of Quebec, in 1673; these persons having sailed down the Mississippi as far as Arkan sas; and arrogating for their sovereign not only the river, but the lands lying adjacent and its tributary streams. The English claimed the disputed territory by virtue of an Indian conquest, by which the Iroquois or Six Nations held the lands conquered by their ancestors; which lands, for a consideration of four hundred pounds, they afterward sold, by a bar gain made at Lancaster in 1744, between Commissioners from Pennsylvania, Maryland, and Virginia, and their own chiefs. This purchase included all their right and title from the west of the Allegheny to the Mississippi River. The truth was, that the In dians who made this treaty were neither in possession of the ceded territory at the time, nor were they sober when they made the alleged transfer. For these reasons France and England eventually commenced hostilities; and a contest was begun by which France lost all her American possessions, and England the greater part of them.

At this period the inhabitants of the colony of Pennsylvania held a monopoly of the trade with the western Indian races, exchanging peltry, trinkets, powder, shot, rum, and blankets, for valuable furs. No white settlement as yet existed there, and the French had but a nominal authority over tribes of mixed Iroquois, Delawares, Shawnees, and Mingoes, who had migrated from Canada at the beginning of the century, and had taken up their residence on the Ohio River and its tributaries.

Laurence Washington and his brother Augustine were among the influential Virginians who desired to gain a footing in this rich region, and a share in the trade carried on therein. A scheme was set on foot to procure, through John Hanbury, a rich London merchant, permission from the British Government to establish colonies on the other side of the Alleghenies. This met with favor, as forming a barrier to French encroachments, and to their anticipated possession of the valley of the Ohio. A chartered association under the name of "The Ohio Company," was established in 1749; and it received a grant of five hundred thousand acres of land, west of the Alleghenies, between the rivers Monongahela and Kanawha, with power to take up land north of the Ohio, if deemed necessary. No rent was required from them for ten years; but two-fifths of the lands were to be selected immediately, on which, within seven years, one hundred families were to be settled. A fort was also to be erected against the Indians, and garrisoned at their own expense. The concerns of the company were first managed by Mr. Thomas Lee, President of the Council of Virginia, and after his death, by Laurence Washington. Enlightened and liberal as he was, he desired to settle this tract with Germans from Pennsylvania, and to exempt them from the taxes and parish rates which they would have been required to pay on coming under the jurisdiction of Virginia. His views of the prevalent restraints on conscience he regarded as unjust, and he thought those communities in which a narrow policy prevailed, flourished but slowly; while those which were more liberal in their religious views, increased with greater rapidity. The colonization scheme progressed; goods and presents from England, adapted to the Indian trade, were imported; and rewards were promised to veteran warriors and hunters who knew the pathless woods, for revealing the best route to Ohio. The French were in the field before the company was chartered. The Governor of Canada, in 1749, sent Celeron de Bienville, an able officer, with three hundred men, to establish relations with the tribes resident on the banks of the Ohio, and to regain the possession of the country for the French. De Bienville made a judicious distribution of presents, and used his utmost exertions to prevent them from trading with the English. He nailed leaden plates to the trees, and at the junction of the Ohio with its tributaries buried others in the ground, indicating that the lands on both sides, as far as their sources extended, belonged to France. The Indians saw these plates, and divined their purport; and, as a consequence, sought British protection. Celeron ordered some Pennsylvania traders whom he found trafficking with the English, to depart; at the same time writing by them to the Governor of Pennsylvania, James Hamilton, informing him of his mission to the Ohio, and expressing surprise at meeting with English traders where England possessed no rights, threatening to deal with rigor in case they should repeat the act in future.

These threats attracted the attention of the governor and his council to the protection of their trade; and Hugh Crawford was sent out to negotiate with the Indians, to whom they promised that their friendship to the English "would last while the sun and moon ran round the world:" he gave them, at the same time, three strings of wampum as tokens of alliance. The governor valued Indian friendship, and in October sent out George Crogan, whom he thought adapted to gain great influence over the Indians; being a veteran trader, who had already made himself popular among them by distributing presents. Andrew Montour, a Canadian half-breed, was to accompany him as interpreter. They obtained a small present, but were to assemble a meeting of the tribes at Log-town, on the Ohio, in the next spring, to receive a greater gift which the assembly would bestow on that occasion.

Christopher Gist was afterward dispatched by the Ohio Company to explore the lands on the Ohio and its tributaries, as far as the Great Falls; to learn the mountain passes, the bearings and courses of rivers; and obtain information of the Indian tribes. By an Indian path which hunters had pointed out, he left the Potomac on the last day of October for the Ohio. He passed the Juniata and the Alleghenies, reached the village of Shaunopin, on the Ohio, and crossed the part of it now termed the Allegheny, arriving at Log-town, an Indian village, situated a few miles below what is at present the city of Pittsburg. This was the residence of Tanacharisson, head sachem of the mixed tribes, surnamed the half-king, and subject to the Iroquois Confederacy.

Gist returned to Shawnee-town after many adventures, and narrated his success with the confederacy of the Miamees. Great rejoicing was the consequence, and feasting, firing of guns, and congratulatory speeches became the order of the day. His object being gained, he proceeded, and directed his course toward Cattawa, on the Kentucky River; and soon the magnificence of that country opened to his view, long before the great pioneer, Daniel Boone, explored it. He continued his journey up the valley of the Kentucky, and on the first of May ascended a rock sixty feet in height, when the great Kanawha met his view in the distance. He crossed it on a raft, and after many toilsome days arrived on the banks of the Yadkin, his frontier home. He found his house deserted. A massacre by the Indians had taken place in his absence. But an old man assured him of the safety of his family, and he soon rejoined them on the banks of the Roanoke. Meanwhile, the Ottawa ambassadors had returned to inform the French that their flag had been removed from the council-house of Piqua, and that the Miamees had rejected their friends, and defied them; also that the western tribes would meet at Log-town, and conclude a treaty with Virginia. An attempt was made by the French to prevent the treaty, by means of Captain Ioncaire, who had, when young, been captured by a tribe of Iroquois, had been brought up and adopted by them, was accustomed to their habits, and afterward retained great influence among them on his return to civilized life. He was active in the French interests, and appeared at Log-town in company with forty Iroquois warriors. The assembly of the tribes were feasting, rejoicing, and firing guns in honor of Pennsylvania; for Crogan and his interpreter were distributing the presents which had been sent by the governor of that colony. Ioncaire delivered an animated speech to the chiefs in their own language; and advised them to turn away the Indian traders, and never deal with them, under penalty of the displeasure of their father, the Canadian Governor. He deposited in conclusion a belt of wampum of large size. An indignant chief arose and asked: "What right had the Canadian Governor here?" and promised to trade with the English as long as one of them should live. Thus the wampum-belt was rejected. Ioncaire then wrote to the Governor of Pennsylvania, to the effect, that the Marquis de la Jonquière, Governor of New France, had given him orders to prevent the English from making any treaty in the Ohio country; that those territories belonged to the King of France; and that the English had no title to them. Meanwhile, Mr. Gist, under the sanction of the Virginia Legislature, surveyed the lands in the grant of the Ohio country, south of the Ohio, and as far down as the great Kanawha. In this expedition he was met by an old Delaware sachem; and the Indian addressed him this searching question: "The French claim all the land on the one side of the Ohio, the English claim all the land on the other side; now, where does the Indian's possessions lie?" Between the encroachments of the French and the

English, and the influences that have followed them, the aborigines have gradually become extinct; and, in the lands where the red man roamed and sounded the war-whoop, the race has well nigh passed away. Such were some of the events that led to the war between the English and French, in which great bravery was displayed on both sides, and the pathway ultimately opened to the independence of the United States.

CHAPTER IV.

HOSTILE PREPARATIONS OF THE ENGLISH AND FRENCH — WASHINGTON APPOINTED AN ADJUTANT-GENERAL — MOUNT VERNON BECOMES A SCHOOL OF ARMS — ILL HEALTH OF HIS BROTHER LAURENCE — HE ACCOMPANIES HIM TO BARBADOES — LAURENCE WASHINGTON PROCEEDS TO BERMUDA—HE RETURNS TO DIE AT MOUNT VERNON—NEW DUTIES DEVOLVING ON GEORGE WASHINGTON — THE OHIO TRIBES AT LOG-TOWN — HOSTILITY OF THE SIX NATIONS — TANACHARISSON BEFORE THE FRENCH COMMANDANT — HIS SPEECH, AND THE FRENCHMAN'S REPLY — FRENCH INTENTIONS — EFFORTS OF THE OHIO COMPANY — CAPTAIN TRENT APPOINTED ON THE WESTERN MISSION BY GOVERNOR DINWIDDIE—HIS ILL SUCCESS, AND RETURN — WASHINGTON APPOINTED TO SUCCEED HIM — SETS OUT IN NOV. 1753.

HOSTILE preparations were now made on the part of France, to dispute the possession by the English of this western territory. The French launched a large vessel on Lake Ontario, and made ready their outposts on the banks of the Ohio. Their trading-house at Niagara was fortified, and every means was employed to prepare for a contest which was to be decided by the sword. The British colonies were likewise on the alert, and in Virginia in particular; where an adjutant-general was appointed to attend to the organization of the militia, and the proper equipment of the troops. George Washington was at this time made an adjutant-general; and he reflected credit on the post, though he was yet but nineteen years of age. A retired officer, who had served at

Carthagena with Laurence Washington, assiduously instructed him in the military art. From him he learned the manual exercises and some field evolutions. Jacob Van Braam, a Dutchman, and a master of fence, also trained Washington in the use of the sword; and Mount Vernon resounded with the clash of arms, and the din of hostile preparations. But the declining state of his brother's health interrupted the martial studies of George Washington; threatening symptoms of a pulmonary disease made a residence in the West Indies necessary; and thither the two brothers sailed on September 28, 1751. They landed at Barbadoes on the 3d of November. Amid beautiful scenes of tropical verdure, and flattered by the delusive hopes held out by the physicians of that place, Washington selected his abode in a pleasant house with an extensive sea prospect; and the theatre which the place afforded gave him some amusement. He was invited to dine at the residence of the first families; and at that of Judge Maynard, these brothers associated with a company called "The Beefsteak and Tripe Club," where everything was served up in the richest profusion, which greatly excited the admiration of Washington. He was taken ill of the small-pox several weeks after his arrival in the island; but under judicious medical treatment, and his brother's care, he became convalescent in a short time. His face was slightly pitted ever after. On his recovery, he made various excursions, and was struck with the spendthrift habits and recklessness of some of the planters. His astonishment was excited when he learned that persons in that island inheriting estates of three or four hundred acres of land, could be in want.

No radical change in the health of his brother took place, and the invalid resolved to go to Bermuda in the spring; and that till then George should return, and bring back his wife from Virginia. After an absence of four months, George reached home in February. He made observations of a minute nature on both voyages; copied the log-book at sea every day; noted the changes of the winds, the motions of the ship, and every incident that transpired, and gained some practical nautical knowledge. The soil and agricultural products, the commerce, military strength, and governmental regulations of Barbadoes, were all subjected to the most careful scrutiny, and remarks on them he noted in his journal. When his brother first wrote from Bermuda, there were hopes of his recovery, and he still desired his wife to join him. But another letter which followed, was more desponding, and prevented her going out. He talked of "going home to his grave," and this dark foreboding was full of the saddest meaning. He returned home in the summer, and reached it in time to die in the midst of his family; attended by his brother, on whose paternal affection his heart seemed greatly to repose. He died in his thirty-fourth year, July 26, 1752, leaving a wife and daughter.

George Washington, by the death of his brother, was placed in a new position. The latter left large estates, of which he was made the guardian; and in case his niece should die, the will specified that Mount Vernon should be possessed by her mother during her lifetime, after which George should become the owner. He was appointed one of the executors of the will; and though but twenty-two years of age, such was the confidence he inspired, that the whole management of the estate devolved upon him, and he executed his trust with fidelity.

The Ohio tribes of the Delawares, Shawnees, and Mingoes met at Log-town at the appointed time; but the chiefs of the Six Nations would not convene with them, proudly delaring that it was not their custom to treat in the woods, and that if the Governor of Virginia wanted to meet them, he should send them a present from their great father, meaning the British monarch; and adding, that they would meet him at Albany. A treaty was eventually concluded by Colonel Fry and the Virginia Commissioners at Log-town, by which the tribes engaged not to molest the English settlers; and the half-king advised his brothers to build a strong house at the fork of the Monongahela. Mr. Gist laid out a town, and building a fort at Shurtee's Creek, east of the Ohio; began a settlement near the Youghiogeny, in which he assembled eleven families; while the Ohio Company established a trading-post at Will's Creek, now the Cumberland River. French aggressions greatly offended the Ohio tribes, and the half-king went to the French posts on Lake Erie, to remonstrate with them. He addressed them as follows: "Fathers, you are the disturbers of this land by building towns, and taking the country from us by fraud and force. We kindled a fire a long time since at Montreal, where we desired you to stay, and not to come and intrude on our land. I now, advise you to return to that place, for this land is ours." Tanacharisson proceeded to tell the commandant, that if the French had behaved as the English, the tribes would have traded with them; but that they could not be permitted to build fortified places, in a country which the Great Spirit had allotted to the Indians for their residence; that he desired to keep both parties at arm's length; that he would support the most friendly party; and was not afraid to order them off the land. The commandant responded contemptuously, in comparing the Indians to mosquitoes, of which he had no fear; declared that the land did not belong to the Indian; that his own forces were like the sands of the sea; and giving back his wampum, he flung it at him.

The deeply-insulted Tanacharisson felt grieved at heart; he beheld future ruin impended over the Indian; and put his trust in the English as their only protectors. The French, it was said, intended to erect a chain of military forts to connect Canada and Louisiana, and thus confine the English between the Alleghenies.

The Ohio Company soon had reason to complain to Lieutenant-Governor Dinwiddie of the hostility of the French and Indians. Captain Trent was dispatched to the French commander on the Ohio, to remonstrate, and he also carried presents for the Indians He stopped at Log-town a short time; then went to Piqua, and found that the place had been attacked by the French, their Indian allies, the Miamis, defeated, Piankesha slain, and the French flag floating over the ruins. Trent became disheartened, and immediately made the best of his way homeward.

Dinwiddie now looked around for a suitable person to undertake this mission. Washington was the person whom he selected. It is true he was only twenty-two years of age; but public confidence had already obtained for him a reappointment as adjutant-general, and his acquaintance with the dangers and mysteries of the wilderness eminently fitted him for the arduous enterprize. His instructions were, that he should proceed to the Ohio, convene the Indian chiefs at Log-town, learn the localities at which the French were stationed, and obtain an Indian escort for the rest of the journey. At the chief French post he was to present the letter and credentials which he bore from the Governor of Virginia, to the commandant, and require an answer in the name of His Majesty, the British king. He was also to ascertain what French troops had crossed the lakes; the reinforcements which were expected from Canada; the number and localities of the forts, with their distances, and garrisons; and lastly, to procure all possible information respecting the intruders, their state or condition, and the objects which they had in view. He commenced his journey provided with the proper credentials, having the seal of Virginia affixed, on the last day of November, 1753. The distance to be traversed extended about five hundred and sixty miles, over rugged and pathless mountains, and through lonely and cheerless wildernesses, where civilization had not yet appeared, or developed any of its genial influences.

CHAPTER V.

WASHINGTON'S JOURNEY TO THE OHIO — ADVENTURES AND OBSERVATIONS ON THE MONONGAHELA — HIS COMPANIONS — LOG-TOWN AND THE SACHEMS — INDIAN DIPLOMACY — IONCAIRE — ARRIVAL AT VENANGO — THE RESULTS OF CONVIVIALITY — THE WAMPUM — LA FORCE, THE COMMISSARY — CHEVALIER LEGARDEUR — AFFAIRS AT THE FORT — EFFORTS TO SEDUCE THE SACHEMS FROM THEIR ENGLISH ALLIANCE — TRYING DELAYS — DIFFICULT NAVIGATION OF FRENCH CREEK — WASHINGTON ARRIVES AT VENANGO — THE HALF-KING'S FAITH IN HIS ENGLISH BROTHERS — THE HOMEWARD ROUTE — ITS DIFFICULTIES.

WASHINGTON commenced his perilous journey as soon as he received his appointment; and at Fredericksburg engaged his old master of fence, Van Braam, to accompany him and act as his interpreter. At Alexandria he procured the necessary supplies for the journey; having reached Winchester on the frontier, he purchased horses, tents, and other parts of the outfit; and passing through a road recently opened to the Cumberland River, then called Will's Creek, he arrived on its banks on the 14th of November. Here he engaged Mr. Gist, the pioneer of the Ohio, as pilot in his expedition, John Davidson, an Indian interpreter, four frontiers-men, of whom two were traders; with these and Van Braam he advanced through a wild country, which the recent rains had rendered almost impassable. On the

Monongahela he learned from John Frazier, an Indian trader who kept a gunsmith's shop in the Indian village of Venango, from which the French had expelled him, that the French general who had commanded on the frontiers was recently dead; and that the army had retired into winter quarters. The rivers being swollen, Washington sent the baggage down the Monongahela, in a canoe, in the care of two men, who had orders to meet him on the Ohio, at the confluence of the Monongahela and the Allegheny. Here he made a careful reconnoissance, and was impressed with the advantages which the place possessed for the site of a military fort, for the purposes of defence, and as a dépôt for supplies. At a later period a fort erected on the spot by his advice, became distinguished in the annals of two wars; and Fort du Quesne, so noted in frontier history, when tested by French engineers of experience and ability, proved the correctness of the military eye of Washington.

Here he visited Shingis in his village — the chief sachem, or king of the Delawares, one of the greatest of the native warriors — who had once raised the hatchet against the English, but who now accepted the invitation given him to be present at the council at Log-town. When they reached that village on the following day after sunset, on the 24th of November, Washington found the half-king absent at Beaver Creek, hunting; and he sent runners to invite him and the other chiefs to a conference. Next day there came to the village four French deserters, who gave Washington all the information which they possessed respecting the French force at New Orleans, their forts on the Mississippi, and at the mouth of the Wabash; of all which he made notes in his journal. From the sachem, on his arrival, he learned of the interview which had taken place between him and the French commandant; and that the French had erected two forts, of which the largest was on Lake Erie, the other on French Creek. The road to them was now impassable; the nearest fort would not be reached in less than six days, and the journey would be required to be taken by way of Venango. The chiefs met Washington at the council-house on the next day, to whom he explained his object, and asked their advice and co-operation. At the conclusion of the conference, he gave them that indispensable ingredient of Indian diplomacy, a string of wampum. According to custom, the chiefs sat a long time after he had concluded his address, as if deliberating on what he had said, or as if expecting to hear him continue.

At last the sachem arose, and assured Washington on behalf of the tribes, that they considered the English as brothers, and one people, and intended to return the French the wampums, or "speech belts;" which, in Indian diplomacy, signified a dissolution of all friendly relations. An escort was promised Washington, composed of Delawares, Mingoes, and Shenandoahs; but a three days' preparation was required for the journey. The delay was very inconvenient to Washington, who had yet to learn the characteristics of Indian diplomacy; and he ascertained that a speedy departure would be offensive to Indian dignity. News arrived, at this crisis, that Captain

Ioncaire had convened a meeting at Venango, of the Mingoes, Delawares, and other tribes, and informed them that, for the present, the French had entered into winter quarters, but would fight the English in the spring; and advised them not to interfere, or the French and English would combine, and after exterminating them, make a division of their lands. The sachem and the other chiefs were anxious to get from Washington the true purpose of his errand to the French commandant; and they declared that they had done as required by the Governor of Virginia.

Washington set out on November the 30th, 1753, with his own party, and in company with an Indian hunter, the sachem, and another venerable sachem named Jeskakake, which means a "belt of wampum," and White Thunder. Although the distance to Venango was only seventy miles, it took the party until the 4th of December to reach it. The French colors were displayed on their arrival; and in reply to an inquiry of Washington, he was informed that the French commandant Ioncaire had control of the Ohio. That officer, when he ascertained the business of Washington, advised him to apply to the commander of the next fort for an answer to the letter; and, meanwhile, gave him an invitation to supper at head-quarters. The use of the bottle soon dispelled the prudence and disarmed the sagacity of his hosts; for restraint was abandoned, and they avowed that it was their intention to take the territory and forts on the Ohio, and that they could do so; for though the English could raise double their number of troops, they were too slow in their movements to accomplish anything. Washington preserved his sobriety, and listened to their drunken revealings, while Van Braam was employed in repeatedly pledging them. Washington, as usual, took notes of all that passed, especially in reference to the number and distribution of the French forces, the forts and their localities, with the facilities which existed for their supply. The rain was too severe on the next day for the party to proceed, and Ioncaire wondered why the sachem had not appeared at headquarters, and was enraptured to behold his Indian brothers. He made them presents, and entertained them abundantly with liquor; so that the poor half-king Jeskakake, and White Thunder, soon forgot everything in the stupefaction of a happy oblivion. The unfortunate sachem was sadly mortified on the next day, and could not be kept from making a speech, much to the same effect as that before the French commandant; and in conclusion he offered to return the French "speech belt," which Ioncaire would not receive, but desired him to take to the commander of the fort. It was only on the 7th of December that Washington could proceed, in consequence of the attempts and stratagems of Ioncaire to detain the sachems, or bring them over to his views. A wily French commissary, named La Force, accompanied them — a resolute and active person, who made considerable mischief, and in the end met his just reward.

Four days' travel, in the midst of snow and rain, brought the adventurers to the fort; it was placed on an island, fifteen miles south of Lake Erie. A hollow square, formed by four houses, with a defence of bastions and palisading twelve feet high, with holes for cannon and small arms, were its chief elements of strength, together with a forge, stables, and log-houses for the soldiers. Chevalier Legardeur de St. Pierre was the commandant — a ceremonious gentleman of the old school, combining the politeness of the courtier with the exactness of the soldier. As soon as Washington had presented Governor Dinwiddie's letter and his own credentials, he was disposed to proceed at once to business; but the Chevalier requested him to retain those documents till his predecessor, Reparti, should arrive. That individual soon came, and Van Braam then read and translated the letter, in which Dinwiddie complained that the French had intruded into the dominions of the British crown, had erected forts in Ohio, and made settlements in Western Virginia.

The writer desired to be informed upon whose authority the French commander had marched from Canada and made this invasion; and he hoped that he would not pursue a course inimical to the friendly relations previously existing between the British monarch and the French king. He commended Washington to his confidence and attention. While the Chevalier and his officers were deliberating upon their answer to this missive, Washington was taking notes of the fort, its plan, strength, and dimensions. He ordered his people to see what canoes were ready for service, and how many were in process of construction. He discovered that measures were being taken to withdraw the half-king and other sachems from the English alliance; and Washington advised them to deliver up the "speech belts" to the French, as they had before promised to do. The Indians asked an audience of the French, and a private one was accorded to them. The wily Chevalier evaded the acceptance of the proffered wampums, and declared that he had a present to send to Log-town, and wished to live at peace with all the tribes on the Ohio. Several circumstances induced Washington to make his stay at the fort as brief as possible. He was informed that every British subject was to be seized, who traded on the Ohio; and Captain Reparti told him that some Indians had carried a white boy as captive past the fort, and had borne several scalps of white men. The Chevalier gave him the sealed reply to Dinwiddie's letter on the 14th, and on the 15th he prepared to return by Venango; but all his movements were impeded by a secret influence.

Every means was now employed to seduce the sachems, and put the Indians at variance with the English. The commandant caused the canoes to be supplied with abundant provisions and liquor, dissembling all the artifices he practised for the detention of the party; and when Washington complained that their delay detained him, as they were a part of his company, he declared that it was not his intention to hinder their departure. He then in vain endeavored to persuade the sachems to start; but the secret was that they had been promised a present of guns if they delayed till morning; and afterward, when they received them, attempts were made to intoxicate them. Just at that moment, Washington informed the half-king that his royal word was pledged to depart; and the sachem, after due importunity, complied, and leaving the tempting liquor, embarked. The navigation of French Creek was full of peril from the floating ice, by which the frail skiffs were often in danger of being staved. The party had frequently to leap into the water, and draw the canoes over shoals; and in one place to convey them across a neck of land for a quarter of a mile. At last they arrived at Venango.

Washington and the sachems then separated, as White Thunder had injured himself, and the others desired to wait at Venango for several days to convey him down the river. Washington was apprehensive that the wily Ioncaire would ply the liquor to seduce them from the alliance, and warned the half-king of that danger. But he desired him not to fear, as he had given up the French, and would adhere to his English brothers. His sincerity afterward stood the test, for he faithfully kept his word. On December 25th, Washington and his party set out from Venango to complete their homeward journey, with a long and difficult undertaking before them. It was feared that the jaded pack-horses would break down; and Washington, dismounting, set the example to the party of using the saddle-horses for transportation. The whole company now travelled on foot. The cold increased in intensity, and the horses were scarcely able to proceed on their difficult and laborious pathway.

CHAPTER VI.

PERILS IN THE WILDERNESS—MURDERING-TOWN—INDIAN TREACHERY — A NIGHT OF GREAT ANXIETY — FEARFUL DANGER ON THE ALLEGHENY—FORTUNATE ESCAPE—QUEEN ALIQUIPPA, THE WATCH-COAT, AND THE FIRE-WATER — WASHINGTON CROSSES THE BLUE RIDGE — CHEVALIER DE ST. PIERRE'S REPLY—THE MISSION OF CAPTAIN TRENT TO OHIO — WASHINGTON RAISES RECRUITS — DINWIDDIE FINDS THE VIRGINIANS GROWING DIFFICULT TO GOVERN—HIS EFFORTS TO RAISE RECRUITS — CAPTAIN VAN BRAAM — TRIALS IN TRANSPORTATION — CONTRECŒUR AT THE FORK OF THE OHIO.

WASHINGTON was impatient to return home. He put the cavalcade under Van Braam's direction, and, accompanied by Mr. Gist, with his pack on his shoulder, and his gun in hand, he hastened on to Beaver Creek, otherwise called Murdering-town, having once been the scene of an Indian massacre. Here he planned his route, struck through the forests, and hoped to be able to cross the Allegheny River on the ice. At Murdering-town, a party of Indians appeared to wait for them; and an Indian proposed some very inquisitive questions respecting their journey. Their way was through a trackless wild, and it was thought expedient to employ one of the Indians as a guide. Several circumstances tended to excite suspicion in the minds of the travellers in reference to this person, and an ambuscade was apprehended. They found themselves at length in a wide meadow, made brighter by the reflection of the snow on the ground. The Indian guide, who had preceeded them fifteen paces, at length turned suddenly around, aimed at them, and fired. Washington was startled, but was not wounded, and on asking Gist whether he was injured, his answer was in the negative. They ran and overtook the Indian as he reloaded; seized him, and wrested his weapon from him. Gist would have dispatched the traitor; but Washington would not permit him to be slain, and pretending that the firing of the gun was an accident or signal, the Indian asserted the truth of this view of the case, and said his cabin was at no great distance. Gist replied that he might return home; but that they would remain there all night; giving the Indian at the same time a cake of bread, and saying that he must furnish them with some meat in the morning. The Indian then withdrew, and did not return. Whatever his designs may have been, he was apparently glad to be released. They continued their journey, however, and in the evening reached the banks of the Allegheny. They had expected to find the river frozen over. It was so, indeed, for fifty yards; but quantities of broken ice were floating in the channel. A night of great anxiety ensued. They encamped on the borders of the river, and at daylight they attempted to construct a raft with an axe, which labor employed them a whole day. They then launched and tried to propel it; but as they moved it with setting-poles, it became entangled between cakes of ice, and they were placed in imminent peril. Washington, with his pole at the bottom, made great efforts to stay the raft till it could be released from the ice; but by the rapidity of the current the frozen masses struck with such violence against the pole, as to throw him into the water where it was of great depth; and where he would have been drowned, had it not been for the tenacity with which he clung to a portion of the raft. At length they reached the opposite shore, and passed the following night upon the snow. They then hurried forward to the house of Frazier, the Indian trader, on the Monongahela, where they heard of a family of whites on the banks of the Great Kanawha, who had been murdered by some Ottawas in French interests. Near this spot lived Queen Aliquippa, not far from the mouth of the Youghiogeny, and they made their way to the royal wigwam. Washington then paid a visit of ceremony to this princess, and gained her favor by a present of an old watch-coat and a bottle of rum, which appeared to be highly prized by that potentate. They reached the residence of Gist, on the Monongahela, on Jan. 2d, 1754; and Washington parted from him, on his homeward journey, crossing the Blue Ridge. He delayed for a single day at Belvoir, and reached Williamsburg on the 16th of the month; where he delivered a full and accurate account of his mission to Governor Dinwiddie.

This expedition became the foundation of the fortunes of Washington, and made him the object of general applause in Virginia. The great courage and singular perseverance amid the perils of the wilderness, which he had displayed, when surrounded by fearful dangers among ruthless savages, and in the prosecution of his journey through almost impassable routes; his extraordinary hardihood in sleeping on the ground in inclement weather and in the open air, in the vicinity of a treacherous foe; all pointed him out as a man of remarkable capacity, energy, and resolution; and gave him the reputation which placed him subsequently on an exalted pinnacle of responsibility and fame.

The Chevalier de St. Pierre returned a courteous answer to the letter of the Governor of Virginia, and said that he would conform to the instructions of his general, and with that inflexible resolution which could be expected of the best officer. The Governor and Council of Virginia came to the conclusion, that this punctilious letter was but evasive; and that the French were preparing to take military possession of the Ohio Territory in the spring. Captain Trent was sent to raise one hundred men to finish the fort begun by the Ohio Company; and he is supposed to have been chosen, notwithstanding his former failure, on account of his being the brother-in-law of George Crogan, the Indian trader, who was thought to have much influence with the Indians. Washington was authorized to raise a force at Alexandria; to procure the supplies for the fort at the Fork, and ultimately to take command of both companies. He was directed to consult George Crogan and Andrew Montour, the interpreters, who were looked on as oracles in Indian matters.

Dinwiddie endeavored to combine all the governors against the common foe; and to effect alliances with the Cherokees and Cahawbas; the Ottowas and Chippewas being already in the French interests.

The colonists made various excuses for not sustaining the purposes of the governor; he convened the House of Burgesses, but met grievous disappointment from the mistaken pride of independence which inflamed them. Some questioned the king's right to the territory; and others objected to granting supplies, lest such means should be looked upon as an act of hostility. The governor complained bitterly of their republican way of thinking, and said that "he feared that it would render them more and more difficult to be brought to order." The event proved that he was no false prophet. The number of troops required was three hundred, and these were to be divided into six companies, of which the command was offered to Washington, who declined; and Colonel Joshua Fry, a man of influence and ability, obtained it. Washington was appointed second in command. A bounty of land offered by Governor Dinwiddie, greatly assisted the recruiting, which had at first made very slow progress. But it was more difficult to get officers than soldiers; and many of those appointed did not appear. Washington was left almost alone to manage and train the raw recruits. In his emergency, he made Van Braam, his old master of fence, captain; and set off for the new fort on the Ohio, on the 2d of April, 1754, with two companies, containing about one hundred and fifty men. Colonel Fry was to conduct the rest. While on the march, Washington was joined by Adam Stephens, an officer who was destined to serve with him some years after this period. He could with difficulty obtain the necessary horses and wagons at Winchester, and was obliged to impress them. The farmers gave their worst horses, and these were of little service. With great toil the cannon and baggage were transported; but the hope was, that at Will's Creek Trent would have pack-horses in readiness. But Trent proved himself to be a worthless person, and failed to fulfil his commission. There was a report of his capture by the French, but the rumor was entirely false.

Captain Contrecœur had sailed down the Venango with a thousand men, and had taken possession of the fort—the whole garrison not consisting of fifty men. The news of its capitulation was carried to Washington by an ensign. He was accompanied by two warriors, one of whom conveyed an address from the half-king to Washington, and the other a belt of wampum for the Governor of Virginia, which Washington forwarded with one of the warriors. He retained the other warrior, whom he sent to the half-king with messages of a conciliatory nature for the chiefs and sachems of the Six United Nations. He called a council of war, in which they resolved to fortify themselves at the store-houses of the Ohio Company, at the mouth of Redstone Creek, and there watch the enemy. Washington sent sixty men in advance, and wrote to Dinwiddie for mortars, grenades, and heavy cannon. He now experienced the trials of his new situation, and gained a foretaste of the perplexities and difficulties which, in future, awaited him from the foe, and from the inefficiency of his own friends in legislative councils. Trent and Frazier began to be severely censured. The first was stigmatized as a coward. The other was not so guilty in his neglect of duty, and he was recommended by Washington as adjutant at a future period. The different colonial assemblies were very slow at this time in voting supplies — a fault which produced incalculable injury to their interests in this war with France, and still more in the days of the American Revolution.

CHAPTER VII.

THE MARCH TO "LITTLE MEADOWS" — CORRESPONDENCE WITH DINWIDDIE AND LORD FAIRFAX — THE DISINTERESTED VIEWS OF WASHINGTON — FRENCH EMISSARIES — MESSAGE FROM THE SACHEM — THE GREAT MEADOWS, AND SKIRMISH WITH JUMONVILLE — ITS RESULTS — WASHINGTON'S FIRST BATTLE — SCARCITY OF PROVISIONS — DEATH OF COLONEL FRY, AND PROMOTIONS — CAPTAIN MACKEY AND THE INDEPENDENT COMPANY — PRAYERS IN CAMP — FIGHT AT GREAT MEADOWS, AND SURRENDER OF FORT NECESSITY — THANKS VOTED BY THE HOUSE OF BURGESSES TO THE TROOPS — EXCEPTIONS MADE, AND REASONS FOR THEM — END OF WASHINGTON'S FIRST CAMPAIGN.

WASHINGTON commenced his march towards Will's Creek on April 29th, 1754, at the head of one hundred and twenty men. It was found difficult to travel through rugged mountains, and the dismal forest known by the epithet of the Shades of Death; but on the 9th of May the party, after experiencing immense difficulty in dragging the artillery of Colonel Fry, arrived at Little Meadows. Various incidents occurred to indicate that the French were in motion; and Washington soon discovered that they were constructing a fort in the place he had noted as the best adapted for that purpose. He suspected that the French emissary, La Force, was acting the part of a spy, as he had been seen lurking about near Laurel Hill with four soldiers; and in the reports of presents bestowed upon the Indians, he found that the sachem was in his interests, and on his way with fifty warriors to meet him. On their arrival at the Youghiogeny, after excessive toil, Washington found leisure to write to Governor Dinwiddie, respecting the embarrassing state of affairs, in consequence of the want of liberality in the Virginia Government, with respect to the provincial soldiers and officers, who received less pay than the regular army, and had to fare entirely on salted provisions. Nothing prevented the officers from throwing up their commissions, but their reluctance to endure the shame of shrinking from danger. These were also the sentiments of Washington. He did not object to serve voluntarily, but he declared that he would rather toil as a day-laborer for a subsistence, when necessity should demand it, than serve under such disadvantageous circumstances. He, however, remarked that, possessed as he was of a constitution hardy enough to endure the severest trials, he would not flinch, and in any case would be the last man to leave the Ohio. In a letter to Lord Fairfax he manifested his indifference to performing the service of a volunteer, or otherwise as might be required; and characterized the motives which influenced him as being pure and noble, his only aim being the service of his king and country.

Hearing that the foe were in the act of crossing the Youghiogeny, at the distance of eighteen miles from his post, he took up his position in the Great Meadows, cleared away the bushes, and declared, after making an intrenchment, that it was "a charming field for an encounter." Six men were missing when the roll was called, for desertions had already begun He detached seventy-five men after La Force, whom he regarded as subtle and mischievous; and, determined to anticipate the hostile force that had hovered around him for some days, he took forty men, and with them reached the camp of the half-king at sunset. He was received with great apparent manifestations of friendship; and with a brother sachem, Scarooyadi, or Monacatoocha, accompanied Washington to the trails he had discovered, and putting two Indians on them, they traced them to a French encampment. He came upon them suddenly, with the half-king and his warriors, in perfect silence. The French ran to their arms, and a brisk conflict took place during the quarter of an hour, while the party received the enemy's fire. The balls whistled around Washington, killing one man and wounding three others. The French lost several men and then retreated; and being hotly pursued, twenty-one were taken captive, and but a single Canadian escaped to carry the tidings back to the fort. Washington prevented the Indians from scalping the prisoners. He considered his own escape as providential. Ten of the French were killed; one was wounded. Jumonville, the French leader, fell at the first fire, being shot through the head. He was an officer of merit, and his fate was much deplored. An officer named Drouillon, and La Force, were the most important of the prisoners who were taken. They pretended that they were advancing to summon Washington to leave the French territories; but a letter of instruction to Jumonville proved the contrary to have been the fact. They were in reality spies, and suffered the penalty of prisoners of war; were conducted to Great Meadows, and sent to Governor Dinwiddie, then at Winchester, with a caution to be on his guard in his communications with them.

Washington was now in a perilous situation, as Contrecœur had nearly a thousand men at the fort under his command, exclusive of Indians. He wrote to Colonel Fry at Will's Creek, to send on reinforcements; but he also declared his determination to fight with numbers very unequal, and not to yield to the foe. The sachem was intent on the fight, and would have all his allies present. He sent them the scalps of the slain Frenchmen, with hatchets and wampums, and summoned his warriors to meet him at Redstone Creek. He left them for his home, promising to send for the Mingoes and Shawnees, and on the 30th to bring back thirty or forty warriors to the camp. Washington wrote to Dinwiddie on the 29th, saying that he expected to be attacked; and that if he should hear of his being beaten, he would be told, at the same time, that they had performed their duty, and had fought to the last. Washington, in a letter to a relative at this period, is said to have described the late affair, and his escape from harm: "I heard the bullets whistle, and, believe me, there is something charming in the sound." Horace Walpole termed Washington "a brave braggart;" and the affair having reached the ears of King George II., he said: "He would not say so if he had been used to hear many"—an opinion confirmed by Washington himself after he became more experienced in deadly encounters. Being asked at a later period if he had ever said so, he replied, coolly: "If I did, it was when I was young."

In consequence of the mismanagement of the commissariat, provisions began to be scarce in the English camp, and the troops were six days without flour. Washington wrote to Crogan to send all that he could furnish, which was the more needed as several Indian allies, with their wives and children, had arrived. Colonel Fry had expired at Will's Creek, and was succeeded by Colonel Innes, of North Carolina, in the command. This appointment gave satisfaction to Washington, as he was an experienced officer, and had served at the siege of Carthagena with his brother Laurence. But the colonel never came into the camp. By the death of Fry, Washington was really in command of the regiment. He appointed Captain Adam Stephens major, and wrote to Dinwiddie in favor of Van Braam. The palisading was completed which had been commenced some time before, and this work they called Fort Necessity, from their being pushed for provisions during its construction. Fry's men at length came up, and then the force amounted to three hundred. Dr. James Craik, a Scotchman, and destined to become one of the most confidential friends of Washington, accompanied them as the surgeon of the troops. An independent company of one hundred men, under Captain Mackey, was expected soon to arrive. The name "independent" did not please Washington, who, in writing to Dinwiddie, wished to know whether Mackey would be under his "command or independent of it, and hoped he would have more sense than to insist on any unreasonable distinction;" for, though he had his commission from the king, and a wide difference, so far as salary was concerned, existed between them and the provincials, yet the latter were as loyal to their sovereign, "and as willing to sacrifice their lives for their country's good as the others." Washington's early military instructor, Adjutant Muse, was made major of a regiment, and brought with him nine swivels and a supply of ammunition. Montour, the Indian interpreter, now a provincial captain, accompanied him. Mr. Gist was ordered to bring on the artillery, and sixty horses were sent to Will's Creek for the transportation of more provisions.

Washington, with great ceremony, and wearing a medal prepared by the governor expressly for such occasions, distributed the presents and wampums among the Indian chiefs, and decorated them and the warriors with the medals which their father, the King of England, had sent them. The son of Queen Aliquippa was among them, and was admitted into the war counsels of the camp at her request, receiving the name of Fairfax, while the sachem received that of Dinwiddie. The sachems returned the compliment, and named Washington Conotaucarious — an epithet the import of which is now unknown. Washington, at the suggestion of William Fairfax, had public prayers read in his camp, and performed the office of chaplain with great propriety of demeanor. At a later period, in the struggles of the colonies for national existence, he prohibited profane swearing; and we shall find him, on another occasion, bowing the knee before his Maker, and invoking the Divine direction. Some French deserters informed him that the fort at the fork was at length completed, and was called *Duquesne*, in honor of the Canadian governor; that it was garrisoned with five hundred men, a reinforcement of two hundred was expected, and in a fortnight nine hundred more; and that it was proof against all attacks, except that of bombs discharged from the land side.

Washington manifested the utmost discretion in not coming into collision with Captain Mackay on any matter involving military authority, and wrote to Dinwiddie to prescribe minutely their relative positions. The captain's men, on the march to Redstone Creek, would not be permitted by him to work on the road, unless they received a shilling sterling a day; and as Washington would not pay this sum, he undertook to finish the road with his own men, and left the captain and his force as a guard at Fort Necessity. With great perseverance and diligent labor, warily guarding against surprise, the advance was gradually made, and the road constructed. At Gist's establishment, thirteen miles from Fort Necessity, he was informed that ample reinforcements had been sent to Duquesne, and that a detachment would be dispatched against him. He at once halted, intrenched, called in the foraging parties, and requested Mackay to join him as soon as possible. On his arrival he summoned a council of war, in which it was agreed that a retreat should be made immediately. Washington gave up his horse, on this occasion, to assist in transporting heavy munitions of war; and he paid the soldiers for carrying his own baggage. The officers followed his example; and in a sultry day, the roads being rough, and the men subsisting on short commons, pinched with hunger, they received no aid from the captain's men, the "king's soldiers," who would render no assistance in the labors of the retreat. They reached Great Meadows on the 1st of July, and here the exhausted Virginians could carry the baggage and swivels no further. An intrenchment then was made; reinforcements were sent for from Will's Creek, and supplies of provisions procured.

Captain de Villiers, brother-in-law of Jumonville, had sallied from Fort Duquesne with five hundred French and several hundred Indians, intent on revenge and slaughter. He fired into the works of Washington at Gist's settlement, and finding them empty was about to return, when a deserter told him that the troops of Washington were in a starving condition at Great Meadows. He then immediately advanced thither. During this interval Washington was doing his utmost to fortify Fort Necessity, which had not been done by Mackay and his men. Trenches and palisades protected it, and its dimensions were one hundred feet square, in a level, grassy plain near the middle of the Great Meadows. It was two hundred and fifty yards wide, and a breastwork was erected by the soldiers, inspirited by the exertions and example of their chief; who, in this moment of peril, asked no aid of the South Carolina men, but himself assisted in felling trees, hewing branches, and piling up the trunks as a bulwark against the approaching enemy. The Indian allies at this critical moment abandoned him, being offended at their subjection to command, disheartened at the feeble preparations, and because their chief was not sufficiently consulted. Their real motive was to put their families in a more secure retreat. A wounded sentinel informed the troops that the French were upon them. Washington drew up his men on level ground, and musketry was soon heard at a distance. He fell back into the trenches, and ordered his men to fire as soon as they could see the foe. Thus an irregular skirmishing was kept up during that day. Under the cover of the woods, the French continued to fire at the distance of sixty yards. The rain also fell rapidly, and rendered the guns in many cases unfit for use, dispiriting and half drowning the men. At 8 o'clock in the evening the French asked a parley, and fearing that it might be merely to examine the fort, Washington at first hesitated. The request was again made; and it was desired that an officer, under their promise of safety, might be sent to them. Jacob Van Braam was the only one who could perform the service, as the engineer, Chevalier de Peronney, who was familiar with French, was then disabled by wounds. The terms of surrender, twice brought by Van Braam, were rejected; and the third time he came with written articles in French, which, as no writing materials were to be had, Van Braam translated *viva voce*. The rain still fell copiously, and he read from a paper to which he held a candle, the light of which was almost extinguished by the water. The translation was made, one article after another, in the presence of Washington and his officers, who endeavored to unravel the meaning from the imperfect English of the captain. A clause by which it was stipulated that all the military stores and arms were to remain in the possession of the French, was objected to and changed. The chief articles, as understood by Washington and his officers, were, that no annoyance on the part of the French or Indians would obstruct their return to the settlements, and that they should retire with the honors of war, and take everything with them but the artillery, which should be destroyed; that their effects should be left at some secret place until sent for; that they should promise, on their honor, not to construct any buildings or improvements on the land of the King of France during one year; that the prisoners should be restored, and that till then Van Braam and Stobe should remain as hostages. Washington agreed to these terms, and his men accordingly retired with the honors of war; but had scarcely begun their march when the Indians began to annoy them. He sent a few men after several stragglers who had been wounded, and remained at Fort Necessity, near which he encamped. In the engagement which had taken place, twelve men were killed, and forty-three wounded, out of three hundred and five, officers included. The number of killed and wounded in Mackay's company is unknown. The loss of French and Indians is supposed to have been far more considerable.

The fatigued and disheartened troops, encouraged by Washington, at length reached Will's Creek, and there found abundant provisions and military stores.

Here he left them; and in company with Mackay, proceeded to the governor at Williamsburg, to render his military report. The Virginia House of Burgesses returned a vote of thanks to Washington and his officers for their bravery, and gallant defence of their country; and a distribution of eleven hundred dollars was made to the privates in the expedition. Major Stobe and Jacob Van Braam were excepted from the vote of thanks; the former on the charge of cowardice, the latter on account of his misrepresentation as an interpreter. Crogan and Montour were found to be different from what they pretended. The two, with all their boasting, had not sent thirty warriors into the camp as fighting men. Such was the beginning of Washington's military career. He had brought his first campaign to a close, and had displayed the prudence, address, and courage of a veteran commander. Amid dangers and sufferings scarcely ever exceeded, he had both gained the esteem and secured the obedience of the soldiers, under the most trying and perilous circumstances.

CHAPTER VIII.

GOVERNOR DINWIDDIE AND HIS VIEWS OF THE WAR — DIFFICULTIES WITH THE ASSEMBLY — GRANTS FROM ENGLAND, AND CHANGES IN THE ARMY—WASHINGTON THROWS UP HIS COMMISSION—HIS RETIREMENT TO MOUNT VERNON—WAR BETWEEN THE ENGLISH AND FRENCH —BRITISH PLAN OF THE CAMPAIGN—GENERAL BRADDOCK APPOINTED COMMANDER—COMMODORE KEPPEL AND HIS SQUADRON—THE EFFECT OF WARLIKE PREPARATIONS ON WASHINGTON—HE JOINS THE STAFF OF BRADDOCK—HIS FLATTERING RECEPTION, AND APPRECIATION BY THE GOVERNORS IN CONGRESS—PREPARATIONS FOR THE EXPEDITION —MEETING OF OFFICERS AT ALEXANDRIA — SIR JOHN ST. CLAIR AND HIS THREATS — THEIR EFFECTS — GEORGE CROGAN AND HIS INFLUENCE — CAPTAIN JACK.

THE French having relaxed their efforts at Fort Duquesne, a letter was conveyed by an Indian to the commander of the English, to say that two hundred men were there, and as many expected; that detachments of men and Indians had been sent off, and all that remained in the fort were Contrecœur and the guard of forty men and five officers; that a hundred Shawnees, Mingoes, and Delawares could surprise and take the guard, and, by shutting the sally-gates, render the fort certain of being captured. This letter was sent to Crogan, who dispatched it to the Governor of Pennsylvania, by whom it was sent to Governor Dinwiddie. The latter entertained the wild project of taking the fort. He therefore wrote to Washington, who early in the month of August had joined his regiment, and assisted in the erection of Fort Cumberland, to march to Will's Creek, and leave word for the officers to follow as soon as they had obtained a complement of men. Such a scheme, at that season of the year, and under such circumstances, was known by Washington to be perfectly chimerical; and his letter to a member of the House of Burgesses at this time, which doubtless Dinwiddie read, had the effect of causing him to give up the rash undertaking.

Dinwiddie was entirely ignorant of military affairs. Some of the North Carolina troops having found none of the necessary supplies when they reached Winchester, at once disbanded and went home. The House of Burgesses were dilatory in granting supplies; and they thought the best way would be, to have such contributions furnished by act of Parliament, as were necessary to arrest the advance of the French; and also by imposing a poll-tax of two and sixpence a head, independently of the Assembly. Certain grants were made by the House of Burgesses in October, 1754, for the public service; an allowance of twenty thousand pounds; and half that sum, with arms for the troops, were sent from England.

As difficulties had often occurred in reference to military precedence, among troops of various kinds, the governor reduced them all to companies, in such a manner that no officer in a regiment was higher in rank than a captain. Washington therefore left the service; and soon afterward Governor Sharpe, of Maryland, desired to secure his assistance. He sent a spirited letter to Colonel Fitzhugh, exhibiting his views of military matters, and his disinclination to hold a commission inferior to that which he held before. About this period an order came from England which commanded the officers who bore the king's commission to take precedence in rank over those who were commissioned by the governors of the provinces; and provided that, when serving with a general and field-officers commissioned by the king, the general and field-officers of the provinces should give them the precedence. These arrangements did much to prepare the way for colonial rebellion and subsequent independence. Washington was much mortified by Dinwiddie's refusal to give up the French prisoners as had been stipulated; and when visiting Williamsburg, was grieved to find La Force in prison. His remonstrance was lost on the obstinate Dinwiddie, who would not liberate the captives. La Force afterward broke prison, and escaped about thirty miles from Williamsburg. Asking a countryman how far it was to Fort Duquesne, he was betrayed, brought back, and chained in a dungeon. All this operated injuriously on Stobe and Van Braam, who were also in durance. Stobe ultimately escaped into the country; but Van Braam, who likewise fled, was conducted back, and afterward shipped to England.

Washington, on resigning his connection with the army, paid a visit to his mother, and rendered all the service in his power to her and his family, faithfully discharging the duties devolving on him. He then gave himself up entirely to agricultural pursuits, at his beautiful estate of Mount Vernon; but his country called him again to arms, and she never uttered her voice to him in vain. The French ambassador, the Marquis de Mirepois, had not been deceived by the vain dissimulation of the British ministry, and he returned indignantly to France. It was found that war was inevitable between the French and English; and in 1755 a plan of campaign was devised by the Government of Great Britain, having a fourfold object in view; namely, to expel the French from Nova Scotia, to dislodge them from Crown Point on Lake Champlain, from the fort erected on Niagara, and to drive them from the frontiers of Pennsylvania, as well as to recover possession of the valley of the Ohio.

The Duke of Cumberland was commander-in-chief of the British army at that time; and by him Major-General Edward Braddock was appointed generalissimo of the American forces against the French. This officer was a veteran, and the duke considered him as admirably fitted for the post, as he was an excellent tactician—which, however, was a different species of qualification from that required of a commander in a new and unsettled country. General Braddock was faultless on parade, a brave officer, and an experienced soldier; but one of his defects was an unbending obstinacy and pertinacity of purpose. He was, however, appointed to command the expedition which was the most important of all the campaigns that were destined to be fought on the frontiers of Virginia and Pennsylvania. The quartermaster-general, Lieutenant-Colonel Sir John St. Clair, had studied the field of operations before the arrival of Braddock. The road, which lay through the region where Wash ington had already campaigned, seemed to him to be almost impassable by an army; and he wrote to Governor Morris, of Pennsylvania, to have the road cut or repaired to the head of the Youghiogeny, and another opened from Philadelphia to aid the transportation of supplies for the army. The governor applied to the Assembly, and had a commission appointed to make a survey, at the head of which was the Indian trader, George Crogan. Commodore Keppel, with his squadron of two ships-of-war, and several transports, had anchored in the Chesapeake; the land forces which they brought consisted of two regiments of five hundred men each, a train of artillery, and the necessary munitions of war. The regiments were commanded, the one by Sir Peter Halket, the other by Colonel Dunbar; and they were to be increased to seven hundred men by the addition of Virginia companies which had been enlisted. Alexandria was the place of rendezvous for the ships and levies. Indian allies were to be employed, and Mr. Gist led General Braddock to believe that four hundred Indians would join him at Fort Cumberland. Sir John St. Clair had contracted with the settlers at the foot of Blue Ridge for two hundred wagons and fifteen hundred horses, to be ready at Fort Cumberland early in May; and Governor Sharpe was to send a hundred wagons. Keppel furnished four cannon for the attack of the fort, and thirty seamen; and all the arrangements, according to Captain Robert Orme, an aid-de-camp of Braddock, seemed to promise the greatest success.

General Braddock having proceeded to Alexandria,

found the Virginia levies arrived, and the troops disembarked. The sounds of warlike preparation roused the martial spirit of Washington, in the peaceful shades of Mount Vernon; and he felt an ardent desire to join the expedition as a volunteer. This disposition reached the ears of General Braddock, who had been informed of his merits; and he directed Captain Robert Orme to invite Washington to join his staff; who wrote in such a generous and kindly spirit to him, that it created a friendly feeling between them ever afterward. The appointment offered no command nor emolument, and required a good deal of expense and self-sacrifice; nevertheless, it would obviate the disputed questions of military rank, gratify his passion for arms, and give him practical experience in a well-organized corps, admirably disciplined, and under a skilled tactician. His mother did her utmost to prevail on him to decline the service, and having ascertained his value at home, desired him not to expose himself to danger; but with all his respect for her, he could not resist the appeal to his warlike sympathies. He reached the head-quarters of General Braddock at Alexandria, where he was heartily welcomed by his young associates, Captains Orme and Morris, aides-de-camp of the general.

Washington was pleased with the flattering reception he received from the general; and found him honorable and generous, though haughty and obstinate, and in matters of military discipline very exact. Four governors were then assembled at Alexandria, representing Massachusetts, New York, Maryland, and Pennsylvania; and Washington was highly appreciated by them all. In a grand council held on April 14th, 1755, the general's commission was read, and his instructions from the king in reference to the necessary fund for the expenses of the war. The governors found it impracticable to obtain any such fund from their assemblies, having tried the experiment in vain; and they gave it as their opinion that the preparations for military expenses in America could not be had without the aid of Parliament; they suggested that the ministers should find some way of compelling contributions; and in the meantime, that the general should use his credit with Government to obtain means for current expenses to carry through the expedition. The congress closed, and but few wagons had arrived. Recollecting the difficulties of the way, the huge preparations of war, and the heavy materials which were to be transported across the mountains, Washington was struck with wonder and dismay. "If our march be regulated by the slow movements of the train," said he, "it will be tedious, very tedious indeed." He was in the right; but Braddock smiled sarcastically at the apprehensions of the inexperienced young officer.

Sir John St. Clair, in the meantime, became incensed because the Government road had not been commenced; and declared that the want of roads and of the provisions which had been promised by Pennsylvania, might ruin the expedition. He raved furiously, and threatened to burn the houses of the inhabitants, if defeated by the French; and declared that he would go through the province with sword in hand, and treat Pennsylvania as a disaffected and rebellious province. This ebullition produced such an effect on the commissioners, that they wrote to Governor Morris, urging him to set people to work upon the road, and send flour to the mouth of the Canacocheague River; and in reply, by his secretary, the orders were given to proceed, adding that the expenses should be paid at the next meeting of the Assembly. George Crogan was, in the meantime, commissioned to convene at Aughquick, in Pennsylvania, all the mixed tribes of the Ohio, to distribute wampum belts among them, and induce them to join General Braddock on his march. Crogan engaged to enlist a large number of Indians; and he secured the services of a resolute band of hunters, under the command of Captain Jack. This person was a remarkable character, who had been a captive among the Indians for many years, knew their customs, was regarded as one of themselves, and whose name inspired terror into their minds. He promised to join the forces of Braddock on the march, and Crogan engaged to attend in company with them.

CHAPTER IX.

GENERAL BRADDOCK — HIS DIFFICULTIES ABOUT MEANS OF TRANSPORTATION—ASSISTED BY BENJAMIN FRANKLIN—DR. HUGH MERCER—CAPTAIN GATES—THE ROADS—SIR JOHN ST. CLAIR—PATRIOTISM OF WASHINGTON—HE IS SEIZED WITH A VIOLENT FEVER—HE RECOVERS — REACHES THE CAMP — PLAN OF ATTACK ON FORT DUQUESNE — WASHINGTON'S ADVICE—BLIND OBSTINACY OF BRADDOCK—RUINOUS CONSEQUENCES — DUNBAR — DEFEAT AND DEATH OF GENERAL BRADDOCK—THE AGGRAVATED DISGRACE—EXULTATION OF CONTRECŒUR.

VERY great inconvenience was experienced by General Braddock, in consequence of the failure of the Virginians to fulfil their contracts. He had the good fortune, however, to meet with Benjamin Franklin, who had been sent out by the Assembly of Pennsylvania, ostensibly in the capacity of postmaster for the transmission of letters between the general and provincial governors, but in reality to make an attempt to remove the impression which he entertained of their being opposed to the war, as they had neglected to fulfil his orders. Franklin undertook to procure wagons for the expedition, and a contract was made with him for four hundred and fifty conveyances, with four horses for each of them, and for fifteen hundred pack-horses. The patriotic Franklin, with that promptness for which he was remarkable, obtained the wagons on his own responsibility from the Pennsylvania farmers, and they arrived in due time; when

General Braddock remarked, that that was the only instance in which he had not experienced deceit and knavery on the part of the colonists. Franklin, in his autobiography, makes mention of the blind confidence with which Braddock hoped to take Duquesne, Niagara, and Frontenac; for he did not think the first would detain him over four days, at the furthest.

That officer entertained no conception of the difficulties of such a march, through a wild country, with hostile Indians on every side, with so much baggage and with so many superfluities. Indeed, Washington, who had joined him at Fredericktown, and was appointed one of his aides-de-camp, assured him of the great hardships which must be suffered in an attempt to cross the mountains in carriages. He advised him to use pack-horses; and declared that the most hazardous part of the expedition would consist in the transportation. Braddock, however, persisted in his own opinions. The general cut a dashing figure, with his chariot, and his body-guard galloping in attendance; but he soon found that it would not answer, and then gave them up. On the 19th of May the arrival of levies swelled the force to fourteen hundred men, besides two provincial companies, numbering thirty men each. Captain Stewart commanded the Virginia light-horse; and one of those who commanded two companies was Horatio Gates, in the capacity of a captain. Drs. Hugh Mercer and James Craik were attached to the expedition.

At Fort Cumberland Washington had an opportunity of seeing a fully disciplined army, and the mode of camp life. The army lay at the fort for some time, detained by the want of supplies, and because the roads were not yet completed. Mr. Peters required guards to protect him from the Indians, in making the road to Philadelphia. But the general could not see the necessity for them; nevertheless, guards were at length found to be indispensable. The Indian reinforcements so confidently expected never arrived; and Crogan brought but fifty warriors from Aughquick. These were treated liberally, and presents were made them; all went well for a time, but the warriors had brought their families with them, and the women were fond of loitering about the camp. Some of these were possessed of considerable charms, and the officers were said "to be scandalously fond of them." Jealousies at length arose, and the squaws were prohibited from approaching the camp; but this precaution was not sufficient, and they had to be sent back to Aughquick. Several warriors went with them, and the three Delaware chiefs returned to the Ohio. Washington had been told by Crogan that the warriors deserted because they were slighted in not being employed; but the governor was pertinacious, and adhered to his own opinion, in spite of all the representations which were made him. Frequent disputes had arisen between the general and Washington, on account of the former representing that the army contractors were without honor, in consequence of their having failed in fulfilling their undertakings, and he applied the same stigma to the country at large.

Washington was seized with a violent fever on the

third day of the march; so that he was compelled to ride in a covered wagon. The general consulted him in private, and then he urged him to leave the baggage and heavy artillery behind, with a body of troops; and to send a number of pieces of light artillery, with some chosen soldiers, to make an attack on Fort Duquesne. In support of this advice, he represented that the French were then very weak on the Ohio, but were expecting additional troops daily. He asserted that a rapid movement might enable them to carry the fort; but, if the army were to remain together, the march would be delayed, the rains would make the roads impassable, the French would be reinforced, and the contest would become involved in doubt and hazard. The general approved of the advice. In a council of war, it was resolved that twelve hundred men, headed by Braddock, should assault Fort Duquesne, while the rest of the regulars, and the heavy baggage, should proceed under Colonel Dunbar. At the great crossings of the Youghiogeny, the illness of Washington prevented him from going further, as the physician thought it would be attended with danger to his life. With great reluctance he obeyed the command of the general to remain where he then was, and he gave him his word of honor that he should be able to rejoin the army before it reached the fort. Orme promised to inform him by letter of all that passed in the meanwhile. The faithful servant of Washington, John Alten, was also taken ill at the same time, which added to his annoyance, as he was unable to render his master any assistance in his sickness. Washington joined the general, however, in a covered wagon, the day before the battle on the Monongahela, and, though he was yet very weak, assumed the duties of his position. To obtain a plan of attack, the surrounding country had been reconnoitred. The fort and camp were on the same side of the river, but an interval of two miles was between them. The Monon gahela was on the left, and on the right a mountain of considerable altitude. The route selected was to cross the river opposite the camp, pursue for about five miles the western bank of the river, cross it to the eastern side, and march on the fort. Lieutenant-Colonel Gage was to cross, advance to the second ford, and recrossing, protect the main army in its passage. Washington rejoiced to behold a splendid army arrayed in the glittering panoply of war; and as he gazed upon it, it inspired him with new life and vigor, and his ailments were forgotten.

The advance under Colonel Gage crossed on the 9th of July, 1775, before daybreak. Sir John St. Clair, with two hundred and fifty men, with implements and two six-pounders, followed to prepare the way for the artillery and baggage. All at length had crossed, and the army waited at a small stream called Frazier's Run, for the general to dispose the troops in order of march. Gage was ordered to lead the advance; St. Clair, the working-party and the six-pounders; and the general was to bring up the main body; while the Virginian troops were to form the rear. Half a mile from the river the ground was covered with grass and low bushes, with no opening except the road, flanked by the deep dells, hid by thickets and umbrageous trees.

Washington had desired the general to send forward the Virginia rangers, or Indian scouts, to explore the vicinity; but he persisted in his own plan of operations, and rejected the counsel. The result was as might have been expected. When about to join the main body, the advance had been fired into, and fiercely attacked. Succor was sent on to them, by the vanguard of about eight hundred men. The rest, four hundred in number, protected the baggage. Fearful yells now resounded through the forest, amid continual discharges of fire-arms. The advance had been attacked by French and Indians. The French commander fell, but the rifle of the Indian was at work; and the grenadiers were either killed, or driven back in confusion on Gage's men, who were ordered to fix bayonets and prepare for battle. The savages, uttering horrible yells, fired in safety from the ravines, and it could only be known where they lurked from the smoke of their guns. The troops fired wherever they saw the smoke, and could not be held in restraint, nor made to obey orders, being frightened more by the yells than by the rifles of the invisible enemy; and they continued shooting at random, by which means they produced but little execution. The unequal contest became more and more desperate. Many officers and men fell; Col. Gage was wounded; the advance retreated upon Sir John Clair's force, which was equally panic-stricken; and Col. Benton with the reinforcements, while drawing out his men, could not hold them in check. When the retreating detachments fell upon them, they were put to confusion.

General Braddock in vain endeavored to rally his troops, and ordered the officers to marshal them in small divisions; but the soldiers refused to obey, while the Virginia troops, from behind the trees, imitating the tactics of the foe, picked off many of them, and afforded some protection to the helpless regulars. Washington advised the general to make the regulars pursue the same plan; but he formed them into platoons, and those of them who fired from behind the trees he struck with the flat of his sword; while some of the Virginians who fought from their shelter, were shot by their own soldiers aiming wherever the smoke was seen to arise. The most gallant bravery was displayed by the English officers; they dashed forward in groups to inspirit the troops; but many were shot down by the savage enemy, and some even by their own men. The slaughter became dreadful; while the yells of the savages increased as they rushed forward, brandishing their tomahawks, with which they scalped their miserable victims. The aides-de-camp Orme and Morris were soon disabled, and the whole duty of conveying orders devolved upon Washington. He behaved with the most consummate bravery, in the midst of dangers the most imminent and fearful; having had two horses shot under him, and his coat riddled with four bullets. Hastening to the main body, to bring the artillery into action, he sprang from his horse, turned and pointed a field-piece against the enemy, and directed its charge into the woods. All was in vain. The men deserted the guns. Sir Peter Halket was shot at the head of his regiment. The unfortunate Braddock was still in the centre of the field, brave to the last; but his fortitude was useless, and it was impossible to retrieve the fortunes of the day. The majority of the Virginians were slain; the general's secretary fell at his side; five horses were shot under him; and a bullet pierced his arm and his lungs. At length Braddock fell to the earth, and was carried off the field in a tumbril. The rout then became general, and nothing but the avarice of the conquerors detained the victorious savages from the pursuit. The army, thus discomfited, continued its flight, until it crossed the river.

Out of eighty-six officers, twenty-six were slain and thirty-six wounded; and the killed and wounded, in rank and file, were not less than seven hundred. A hundred men halted near the ford, where the wounded general lay with his disabled aides-de-camp and several officers, still able to give orders, and hoping to keep his position till he was reinforced. Some of the men were advantageously posted near him, but most of them had deserted him. Washington, in the meantime, proceeded to the camp of Colonel Dunbar, forty miles distant, to obtain the escort of two companies of grenadiers, with wagons, provisions, and hospital stores. When he arrived in the camp he found that the evil tidings had preceded him; and as he returned with the convoy and supplies, at thirteen miles distance, he met Gage conveying General Braddock and the wounded officers. They rested one day at Dunbar's camp, and on the 13th resumed the march, and reached the Great Meadows the same night. Braddock remained silent during the first evening, and through the day succeeding the battle; and only uttered an occasional ejaculation amid his agonies. He died on the 13th at Great Meadows. At that spot he was buried with funeral honors; and Washington read the burial service over his grave.

After the funeral of General Braddock, Washington sent a message to Fort Cumberland to procure horses for the disabled officers, and suitable quarters for them on their arrival. He wrote meanwhile to his mother and brother, praising the valor of the Virginians, and condemning the cowardice of the regulars. Dunbar might have retrieved the day, having had fifteen hundred men under his command; but his camp became confused when tidings of the defeat reached him; he destroyed his military stores to facilitate his flight; and then hastened with his retiring forces to Philadelphia.

The field from which Washington had escaped presented an awful spectacle; the dead and dying were stripped and plundered by white and red men alike; and the murderous tomahawk and the scalping-knife terminated many a life which hung by a thread. This disgraceful defeat agreeably surprised the French general, De Contrecœur, who was in transports at the unexpected success. The force which had been sent out was not the main army, but consisted of seventy-two regulars, a hundred and fifty Canadians, and six hundred savages, of whom Captain de Beaujeu was the leader. The whole number of slain, including French and Indians, did not exceed seventy.

This unfortunate defeat of Braddock's created, for the first time, the impression that British troops had not that irresistible prowess which had universally been ascribed to them; and became one of the most powerful causes in producing the steady and unflinching resistance made by provincial troops against a regular army, which afterward occurred during the Revolution.

CHAPTER X.

WASHINGTON IN COMMAND — INDIAN RAVAGES — PANIC AT WINCHESTER — THE SAVAGES RETURN TO THE OHIO — THE FATE OF THE EXPEDITIONS AGAINST NIAGARA AND CROWN POINT — MILITARY PRECEDENCE — THE DECISION OF GENERAL SHIRLEY — EARL OF LOUDOUN — DANGERS AT GREENWAY COURT — GREAT ALARMS AT WINCHESTER — TENDER SYMPATHIES OF WASHINGTON — ILLIBERALITY OF THE VIRGINIA PRESS — ITS EFFECTS — APPRECIATION OF WASHINGTON BY THE SPEAKER OF THE HOUSE OF BURGESSES — PARSIMONY OF THE ASSEMBLIES — WASHINGTON'S ADVICE ABOUT THE FORTS — GREAT INEFFICIENCY OF THE MILITARY — DINWIDDIE'S AMBIGUITY — FALL OF THE FORT AT OSWEGO.

WASHINGTON reached home on the 26th of July, 1755, having suffered much, both in health and fortune, by the campaign. He complained, in a letter written about this time, of the ill success of his former expedition; in which, after serving with zeal, and meeting with reverses, his commission was taken from him after his return; that then, in his second expedition with Braddock, he had lost everything. Little did he imagine the benefit his country should afterward derive from his experience. Volunteer companies now began to be formed, to repel the hostile inroads of the French and Indians; and Washington was again ready to serve his country, but not on the same terms. He therefore received a commission, by which he was appointed commander-in-chief of all the forces raised or to be raised in the colony; three hundred pounds were voted him on account of his late losses in battle; and in a letter to his mother he afterward expressed his zeal for the public service. Governor Dinwiddie, it was thought, ceased to regard Washington at this time with friendly feeling, on account of his popularity in obtaining this command, which he had intended for Colonel Innes; and it is worthy of note, that Washington was honored with this early mark of the confidence of Virginia, not from any splendid triumph which he had achieved, but on account of his persevering fortitude amid reverses, and for his bravery in the time of trial; as well as for his wisdom in suggesting advice which, if followed, would have saved the army.

Washington fixed his head-quarters at Winchester, and here he was brought again into relations with Lord Fairfax, lieutenant of the county, who had organized a troop of horse, and previously aided Washington with his counsels and his sword. An express arrived, that the frontier was harassed by a body of Indians, who were murdering the inhabitants, approaching Winchester, and threatening to invade the valley of the Shenandoah. In the absence of Washington at Williamsburg, Lord Fairfax sent the militia of Fairfax and King William's county to the defence of Winchester. Washington soon returned, and had it not been that only twenty-five of the militia could be induced to march, would have proceeded at once to attack the savages. He met with great difficulties from want of co-operation, and was compelled to impress wagons for the service; the military laws also required to be modified, but applications to the governor for this purpose were at that time fruitless. The fright and panic at Winchester were intense beyond description; the Indians were said to be only twelve miles distant, and the people fled for their lives. The most exaggerated accounts were brought in; and Washington found, as he sallied forth with forty men and the militia, that the whole alarm was occasioned by the vociferations and pistol-firing of three drunken troopers, whom he sent back as prisoners. The Indians, about one hundred and fifty in number, being glutted with carnage, spoils, and captives, had returned to their homes on the Ohio, and all was again quiet on the frontiers.

A reward was offered by the colonial governor for the head of Shingis, who was said to be the chief author of these ravages; but the old sachem had been true to the cause, and Scarooyadi, his successor, imitated him in his loyalty to his English brothers. Washington cultivated Indian friendships as being of immense benefit to the service, without which he felt himself unable to cope with the savage foe.

About this period Washington was informed of the fate that attended the other enterprizes which had been undertaken by the English. That against Niagara failed, after the defeat of Braddock. General Shirley, who commanded the troops, found them stricken with alarm; many of them deserted; the long autumnal rains overtook and disheartened the remainder; and with military incapacity the enterprise was eventually abandoned. Seven hundred men were left in garrison at Oswego. General Johnson, with a body of six thousand New York and New England troops, conducted the expedition against Crown Point, and marched as far as Lake George. He was informed that a French army, under the Baron Dieskau, was marching against him; and having erected a fort, he sent forward one thousand men to oppose the foe. The discharge of heavy musketry quickly gave evidence of an encounter, and the firing became hotter as the men under Colonel Williams returned in full retreat. Soon the fugitives, pursued by the Indians, yelling the war-whoop, appeared; and the camp was overwhelmed with terror, when Dieskau was seen at the head of his forces. The artillery continued to fire upon the French and Canadians; the English recovered from their panic, and did dreadful execution with the artillery and small arms; the breast-works were scaled; a medley fight ensued; the enemy were routed; and the brave baron was among the slain. Johnson was wounded in the action, and did not therefore follow up his victory. He built a stockaded fort, and called it William Henry; but when it was completed, it was too late to proceed against Crown Point. The English Government subsequently conferred on him a baronetcy and five thousand pounds.

Thus ended all the projected expeditions. Washington then devoted his attention to the militia laws, and by his efforts several important improvements were made tending to perfect the military discipline of the troops. They were taught, also, to imitate the Indian method of fighting; and new roads were opened for the transmission of supplies and reinforcements. Questions of military precedence still occurred to annoy Colonel Washington; and a certain Captain Dagworthy, a Maryland officer who had served in Canada, who had received a king's commission, but had since commuted for half-pay, refused to obey the orders of any officer, of whatever rank, who was commissioned by a provincial governor. Differences arose in consequence of this declaration, and Washington refrained from mixing himself up with the dispute; but he determined that, if a Maryland captain should take precedence of him, he would resign his commission. The whole matter was to be referred to General Shirley. Washington, accompanied by several officers, travelled through Philadelphia and New York to Boston. He was successful in his mission, and Dagworthy was compelled to yield the precedence to the commander-in-chief of the Virginia forces. Shirley was soon after recalled, being superseded by General Abercrombie, who brought two regiments with him. A plan long since entered into rendered the Earl of Loudoun general commandant in America, with almost vice-regal power; by which arrangement, the other military men being made subordinate, the ministry hoped to unite the colonies under military rule, and compel the assemblies to contribute a common fund, subject to the control of one dictatorial power.

The Earl of Loudoun now became Governor of Virginia, and colonel of the regiment. The campaign was to commence in the following spring. Washington was said at this time to have been a suitor of Miss Phillipse, who was subsequently married to his friend and fellow aide-de-camp, Captain Morris. Marauders had entered the valley of the Shenandoah;

persons had been murdered by the Indians near Winchester; and it was suggested to old Lord Fairfax that his abode at Greenway Court was no longer secure, and that his scalp would be particularly acceptable to the Indians. He would not depart, however, and the place was fortified by a numerous retinue of white and black attendants. Washington found the inhabitants of Winchester filled with dismay, and resolved to organize a company, and put himself at the head of it. He sent to Fort Cumberland with orders for a detachment from the garrison, and complied with the advice of Lord Fairfax, and other officers, to appeal to the patriotism of the men, and thus procure musterings in private. Only fifteen persons of all those enrolled made their appearance: in the meantime the deepest alarm prevailed, and the forests could only be traversed by experienced hunters. The captain of a scouting party and ten men had been slain in the Warm Spring Mountain; and burning houses, famishing garrisons, and tales of massacre increased the general horror.

The inhabitants of Winchester were wrought up to the highest pitch of terror, and in their deep distress they looked to Washington for relief. He was deeply touched by this display of feeling. Women held up their children, and besought him to save them; and their supplicating sorrow, with the heart-moving petitions made by the men, affected him in such a manner that he declared he could die a sacrifice for them, if by so doing he could secure their deliverance. Yet, in the midst of all this alarm, the Virginia newspapers, while amplifying on the frontier troubles, threw the blame on the army, its officers, and its commander. Such an effect had this deep injustice on the mind of Washington, that the existing danger only prevented his giving up his command. Some complimentary letters, however, were sent him; the Speaker of the House of Burgesses recognized him as being the only person who was able to bring affairs to a prosperous issue; and he desired him still to retain the command. The parsimony displayed at this time by the House was astonishing. When the Assembly voted twenty thousand pounds, and an addition of fifteen hundred men, the appropriation was applied by Dinwiddie in a way almost useless, in erecting forts through the Allegheny Mountains, from the Potomac to South Carolina; neglecting the prudent advice of Washington, who urged the impolicy of their construction at so great a distance from each other as to render them inefficient. His plan was to erect them within eighteen miles of each other, that they might preserve a *surveillance* over the adjacent country; and to be garrisoned with eighty or a hundred men each, so as not to leave the fortresses too weak, should detachments from them be required. He also recommended that a fort should be built at Winchester, whose central position would render it a fit place for military stores; where the families of commanding officers could reside, and it thus be made a frontier citadel. He further advised that forts be erected upon the frontiers at convenient distances, three or four in number; and he condemned the use of Fort Cumberland as being out of the way, and therefore inefficient. Many other useful counsels were given by the young commander, but neglected by Dinwiddie, who persisted in a frontier line of twenty-three forts. Nevertheless, he erected the fort at Winchester recommended by Washington. During the summer the works at Winchester were commenced, and carried on with as much expedition as could be expected, considering the imperfect nature of the organization. In honor of the commander-in-chief, it was named Fort Loudoun. The other forts were begun, and drafts from the militia sent to garrison them. The service was perilous, and several persons were murdered in a defile by the Indians, a short time after Washington, who superintended these operations, had passed through.

In an autumnal tour made with Captain Hugh Mercer, Washington attempted to raise a force with which to oppose the roaming Indian bands; and such was the inefficient state of the militia, that after waiting a few days, only five men could be mustered for this service. Matters were but little improved where the militia took up arms. Their term of service had half expired, as December was the limit fixed by the act of the Legislature; provisions had been lavishly wasted; half the time was taken up in marching out and returning home; cattle were unceremoniously seized for the use of the troops, which naturally increased the popular disaffection. Numerous instances occurred in which the want of defence in the garrisons was apparent. Indians, at one fort, seized several children and bore them off. Another fort was surprised, and some of the garrison put to death; and when Washington visited a certain fort, the men were found firing at a mark, in this way wasting the ammunition which might be necessary for the protection of their lives. He describes himself as setting out, on one occasion, from Catawba with thirty men, who were chiefly officers, who made continual sport of order, circumspection, and vigilance; and he remarks that it was fortunate no enemy appeared, or their lives might have been lost through the noisy turbulence of these "*gentlemen soldiers.*"

The service of the year 1756 was full of perplexity to Washington, in consequence of the enigmatical manner in which Dinwiddie conveyed his orders; and so ambiguous were these orders in reference to Fort Cumberland, which Washington had recommended should be abandoned, that their import was incomprehensible. Dinwiddie at length took offence at some remarks uttered by Washington in reference to frontier service, and made such a representation to Lord Loudoun respecting Fort Cumberland, that an order was issued to keep it manned. The consequence of this resolution was a withdrawal of garrisons from the frontier forts, and of most of the troops from Winchester — a course full of imprudence, and attended with much loss and expense.

The secret was that Dinwiddie bore Washington a secret grudge, because the popular voice had made him commander; and he wished to disgust him with the service, in order that he might resign. Had it not been for the Winchester panic, and the real danger in which the country was involved, he might have succeeded in his purpose; but to Lord Loudoun Washington entrusted the future fate of Virginia.

The fort at Oswego was besieged by the French General Montcalm on the 12th of August, and on the 14th it capitulated. The terms of submission were barbarously violated, and many of the British soldiers were murdered by the savages. General Webb, who went to the assistance of the fort, returned to Albany after he had heard of its capture; and Lord Loudoun, who had made preparations for a great northern campaign in the spring, went into winter quarters in New York. While the relief to Oswego was postponed, an army of ten thousand men was loitering in an idle camp in Albany. Mismanagement in every department of the public service was the calamity of those times; it remained for unfolding circumstances to bring about a better state of affairs, under the propitious agency and influence of Washington.

CHAPTER XI.

DINWIDDIE AND LORD LOUDOUN — WASHINGTON'S RELATIONS WITH THEM—HIS ADVICE RESPECTING THE REDUCTION OF FORT DUQUESNE —FAILURE OF THE EXPEDITION AGAINST CROWN POINT — WASHINGTON'S ILL HEALTH—HE RECOVERS, AND RESUMES COMMAND—EXPEDITIONS IN THE NORTH — EXPEDITION AGAINST FORT DUQUESNE — WASHINGTON'S FIRST INTERVIEW WITH MRS. CUSTIS — HIS OPINION AND ADVICE RESPECTING THE LINE OF MARCH — FORT DUQUESNE — THE ENGAGEMENT — COLONEL BOSQUET — WASHINGTON PLANTS THE ENGLISH STANDARD ON THE RUINS OF THE FORT — HIS MARRIAGE WITH MRS. CUSTIS.

WASHINGTON had reason to suspect that Governor Dinwiddie had impressed Lord Loudoun unfavorably against him; and that erroneous opinions were entertained at head-quarters respecting the state of military affairs under his command. A meeting was to be held at Philadelphia in March, 1757, between Lord Loudoun and the Southern governors, in reference to the defence of the provinces; and Washington having requested permission to attend it, obtained it with a very ill grace from the governor. A month before the meeting, Washington sent his lordship a letter in which he explained the inefficient state of the militia, the errors which led to confusion, and an account of the imperfect state of defence. The purport of the letter was, the ambiguity of the orders received; and the various mistakes and errors for which Washington became answerable in consequence of it; the motives which influenced his conduct in again entering the service; and the hopes which he entertained from the appointment of Lord Loudoun. The reception which Washington met with in Philadelphia, and his being consulted about an attack to be made on Fort Duquesne, evinced the impression which his letter had produced on his lordship. This attack he advised to be made at the same time with that on Canada; but the plan adopted was different, and by this means the defences of Virginia would become weaker than before.

Washington failed in obtaining a king's commission; and his instructions were to co-operate with Colonel Stanwix, to whom he would, in a measure, be subordinate. Colonel Stanwix, a gentleman of great worth, commanded a regiment on the Pennsylvania frontier. The long-meditated reduction of Crown Point on Lake Champlain, was changed for that of the strongly fortified post at Louisburg, on Cape Breton. Lord Loudoun set sail for Halifax with six thousand men, in July, 1757, to join Admiral Holbourne with six thousand troops, eleven ships of the line, and a fleet of transports. The junction was made at Halifax; but the French had anticipated them, and Admiral de Bois de la Mothe had reached Louisburg with a large naval and land force, which, with the well-fortified and well-provisioned works, rendered it imprudent for Lord Loudoun to attempt anything. He returned without a triumph to New York; while Admiral Holbourne made a vain display of his fleet within two miles of Louisburg, endeavoring to draw on an engagement, which La Mothe declined. A storm subsequently shattered his vessels, and he returned ignominiously to England. Thus ended the great northern compaign, which justly excited the derision of the enemy. The rest of this year Washington spent in defending the frontiers with an inadequate force; during which the Shenandoah Valley was almost emptied of inhabitants. Washington had reason to think that false representations had been made to the governor against him; and he wrote a spirited letter, full of noble sentiments, which had little effect with that narrow-minded official. The numerous vexations which he was compelled to endure, made inroads on the strong constitution of Washington; and by the advice of his friend and physician, he returned to Mount Vernon. Dinwiddie sailed for England in January, 1758, little regretted by the colonists, with a character stained by imputations of extortion, avarice, and delinquency, in regard to the disposal of certain sums sent by the British Government, for which he had never accounted.

The health of Washington improved by relaxation, and he again assumed the authority at Fort Loudoun. Mr. John Blair had charge of the government until the arrival of Mr. Fauquier, the successor of Dinwiddie. William Pitt had succeeded to the British Cabinet, and the command in America devolved on Major-General Abercrombie. This officer made a threefold division of the forces; one of which was to march northward under Major-General Amherst, to aid the fleet under Boscawen in the reduction of Louisburg and Cape Breton; another was to be led against Ticonderoga and Crown Point, on Lake

Champlain, by Abercrombie; and Brigadier-General Forbes was to reduce Fort Duquesne. The colonial troops were to be put on the same footing with the regulars, and to be of equal rank. Washington resolved to remain in the service till after the capture of Fort Duquesne; and the forces of Virginia were now increased to two regiments, both destined for that expedition. They contained one thousand men each; one of which Washington was to command, the other was under Colonel Byra.

It is important to trace briefly the two expeditions against Louisburg and the island of Cape Breton, and against Ticonderoga and Crown Point.

Major-General Amherst, with Brigadier-General Wolfe, who afterward became famous, embarked in the fleet of Admiral Boscawen at Halifax, in the end of May, 1758; and on July 2d, reached the Bay of Gabarres, a few miles from Louisburg, whose garrison consisted of twenty-five hundred regulars, three hundred militia, and four hundred Canadians and Indians. Six ships of the line, and three frigates, were anchored in the harbor. An attempt was made to land in boats on the 8th of June, under Brigadiers Wolfe, Whitmore, and Laurens. The landing was effected with great gallantry by Wolfe, amid the surf and the discharge of artillery. The other divisions also landed, and Louisburg was attacked. Amherst was cautious, and a desperate defence was determined on by Drucour, who commanded the besieged. Wolfe, by a vigorous-night attack, took Light-Horse Point, and thereby greatly aided Amherst. Three of the largest of the enemy's ships were fired by a bombshell on July 21st, two others were afterward boarded, sword in hand. The enemy were compelled at last to capitulate; and Captain Amherst, brother of the general, conveyed to England eleven pairs of colors taken at Louisburg, which were suspended in St. Paul's Cathedral.

Abercrombie, with six or seven thousand regulars, and nine thousand provincials, encamped on Lake George. After the return of Major-General Putnam, whom he had sent to reconnoitre, he prepared to advance against Ticonderoga, in Lake Champlain; and the forces, on the 5th of July, were embarked in one hundred and twenty-five whale-boats, and nine hundred batteaux, and the artillery on rafts. When they came upon the enemy behind a breastwork, the French burnt their camp and retreated. The troops remained steady, but the guides being ignorant, they became confused in the forest. A brisk engagement ensued with a detachment of the French, in which the foe was routed. Lord Howe, however, fell, and the command devolved on Abercrombie, who retreated to the place where they had landed. Montcalm had called in the outposts, and fortified himself strongly. The engineers assured Abercrombie that the works were in reality very weak. He accordingly ordered an attack, and in the storming of the works, the troops exhibited the most heroic valor. But all was in vain; they were shot down as they reached the parapet, and in repeated assaults were repelled with terrible loss. Two thousand killed and wounded demonstrated the deadly energy and valor of the French troops. The English were then drawn off, and the disheartened Abercrombie re-embarked the troops and returned across the lake. Frontenac was taken from the French by Colonel Bradstreet, about the same period.

The expedition appointed to reduce Fort Duquesne proceeded slowly. Brigadier-General Forbes, the commander-in-chief, was detained at Philadelphia; and Colonel Bouquet was stationed at Raystown, in Pennsylvania, where about four thousand troops had been collected. Washington disciplined his troops at Winchester, consisting of nineteen hundred regulars, and seven hundred Indians. The force was in need of almost every article of equipment, and he had vainly represented to the authorities the destitute condition of the troops. He set out on his way to join General Forbes at Williamsburg, and to inform the council of the state of affairs, accompanied by Bishop, the well-trained military servant left with him by General Braddock. On this journey he fell in with a certain Mr. Chamberlain at York River, and accepted an invitation to dine with him, with considerable reluctance, as he was in haste to arrive at Williamsburg. At this gentleman's residence he met a lady named Custis, whose charms produced a deep impression on his heart. She was a fascinating and blooming widow, the daughter of Mr. John Dandridge. Her husband had been three years deceased, and had left her two young children, and a considerable fortune. The dinner being over, Bishop made his appearance with the horses; but Washington found the time pass too agreeably, and he determined to postpone his departure until the next morning. He then resumed the way to his destination. The residence of Mrs. Custis was at White House, not far from Williamsburg; and he subsequently employed the time to such advantage, and pressed his suit so successfully, that the widow accepted him, a regular engagement was the consequence, and the marriage was agreed upon to take place as soon as Fort Duquesne should be reduced. Washington was triumphant in love as in war; and at this time his gallant bearing and handsome person must have rendered him very attractive to the most fastidious and exacting of the fairer sex.

Washington was impatient to march, and the more so as he feared the Indian allies would desert him if the delay were prolonged. He equipped his men in the Indian hunting-garb, and Colonel Bouquet thought this would be a good attire for the expedition. Washington regretted that the line of march was not by Braddock's road, but by a new one to Fort Duquesne, on the usual tracks of the Indian traders. He showed that the new road could be opened only by extreme labor, whereas the other could be repaired in a short time, and their destination could be reached in thirty-four days; so that by the middle of October the entire campaign would be concluded. His advice was of no avail; September found him yet inactive in Fort Cumberland; while sixteen hundred men were sent on the advance from Raystown, to work on the road, and the time was thus fleeting uselessly away.

With great toil the road was made to Loyal Hannon, near Laurel Hill Colonel Bouquet detached

Major Grant with eight hundred picked men, and some of Washington's company, in Indian garb, under Major Lewis. This enterprize was conducted with little prudence. The savages were apprised of their approach; the *réveille* was sounded; and having now reached the fort, an observation of the works with a plan, was made in view of the garrison. The infatuation of the British commander was augmented by the silence of the fort, as not a single gun was fired. This was taken as an evidence of fear, when suddenly the garrison sallied forth, and the flanks of the English were attacked by an Indian ambuscade. Bravery was now of little service; the most dreadful carnage ensued in the whole detachment. Captain Bullitt made a barricade with wagons, and his men were posted behind them. The savages pursued the fugitives when they had completed their havoc and plunder; and on their advance Bullitt and his men, at a signal before agreed upon, opened a destructive fire upon the foo, by which they were checked. Bullitt and his troops then made a feint of surrender to the enemy; and when within eighty yards poured a volley among them, and charged with the bayonet. The Indians fled, and the routed detachments returned to Colonel Bouquet's camp at Loyal Hannon, having lost twenty-one officers and seventy-three privates. Colonel Forbes complimented Washington at Raystown on the conduct of the Virginia troops; and Captain Bullitt was promoted. Washington received the command of a division, to keep the advance of the main body, and repel the onset of the Indians.

The commander of Fort Duquesne, when the British

troops were within a day's march of it, embarked at night in boats, blew up the fort, and by the light of the burning ruins sailed down the Ohio. Washington mounted the British flag on the remains of this fortress on the 25th of November, 1758. The army collected and interred the bones of their comrades who had fallen in the defeat of Braddock, and the dilapidated works were again put in a posture of defence, and called Fort Pitt, in honor of the British minister. It was defended by two hundred men detailed from Washington's regiment, and the name has since been changed to Pittsburg. By the fall of this fort the French power on the Ohio was destroyed; danger vanished from the frontiers; and a treaty of peace was concluded with the Indians between the lakes and the Ohio. In the quiet that ensued, Washington laid down his commission, hung up his arms, with the applause of the people, and, amid a joyous gathering of his relatives and friends at the White House, his marriage with Mrs. Custis took place on January 6th, 1759.

The British minister, encouraged by the triumphs of the past, planned the entire subjugation of the French possessions in America, and resolved to expel that nation from Canada. The strongholds of the province were Quebec, Niagara, and Ticonderoga, against each of which an expedition was prepared.

CHAPTER XII.

WASHINGTON IN THE HOUSE OF BURGESSES — HIS RESIDENCE AT MOUNT VERNON — A DESCRIPTION OF HIS CHARACTER — ENJOYMENTS AND PURSUITS IN RURAL LIFE — WASHINGTON'S INDUSTRY — HE EXPLORES THE DISMAL SWAMP — COURTLY HABITS IN THE OLD DOMINION — WASHINGTON THE MODEL OF A VIRGINIA GENTLEMAN.

WASHINGTON remained three months at the White House with his bride, after their union. On his arrival at Williamsburg to take his seat in the House of Burgesses his appearance was greeted with numerous testimonials of respect, and the speaker pronounced a eulogy on the services which he had rendered to his country. When he rose to reply, he could not articulate a word; but blushed and stammered. The smiling speaker opportunely replied: "Sit down, Mr. Washington, your modesty equals your valor, and that surpasses the power of any language I possess." During the remainder of the session, Washington attended the House frequently, and afterward with his wife took up his abode in the peaceful shades of Mount Vernon. Before this time he had felt a desire to visit England; but now he describes himself as "fixed in his seat, with an agreeable partner for life, and hoping to find more happiness in retirement than he ever experienced in the wide and bustling world." His wife's former husband had left two children, a large landed property, and forty-five thousand pounds in money; one-third of which Mrs. Washington possessed in her own right; the remainder was divided in equal shares between the two children, one a boy of six, and the other a girl of four years of age.

A decree of the General Court appointed Washington guardian of the property of the children — a trust which he always discharged with great faithfulness. He felt at this period intense fondness for the pursuits of agriculture. He loved the pleasant retirement of Mount Vernon, and his beautiful mansion commanded a splendid view of the Potomac. Woods yet remained on the estate, and dells with inlets, and streams of water; while here and there, farms tilled with different sorts of culture, and having each their peculiar class of laborers, variegated the scene. Within the ample grounds were the haunts of the deer and the lurking places of foxes; through which, in his youthful days, he had followed the chase with Lord Fairfax, amid all the woody region lying from Mount Vernon to Belvoirs, on the picturesque shores of the Potomac. Here, too, the beloved brother whom he had loved, but who was deceased, had wandered with him in their boyhood days. Such remembrances were dear to his heart; and there, free from the restless dreams of ambition, it was his desire to spend his years in the happy seclusion of rural scenery. Here he who afterward became the great American Fabius, the father and deliverer of his imperilled country, spent several of his happiest years. He was not yet widely celebrated by the trumpet of fame, nor had he gained an exalted niche in her temple. The muse of history had not traced his virtues on the undying page, as the pride and glory of his country; yet here, in this retired spot, were then slumbering the sparks, which were destined afterward to kindle into a torch whose light should cheer and guide his country in the darkest hour of her coming disasters. The mind loves to linger in the pleasant shade and rural scenes in which such eminent virtues had their nursery.

Washington was already opulent. His ample fortune received the accession of a hundred thousand dollars by his marriage. His style of living, at this period, was dignified. A coach and four, with liveried postillions, was the usual conveyance of his wife and female visitors; though he himself always appeared on horseback, and kept the finest stud of horses in the vicinity. It should be remembered that Virginia, in those days, was an aristocratic community, as became the descendants of the cavaliers. A high and chivalrous spirit prevailed, and considerable fondness for ostentation distributed the wealth of the rich around them. Hosts of attendants for almost every purpose thronged a Virginia mansion of that era, the rich fabrics and commodities of London were imported; and luxury generally prevailed.

Washington kept his own accounts, and set an excellent example of diligence and attention to business. To his negroes he was always kind, but he kept them at work. He once watched the labor of four negroes, who, as carpenters, were sawing timber; observed what time was needed to get the tools ready; how long it required to clear away the branches, and then to saw the tree; and by this scrutiny the capability of every man was fully put to the test. So he once assisted his man Peter several days in the invention of a plough; and when a mill was said to have fallen in a thunder-storm, he put himself at the head of his servants, laboriously wheeling and shovelling gravel while the rain fell in torrents, to set bounds to the pressure of the water. He was remarkably fond of the chase, as was mentioned on a former page, and few enjoyed a hunting dinner with greater zest. His custom was to rise early; and he was in the habit of lighting his own fire when he rose before daylight. He took several cups of tea, and some cakes at breakfast, and then mounted his horse. He dined at two o'clock. When the day was wet he read, or arranged his papers, or posted his books.

On one occasion a person who was shooting his ducks, was followed by him, after hearing the report of his gun. He at length came upon him, and the offender raised his weapon in a threatening manner. But Washington wrested it from him, and administered to him such a reproof as prevented him from trespassing again. He sometimes went to Annapolis with Mrs. Washington, and enjoyed the pleasure of cultivated and fashionable society. Dinners, balls, and private theatrical entertainments were then the order of the day, and Washington often took part in the dance.

Mount Vernon was a great resort of visitors, many of whom, attracted by Washington's reputation, went to see him. He received them with the most liberal hospitality. He himself never had any children, but those of Mrs. Washington he protected with the assiduity and affection of a parent. He was at this period, a vestryman of two parishes; and on the rebuilding of the church at Pohiok he assumed a large portion of the expense.

An enterprise was set on foot, about this period, to drain the Dismal Swamp. Washington, with characteristic hardihood, explored it, and found it to be thirty miles long and ten miles wide; gloomy woods of cedar and cypress, hemlock, fallen trees, and moss, were everywhere seen; while here and there were pools, vines, creeping plants, and now and then a bog that shook under him in so dangerous a manner, that he was compelled often to dismount. The Lake of the Dismal Swamp, or Drummond's Pond, he found in the centre, about six miles long, and in breadth not more than three. It was located at the highest point, and formed a suitable reservoir for canals. He noted every particular in his book, traversed the whole region, and having made his encampment on firm ground, finished his exploration, and afterward originated the improvements which were subsequently made in this locality.

We have thus traced Washington through the perils of the wilderness, and amid the thrilling scenes in which he obtained military experience, and learned the art of war. We have seen him face the foe with bravery, and in perilous circumstances exhibit the magnanimity and fortitude of the hero. We have beheld honors bestowed upon him by his native State, and her House of Burgesses; and we have followed him into domestic retirement, and observed his ennobling virtues there, amid tranquil and rural seclusion. Henceforth we shall trace him amid the perils of war, surrounded by the laborious toils of a camp, on the sanguinary fields of battle, and in the supreme offices of power and influence, to which the gratitude of a free people subsequently elevated him.

The treaty of Fontainbleau, which gave peace to the colonies, seemed to afford the hope of its perpetuity. This hope was destined to disappointment; and the Delawares, Shawnees, and other Ohio tribes, with whom Washington had mixed, as well as some of the chiefs who had been his allies, took up the hatchet against the English, laid a deep plot, whose ramifications included a simultaneous attack on all the posts between Fort Pitt and Detroit. After ravaging the frontiers of Pennsylvania, Maryland, and Virginia, and carrying butchery, desolation, and dismay all around, they were only checked by the influence of Sir William Johnson from uniting with the Six Nations, and rendering the triumph of the tomahawk complete. This war, from the name of the leading spirit in it, was known as Pontiac's War.

CHAPTER XIII.

CAUSES LEADING TO THE AMERICAN REVOLUTION — RESTRICTIONS ON COMMERCE AND MANUFACTURES — THE RIGHT TO TAX AMERICA, AND OTHER GRIEVANCES — THE STAMP ACT — SPEECH OF PATRICK HENRY — REPEAL OF THE STAMP ACT — THE OFFENSIVE CLAUSE RETAINED — THE EQUANIMITY OF WASHINGTON — LORD BOTETOURT, HIS CHARACTER, AND DEATH — THE GENERAL COURT OF BOSTON — WASHINGTON MAKES A TOUR TO THE OHIO — HIS AFFLICTION ON THE DEATH OF MISS CUSTIS — DIFFICULTIES AS THE GUARDIAN OF JOHN PARKE CUSTIS — EARL OF DUNMORE GOVERNOR OF VIRGINIA — THE TEA THROWN INTO THE SEA AT BOSTON — BOSTON PORT BILL — WASHINGTON AS CHAIRMAN AND DELEGATE — HIS ENTHUSIASTIC PATRIOTISM — AFFAIRS IN BOSTON, AND EMBARRASSMENT OF GENERAL GAGE.

SERIOUS difficulties were now about to arise between Great Britain and her colonies. The colonial paper having depreciated, the British merchants sent a memorial on the subject to the Board of Trade; who replied that no paper issued by the colonies should be a legal tender in payment of debts. Washington saw the inflammatory tendency of this decision. The colonies revered the mother country, but her selfish commercial policy amounted to monopoly. Foreign vessels were excluded from American ports, and imports were to be made solely from England, in English ships; while exports were required to be sent only to Great Britain or her dependencies. Heavy duties were imposed on articles of trade; manufactures were placed under the most illiberal restraints, or prohibited entirely when likely to come into competition with those of Great Britain. The circumstances which precipitated an open rupture between England and her colonies are familiar to every reader, and need not be repeated here.

Washington was one of the watchmen who guarded the interests of his country, and calmly observed the coming storm from his abode of Mount Vernon. American taxation was opposed by Sir Robert Walpole, the English minister, who said that it would require a bolder man than himself to adopt such a step; but he suggested it indirectly by the imposition of heavy duties. An attempt was made in 1760 in Boston, to collect those duties on certain articles; but it was not permitted to be done. The commission of judges appointed "during the king's pleasure," gave offence, and were resisted first in New York. The exaction of oaths from naval officers against smuggling, had an injurious effect, and the colonists in retaliation refused to purchase British fabrics for clothing; by which means, in one year, in Boston alone, the demand for British goods fell ten thousand pounds.

The "right to tax America" was debated in 1764, in the House of Commons, and decided in the affirmative; and notice was given of this resolution to the colonies, where the intention was expressed of supporting a standing army by the moneys raised by that taxation. An immense number of claims against the colonies, based on twenty-nine acts of Parliament between 1660 and 1764, which Burke justly termed "an infinite variety of paper claims," held the colonies in a species of pecuniary bondage. The Stamp Act became the signal for opposition. By it no instruments would be valid in law or trade, except such as were written on stamped paper, to be purchased only of the agents of the British Government. At the same time all criminal offences were to be tried in the royal or admiralty courts.

Washington was present in the House of Burgesses on May 29th, 1765, when the Stamp Act came up for discussion in that body. His patriotism was at once inflamed. Patrick Henry rose and vindicated the exclusive right of the General Assembly of Virginia to tax the inhabitants of that colony; and declared himself an enemy to the colony which maintained the contrary. It was on this occasion that he fulminated the famous and soul-stirring threat: "Cæsar had his Brutus; Charles the First his Cromwell; and George the Third" (treason! treason! exclaimed some persons near the chair) "may profit by their example. Sir, if this be treason, then make the most of it."

The whole country soon became aroused and inflamed. Events were hurrying forward to a decisive crisis. The enforcement of the Stamp Act in Boston; the excitement in New York; the combination of the merchants of that city, Philadelphia, and Boston, against the importation of British goods till the repeal of the Stamp Act, with "Union" for their watchword; the dismissal of Mr. Grenville from the British Cabinet; Dr. Franklin's examination before the English House of Commons; the repeal of the Stamp Act in 1766, with the fatal clause—the chief bone of contention—remaining, "that the king, with consent of Parliament, had power to make laws to bind the colonies, and people of America, in all cases whatsoever";—all had been duly noted by the vigilant and patriotic mind of Washington. He saw with apprehension the growing discontent, and the people rising against taxation; this feeling was intensified and increased when he heard of the embarkation of two regiments of troops to overawe the people; tidings of the refusal of the "Select men" to find quarters for the soldiers on their arrival; these events and many more, came to his knowledge; but he preserved his equanimity, for the voice of his country had not yet invoked his personal interference. His diary, at this period, evinces the tranquillity which he enjoyed at Mount Vernon, in his agricultural pursuits, his hunting, his duck shooting on the Potomac, his dinners at Mount Vernon and Belvoir with his old friend Lord Fairfax. We find him writing to his friend George Mason, and discussing all the points at issue between the colonies and the mother country; exhibiting in his remarks the grand principles by which his conduct was afterward regulated, and yet showing that he could apply to England incidentally the title of *home*. It was perhaps not yet too late to prevent extremities. Lord Botetourt was appointed governor of the province. Of him Walpole had said that he would turn the heads of the Virginians one way or the other, and either excite their animosities, or captivate them by his personal graces. He entertained many erroneous ideas in reference to the colony, and opened the session of the House in state as the king was accustomed to open Parliament, proceeding to the capitol in his coach drawn by six white horses; and, after delivering his speech, returning to his palace with the same preposterous pomp. But the Virginia legislators were occupied with matters of more serious importance. They came to contend for their rights; they adopted spirited resolutions; they condemned the recent act of Parliament imposing taxes; and declared that the power of doing so was vested in the House of Burgesses alone.

Their fellow-patriots of New England manifested their sympathy with the heroic stand taken by Virginia. As Massachusetts was at that time without a General Assembly, the contest was continued by the Virginia Legislature; and in an address to the king it was asserted, that all crimes and misdemeanors should be tried by his majesty's courts within the colony; at the same time beseeching him to prevent the miseries resulting from sending persons charged with crime to England, depriving them of the privilege of trial by jury, and of producing witnesses in their defence. Dismayed or incensed by these high-toned proceedings, Lord Botetourt dissolved the House of Burgesses. The spirit of resistance being once aroused, was not to be allayed; but his lordship altered his tactics, became a strenuous advocate for the abolition of the taxes, and quieted the Virginians with the assurance that their demands should be satisfied. Meanwhile, the General Court having met in Boston, sent a committee to the Governor of Massachusetts to say, that they could not transact business while the town was invested by sea and land, while cannon were pointed at their door, and a military guard kept the

State House; requesting these obstructions to be taken away during their sitting. The governor replied that he had no authority to do so; the court, therefore, did not sit, and when in session at Cambridge, where they met, the governor sent a message to demand money and quarters for the support and accommodation of the troops. The demand was refused, as hostile to the rights of the colony.

A change took place at this period in the British Cabinet. The Duke of Grafton was succeeded by Lord North. In March an act was passed by which all the duties imposed in 1767 were revoked, *except that on tea.* This measure involved the whole question in dispute; and the people resolved to purchase no more tea till the repeal of the duty. The disingenuous conduct of the ministers had the effect of mortifying Lord Botetourt, who asked for his discharge; but before it arrived, he died of an attack of bilious fever, which overcame a frame already debilitated by vexation. He had become popular with the Virginians; the House of Burgesses decreed the erection of a statue to his memory; and he yet gives name to a county in that State. Washington at this period made an expedition to the Ohio, to ascertain whether the soldiers had obtained the lands promised them. The frontier was then in a disordered state; some traders and squatters were murdered, and further trouble was apprehended. He visited Fort Pitt, then garrisoned by two companies. A hamlet consisting of a few log houses, called the town, composed what is now the populous and flourishing city of Pittsburg. He descended the Ohio as far as the great Kanawha; breakfasted at Log-town; and in the progress of his journey gratified his passion for hunting by the pursuit of deer, and the shooting of wild turkeys. He made frequent notes of the appearance of the country, and of the quality of the soil. After his return home, the hazardous nature of his journey became apparent by another outbreak of the Indian tribes, which took place on the Ohio, in which Colonel Lewis and a number of Virginians were murdered on the banks of the great Kanawha.

The paternal conduct of Washington toward the two children of his wife, has already been referred to. His sensibilities were now put to a severe test by the illness and death of Miss Custis, in her seventeenth year. She had always been of a feeble constitution, and early in the summer of 1773 became rapidly worse. Washington had been absent for a period; and on his return he discovered that a pulmonary disease rendered her recovery hopeless. He was greatly afflicted; and, kneeling at her bedside, he offered the most fervent petitions to the great Disposer of events for her recovery. He remained at home after her death, to offer what consolation he could to Mrs. Washington. Great difficulty had been experienced by Washington in the office of guardian to John Parke Custis, who was the centre of his mother's hopes, on account of the decease of her daughter. He was a sensitive and susceptible youth; possessed a large and independent fortune; and his mother greatly indulged him. An Episcopal clergyman had been his instructor at Annapolis, but he often neglected his studies, and joined the family at Mount Ver non. His education was consequently very imperfect. When his guardian returned from the Ohio, he found that a resolution had been adopted to send him on his travels with his clerical tutor. The scheme was given up at the prudent intervention of Washington, after which he formed a matrimonial engagement. Washington opposed the marriage also, as being too premature, and wrote to this effect to the lady's father, Mr. Benedict Calvert. He then took young Custis to New York, and placed him in King's College, an institution now known as Columbia College. This event occurred previous to the death of his sister; and within a year afterward, before he had attained the age of twenty, he married the object of his affection, on February 3d, 1774. Washington at that time made no opposition to the match, though he was opposed to early marriages as well as to early travel.

The Earl of Dunmore had been appointed Governor of Virginia on the death of Lord Botetourt. Differences with the Assembly caused him to prorogue it; but a convention of it became necessary in March, 1773. A committee of eleven was appointed to obtain accurate intelligence of those acts and resolutions of the British Parliament which affected the interests of Virginia, and also to open communications with the sister colonies. These committees accomplished much for the cause of liberty. Friendly relations were maintained by Washington with Lord Dunmore; and at the time of the lamented death of Miss Custis, he had intended to accompany his lordship on a tour to the western frontiers, but that bereavement interfered with the arrangement.

During several years no tea was imported into the colonies; but orders were issued in 1773 to the East India Company, to send several cargoes to America; and as large quantities had accumulated, it was resolved to force the purchase of the tea on the colonies. Several ships were freighted with the commodity, but the people of New York and Philadelphia would not permit it to be landed. At Charleston it was unloaded, but it was ruined in the damp cellars. At Boston the inhabitants, disguised as Indians, boarded the ships on the night of December 18th, forced open the chests, and threw the tea into the sea. To humble and punish the Bostonians, the concentrated wrath of the British Government was vented by an act called the Boston Port Bill, by which the port of Boston was blockaded, and the custom-house transferred to Salem, in June, 1774. The judges of the courts were to be appointed by the king, and offences were to be tried thenceforth in Great Britain.

Washington had dined with Lord Dunmore on the 16th of May; the House of Burgesses had been convened; and a ball was resolved upon to compliment Lady Dunmore, who had recently joined her husband with her numerous family of sons and daughters. All seemed propitious till the news of the Boston Port Bill arrived, and both pleasure and business were then laid aside. The 1st of June was appointed as a day of humiliation and prayer. On the next day, when in the midst of an animated debate, Lord Dunmore sent for the Burgesses to appear at the council chamber; and in a laconic speech immediately declared the House dissolved. The Burgesses adjourned to the Raleigh tavern, and resolved that the Boston Port Bill was inimical to the liberties of North America; recommended the disuse of all East Indian commodities; declared taxation an attack on the rights of all the colonies; ordered a communication to be opened with the colonies, and recommended a general organization, or congress, to meet annually. Washington and the Burgesses were still on good terms with his lordship, notwithstanding their differences of opinion and policy.

On the 1st of June, 1774, the Boston Port Bill was carried into effect, and General Gage appointed to execute the designs of the British Cabinet, being appointed to the military command of Massachusetts. He thought that with five regiments he could keep Boston in subjection. At the suggestion of the Assembly, a paper called "a solemn league and covenant" was put in circulation by the committee of correspondence. The subscribers were bound by it to cease all intercourse with Great Britain, and with those who refused to enter the compact, till their chartered and invaded rights should be restored. Alarm pervaded the country when it became known that Boston was blockaded. Washington was appointed moderator of a meeting held in Fairfax County, in the end of June; and was chosen chairman of a committee to draw up resolutions, and report them to the general meeting to take place in the court-house on the 18th of July. Bryan Fairfax, the brother of George William, was shocked at the course affairs were taking; and in a letter to Washington advised the sending of a petition to the king. Washington answered that it would be useless, as this had been frequently done already. When the committee assembled, of which Washington was the chairman, resolutions were offered involving the various matters at issue. He was appointed a delegate to the general convention of the province, to meet at Williamsburg on the 1st of August. On the assembling of this convention, he is said to have spoken with great earnestness; which was a proof of his zeal in the cause, as he was not ordinarily vehement in speech. It is affirmed that his enthusiasm rose very high; and that he declared himself ready to raise one thousand men, support them at his own expense, and march at their head to relieve Boston.

General Gage was in great perplexity as to the proper policy to be pursued toward the inhabitants of Boston. They acted with so much coolness and determination, that he did not know how to proceed in reference to them; whereas, had their conduct been disorderly, his duty would have been plain and easy. The commerce of the city was at an end; the wharfs were deserted, and the grass beginning to grow in the streets; but everything was conducted with the utmost decorum, though town meetings took place frequently. These meetings produced, at length, so powerful an effect, as to require an act of government forbidding them; but they still were held, the liberty tree became a rallying place for every popular movement, and a flag hoisted on its summit was saluted by the citizens as the emblem of the rights and purposes of the people.

CHAPTER XIV.

FIRST CONTINENTAL CONGRESS IN PHILADELPHIA—ITS PROCEEDINGS—WASHINGTON AT MOUNT VERNON—GENERALS PUTNAM AND LEE IN BOSTON—THEIR ANTECEDENTS—MAJOR GATES AND THE VISITORS AT MOUNT VERNON—LEE'S FONDNESS FOR SINGULAR PETS—WASHINGTON A DELEGATE TO THE RICHMOND CONVENTION—SPEECH OF PATRICK HENRY—WASHINGTON'S CONVICTIONS CORROBORATED—BATTLES OF LEXINGTON AND CONCORD—THE WAR BEGUN—VIEWS OF WASHINGTON.

PATRICK HENRY and Edmund Pendleton joined Washington at Mount Vernon, and in his company proceeded to Philadelphia, to attend the first Continental Congress, which assembled in that city on Monday, the 5th of September, 1774, in Carpenter's Hall. All the colonies, Georgia alone excepted, were represented on this memorable occasion, which saw fifty-one delegates convened to lay the foundations of a mighty empire. A preliminary question having arisen respecting the way in which votes should be taken, on account of the inequality of the number of delegates from different colonies, Patrick Henry repudiated the idea of sectional distinctions. Said he: "*I am not a Virginian, but an American.*" It was finally determined that each colony should have one vote; and Mr. Duché, an Episcopal clergyman, being invited to officiate as chaplain, engaged in prayer. In the lesson for the seventh day, the Psalter contains the thirty-fifth Psalm, where David prays for the Divine protection: "Take hold of shield and buckler, and stand up for my help. Draw out, also, the spear, and stop the way of them that persecute me. Say unto my soul, I am thy salvation." It has been remarked that Washington knelt on this occasion, while others stood. It was an impressive season, and every-one was affected with the prayer offered up in such peculiar circumstances. The Congress was held with closed doors; but a deep and significant silence prevailed, which was at length broken by the eloquent speech of Patrick Henry, and by the chaste and classical address of Richard Henry Lee.

Congress, by a resolution, declared their opinion respecting the late acts of Parliament, terming them a violation of the rights of the people of Massachusetts, and expressing their resolution to resist in case of necessity. In "a declaration of colonial rights" which they adopted, they claimed all the privileges of Englishmen, and the power of legislating in provincial assemblies. They asserted that the common law of England was their birthright, and regarded the maintenance of a standing army as unconstitutional and subversive of their liberties. The acts of Parliament in the reign of George the Third, known as "the sugar act, the stamp act, the two acts for quartering troops, and the tea act," were specified as infringements of their franchises. The chief measures of this Congress were remarkable for unanimity and acuteness; and the papers prepared by it are acknowledged to be master-pieces of practical talent and political sagacity. What part Washington took in the debates of this session is not certainly known, as the discussions were involved in secrecy. Doubtless they were worthy of himself and beneficial to his country. He returned to Mount Vernon; and his presence there was more necessary to cheer Mrs. Washington, in her loneliness, after the decease of her daughter, as George William Fairfax had returned to England, to take possession of immense wealth to which he had fallen heir. Belvoir, his Virginia estate, was left in charge of the steward of Mount Vernon; an accident subsequently burnt the mansion to the ground, and it was never rebuilt.

A report had prevailed, during the sittings of the Congress, that Boston was cannonaded. The people of Massachusetts had become excited by the presence of a menacing military force, and disciplined themselves, accumulating arms and ammunition in several places, for the purpose of meeting emergencies. Gage ordered all these magazines to be seized, and in particular the arsenal northwest of Charlestown.

News of its capture having spread abroad, thousands of patriots collected, and were with difficulty kept from marching toward Boston. Gage became surprised that so many of the other provinces took an interest in the proceedings occurring in Massachusetts. Commissions that arrived for colonial officers were not accepted; or, if accepted, were soon resigned; and Generals Putnam and Charles Lee appeared on a visit to Boston. Putnam was a veteran soldier; had served at Louisburg, at Fort Duquesne, and at Crown Point. He was taken by the Indians and condemned to be burnt, but was rescued; and after returning again to rural pursuits, his patriotic heart was stirred within him. He was appointed chairman of the committee of vigilance, and the line of his duties led him to Boston. General Charles Lee was an Englishman by birth, had served under Abercrombie and Prideaux, and was distinguished in a number of battles. He had served in Portugal with renown; was aide-de-camp to the monarch of that country; returned to England in 1766, and in 1769 entered the Polish service with the rank of major-general. He arrived in America in 1773, and at once took an active part in the political agitations of the country. He went to Boston, according to his own account, out of mere curiosity to see a people placed in such singular circumstances. A self-elected assembly of ninety members convened at Salem, and voted themselves a provincial Congress, choosing John Hancock as their president. Officers were appointed, and a militia organized, with an order and system which proved formidable to General Gage.

General Charles Lee and Major Horatio Gates were frequent guests at Mount Vernon, after their return to Virginia; and Washington was pleased with their visits at that time, inasmuch as they were skilled in military affairs, and both were interested in the popular cause. Major Gates was an Englishman, liberally educated, and had served as a volunteer with General Edward Cornwallis, Governor of Halifax. He was wounded in the defeat of Braddock; and subsequently, as major of brigade, he accompanied General Monckton to the West Indies, and distinguished himself at the capture of Martinique. He was appointed major of a regiment of foot, and received a commission in the royal troops. He sold out his commission, emigrated to Virginia in 1772, and then became acquainted and intimate with Washington. This singular man had a prodigious passion for dogs, which he trained to take their seats with him at table; because, as he said, he "must have some object to embrace." With Putnam, Lee, and Gates, Washington became afterward closely connected, during the memorable struggle for independence.

Washington attended the second Virginia convention at Richmond in March, 1755, as a delegate from Fairfax County. Patrick Henry, in a speech delivered at that time, said: "We must fight, Mr. Speaker; I repeat it, sir, we must fight! An appeal to arms and the God of Hosts, is all that is left us." Such was also the conviction of Washington, and he suggested a plan for carrying on the war; for though not one of the first to take up arms, he was the person best fitted for marshalling troops, and vigorously carrying on the conflict in the face of danger and difficulty. "It is my full intention," said he, in a letter to his brother, "if needful, to devote my life and fortune to the cause."

Open hostilities at length commenced. Four thousand men had been added to the British troops in Boston. General Gage determined to seize the magazine at Concord, and detached a force on the 18th of April, 1775, to carry that design into effect. Dr. Joseph Warren sent information of the affair to John Hancock and Samuel Adams, and the committee of safety ordered the cannon to be collected, and part of the stores to be removed. Dr. Warren dispatched two messengers by different routes to give warning of the approach of the king's troops. They arrived at Boston before the orders had been promulgated, that no one should leave the town. A lantern was, at the same time, according to a signal agreed upon, suspended from the upper window of a church in the direction of Charlestown; and thus the adjacent country received the alarm. Guns were fired, and the sound of the village bells assured Colonel Smith that the country was rising. He was but a few miles distant, and sent back for reinforcements. Major Pitcairn was sent with six companies, and orders were given to seize the bridge of Concord. Pitcairn was within a mile and a half of Lexington before a horseman had alarmed the village. Drums were beaten, guns were fired, and when he approached the church, about eighty yeomen were equipped and marshalled on the green. Pitcairn rode up, waved his sword, and exclaimed: "Disperse, ye villains! Lay down your arms, ye rebels, and disperse." The order was unheeded, and a discharge of musketry took place on both sides. The fire was irregular, but that of the British produced the greater effect. Ten were killed and eight wounded, and the patriots were put to flight.

When Colonel Smith marched forward within six miles of Concord, the country was aroused, the militia were mustered on the parade-ground near the church, and the Lincoln yeomanry had joined them. News had arrived that the British, in their advance to Concord, had fired on the people of Lexington. Great indignation prevailed in the vicinity, and the whole militia pouring out, formed two battalions. About seven o'clock in the morning the British came in sight of Concord. Two hours were taken up in attempting to destroy the military stores, but with little effect, as the greater part of them had been removed. Meanwhile, four hundred and fifty militia were collected at Concord. About ten o'clock the British approached them, fired upon them, and killed two persons, wounding a third. The Americans returned the fire, and pursued the British across the bridge. The remaining military stores were destroyed, the dead buried, and the wounded put on conveyances. Smith then retreated to Boston. His troops were wearied, and subjected to the most harrassing retaliation on the part of the assembled and hostile yeomanry. Along the public roads, when they passed through the woods, and from behind walls and other structures, they were fired upon, and many of them slain. For some miles they had to march through woods, defiles, or places skirted by fences, and there many were shot down, and others even expired from sheer exhaustion. Colonel Smith was wounded before he reached Lexington; and Lord Percy's brigade of a thousand men, with two field-pieces, met them. His brigade opened their ranks, and forming a hollow square, the exhausted men lay down to rest upon the ground. He commenced to fire with the two field-pieces, and thus kept the Americans at bay. The Provincials had fought without a leader, but now General Heath led them on, and rallied them in martial array. Dr. Warren rode rapidly from Boston, and became one of the most efficient officers on the field. Lord Percy continued the retreat. A galling fire was kept up on his rear by the Americans, who pursued him at every step. He himself made a narrow escape from death, being struck by a ball, which glanced from his waistcoat button.

Washington says of this scene: "If the retreat had not been as precipitate as it was — and God knows it could not well have been more so — the ministerial troops must have surrendered, or been totally cut off." The firing was heard in Boston, and when Gage ascertained the result, he was overwhelmed with surprise that the raw recruits of the Americans could resist, much less defeat, the well-trained and veteran troops of England. The British in this engagement had seventy-three killed, and one hundred and seventy-four wounded; the Americans forty-nine killed, thirty-nine wounded, and five missing.

The whole country now became fully aroused and inflamed. The condition of Virginia at this period was critical. Lord Dunmore had seized the munitions of war in the province. The cry went forth that the freedom of the colonies was at last to be secured; and Washington was designated as the proper person to assume the command of the patriots. He was at Mount Vernon, preparing to attend the second Continental Congress as a delegate from Virginia, when the news of the battle at Lexington reached him, and cast a gloomy shadow over the charming and tranquil scene. These were his thoughts on this crisis: "Unhappy it is to reflect, that a brother's sword has been sheathed in a brother's breast; and that the once happy and peaceful plains of America are to be either drenched with blood, or inhabited by slaves. Sad alternative! But can a virtuous man hesitate in his choice?"

The Revolution rapidly advanced. Thirty thousand men were immediately requisite for the defence of the country; and of these Massachusetts gallantly resolved to raise thirteen thousand five hundred.

CHAPTER XV.

ETHAN ALLEN AND THE GREEN MOUNTAIN BOYS—BENEDICT ARNOLD—CAPTURE OF TICONDEROGA AND CROWN POINT—CANADA OPENED TO THE PATRIOTS—THE SECOND CONGRESS APPOINTS WASHINGTON COMMANDER-IN-CHIEF OF THE CONTINENTAL ARMY—HIS REMARKS ON THE OCCASION—HE SELECTS HIS GENERALS AND OFFICERS—BRITISH REINFORCEMENTS UNDER HOWE—BURGOYNE AND CLINTON—SEIZURE OF THE HEIGHTS OF CHARLESTOWN—BREED'S HILL AND BUNKER HILL—FORTIFICATIONS—SURPRISE OF GENERAL GAGE—THE BATTLE OF BUNKER HILL—ITS RESULTS.

THE appeals made by the circular letters which were issued by the committee of safety, met with prompt attention; and bodies of militia flocked to the standard of the patriots at Boston, from New Hampshire, Rhode Island, and Connecticut. With the troops of the latter came Israel Putnam, who had lately been appointed brigadier-general. The command of the camp at Boston was given to General Artemas Ward, who had served as lieutenant-general under Abercrombie.

Some bold spirits in Connecticut conceived the design of surprising Ticonderoga and Crown Point--an idea secretly favored by the Legislature of Connecticut. The greatest accession of troops came from "The New Hampshire Grants," on which Ethan Allen and his lieutenants, Seth Warner and Remember Baker, had once set the authority of New York at defiance, and formed an association called the "Green Mountain Boys." They now offered their services in the popular cause, and with two hundred and seventy men, under Ethan Allen, an advance was made to Castleton, near Lake Champlain. Detachments were sent to bring all the boats to Shoreham, opposite Ticonderoga. At Castleton Benedict Arnold joined the patriots. He also entertained designs on Ticonderoga, and had been appointed to raise a force of four hundred men in Western Massachusetts. He hastened to overtake the march, showed his commission, and aspired to the command; but the Green Mountain Boys would follow no leader except Ethan Allen. Allen and Arnold reached the fort with eighty men; mounted a hill under the direction of a boy in the vicinity; baffled the first sentry, and granted the life of another on condition of being led to the quarters of Captain Delaplace, the commandant, who was yet in bed. The appearance of the party so unexpectedly, greatly astonished him. "By whose authority do you act?" he exclaimed. "In the name of the Great Jehovah and the Continental Congress," replied Allen. The garrison of forty men were sent, with their captain, prisoners of war to Hartford. The fortress was full of military and naval stores.

Colonel Seth Warner was now sent with a detachment against Crown Point, which surrendered on the 12th of May, 1775. The garrison consisted of twelve men and a sergeant. The captors found in it upwards of an hundred cannon. Arnold now claimed to command Ticonderoga, but was compelled to yield to the greater popularity of Allen. On the arrival of a schooner and some boats, a project was formed to surprise St. John's on the Sorel River, the frontier port of Canada. Cannon were put on board, and Arnold, who was a seaman, took the command; while Allen and the Green Mountain Boys embarked in the boats. Arnold outsailed the latter, captured the garrison of St. John's, consisting of twelve men and a sergeant, a king's sloop carrying seventy guns, two brass pounders and seven men; and hearing that troops were on the way from Montreal and Chamblee, sailed off with his prisoners and prizes. He met Allen, who had been foiled in his attempt at garrisoning St. John's with Green Mountain Boys, as a larger force had arrived. He therefore returned to Ticonderoga. This gave the patriots the command of the Lakes George and Champlain, and opened the way to Canada.

The second Congress assembled at Philadelphia on the 10th of May, 1775, and Washington was appointed chairman of all the committees having jurisdiction over military matters. There was much discussion during the session in reference to the army before Boston, and the subject of the appointment of a commander-in-chief engrossed much attention.

On the 15th of June, 1775, the pay of the commander-in-chief was fixed at five hundred dollars a month. The forces were to be called the Continental Army, and that under General Gage the Ministerial Army. Mr. Johnson, of Maryland, rose and nominated Washington for the post of commander-in-chief. The election was made by ballot, and was unanimous. Washington then rose in his place, and gave expression to his grateful sense of the honor conferred upon him, and his devotion in the service of his country; but he added that, lest some unlucky event should happen unfavorable to his reputation, he desired every gentleman to remember that he declared, with the utmost sincerity, that he did not think himself equal to the command with which he was honored. As to salary, he begged leave to assure the Congress that, as no pecuniary consideration could have tempted him to accept this arduous trust at the expense of his domestic happiness, he did not wish to make any profit by it. He declared that he would keep an exact account of his expenses, which, he did not doubt, they would discharge; and that was all he desired. Four major-generals were appointed. General Ward was placed second in command, next to him was General Lee; the other two were Philip Schuyler, of New York, and Israel Putnam, of Connecticut. Seth Pomeroy, Richard Montgomery, David Wooster, William Heath, Joseph Spencer, John Thomas, John Sullivan, and Nathaniel Greene, were appointed brigadier-generals. Major Horatio Gates, at the request of Washington, was appointed adjutant-general, with the rank of brigadier.

Washington received his commission from Congress on the 20th of June, and, at the request of several officers, made a review of some companies of militia, horse and foot. At this period he was forty-three years of age; and as he sat on his horse, his manly grace and commanding presence delighted every beholder, and he was received with general acclamations.

During the deliberations of Congress, the town of

Boston was blockaded, water was cut off from the country around it, no fresh provisions could be obtained, and much privation was suffered by the city in consequence. Reinforcements, under Generals Howe, Burgoyne, and Clinton, all of whom were commanders of reputation, arrived on the 25th of May from England. General Gage determined to take the field; the province was put under martial law, and pardon was offered to all who would lay down their arms, excepting only John Hancock and Samuel Adams. The proclamation had no other effect than that of putting the patriots on the alert. Their number daily increased, and at length amounted to fifteen thousand men, who were variously distributed. They presented a miscellaneous gathering of four distinct bodies, of whom ten thousand belonged to Massachusetts, under the command of Artemas Ward. His head-quarters were at Cambridge. The troops were mostly undisciplined recruits, and many of them were without military accoutrements. They were distributed over a space of ten or twelve miles Boston, at that period, had a population of seventeen thousand; and the garrison of British troops, well disciplined, amounted to ten thousand. They were hemmed in by the besiegers, and an engagement was desired on both sides, in which each felt confident of success. A project was formed to seize the heights of the peninsula, opposite to the north side of Boston, called Charlestown. Secret intelligence had informed the Americans of the intention of General Gage to seize Dorchester Heights on the 18th of June; and this determined them to hurry forward the project of taking Charlestown Heights. These had lately been reconnoitred by Richard Fridley, an experienced engineer. For this purpose troops were detached from the Massachusetts regiments, including two hundred men under Captain Knowlton, from Putnam's Connecticut troops, and forty-nine artillery-men, with two field-pieces, under Captain Samuel Gridley.

The time agreed on for the attack was the 16th of June; and at sunset twelve hundred men met on the common before General Ward's quarters, with packs, blankets, and twenty-four hours' provisions. After prayers they set out in silence, ignorant of their destination. Colonel Prescott was chosen to command the enterprise, and he carried written orders to fortify and defend Bunker Hill till it was relieved; Colonel Richard Gridley was to plan the fortifications, and reinforcements were to be sent to aid the fatigue party in the morning. The detachment with Colonel Prescott at its head, left Cambridge at nine o'clock, and was joined at Charlestown Neck by Major Brooks and General Putnam. It was here that the wagons, which were full of tools for intrenchment, suggested to the men the first idea of the purpose intended. They now came near the ground, over which the British kept constant watch, having erected a battery almost opposite to Charlestown. Five vessels were stationed so as to command Charlestown Neck. Col Prescott led his men across this isthmus without being discovered, and began the ascent of Bunker Hill, whose altitude is a hundred and twelve feet; the summit being reached by a declivity which extends from the Neck to the top of the hill, about three hundred yards; and then, declining south, connects with Breed's Hill, whose height is about seventy feet. The hill-tops are seven hundred yards from each other. The height being attained, the next point to be decided was, which hill should first be fortified? The written orders designated Bunker Hill, but Breed's Hill was nearest to Boston, and commanded both it and the shipping. After a good deal of debate on the question, as the night waned, it was determined to fortify Breed's Hill, and the enterprise was undertaken with great spirit; but, in consequence of having wasted much time in discussion, it was midnight before they commenced. Prescott assumed the responsibility of the occasion, and sent twice to the water's edge to observe the enemy. All was still quiet there, so that the sentry's cry of "All's well" could be distinctly heard in the streets of Boston, as well as the call of the watch on board the ships of war in the port.

The labor of erecting intrenchments proceeded with such energy and spirit, that by the dawn of day a strong redoubt, with a breastwork partly cannon proof, connected the summit of Breed's Hill with the slough. The purpose of Prescott was accomplished; but in the morning the Lively, the nearest ship, brought her guns to bear, and fired upon the hill. Other ships in the port did the same. One man was killed; and when the question was propounded to Prescott what was to be done, his laconic answer was: "Bury him." His fall had an effect on some of his comrades, who left the hill, and did not return. The cannonading disturbed the morning slumbers of the Bostonians, and of General Gage, who could scarcely believe the testimony of his senses. Seeing the tall figure of Prescott, he was anxious to know his name, and whether he would fight. Being answered in the affirmative, he replied: "Then the works must be carried." He summoned a council of war, in which a majority, among whom were Clinton and Grant, advised that troops should be landed on Charlestown Neck, and attack and dislodge the Americans, under the cover of the batteries. Gage objected to this plan, because it would place his army under two fires. He considered it better to push directly up the hill; and thought that in a hand-to-hand encounter, raw militia would be wholly inefficient in comparison with his disciplined troops.

The bustle of military preparations at length informed the wearied Americans that the town of Boston was alarmed, and that disciplined soldiers were mustering to attack the rudely-fortified height. After some delay, Colonels Stark and Read marched to the relief of Prescott. Each soldier received two flints, fifteen balls, and a gill of powder; which, as it had not been put up in cartridges, had to be carried in powder-horns, or loosely in the pocket. The balls, also, had to be suited to the calibre of the different guns, as in many instances they varied in size. The troops on Breed's Hill gallantly bore the fire from the ships and the battery on Copp's Hill, returning an occasional shot, the men fortifying themselves more strongly; and at 11 o'clock, having placed their intrenching tools in the rear, with anxious impatience they awaited reinforcements and supplies. Some misunderstanding arose between Generals Putnam and

Prescott about the intrenching tools. They were afterward taken to Bunker Hill, and an important breastwork was erected under the direction of Putnam. Twenty-eight barges, with a large detachment of grenadiers, rangers, and light infantry, under the command of Major-General Howe, making a splendid appearance, in well-appointed military equipments, were seen at noon crossing in parallel lines from Boston, while a heavy fire proceeded from the ships in the port. General Howe paused on Breed's Hill. The troops were more strongly intrenched than he had expected, and he sent to Gage for additional forces and ammunition. In the meantime, "grog" was served out to the British troops; and the American soldiers, by this time both hungry and thirsty, saw the foe eating and drinking. Their own refreshment consisted in fortifying their position better; and Putnam, meantime, sent Captain Knowlton to cover a pass which, if unguarded, might enable the enemy to turn their flank, and seize on Bunker Hill. A double fence was constructed by pulling up the posts and rails of other fences, and filling the intervening space with newly-mown hay. While this work was being accomplished, Putnam sent his son, Captain Putnam, to hasten the march of the troops from Cambridge; and meanwhile the veteran Stark arrived with five hundred men. Warren, who had opposed the occupation of the heights, arrived at two o'clock, to aid in their perilous defence. He declined the command at the post offered him by Putnam, and ultimately took his stand at the redoubt. Nearly seven hundred feet intervened between the redoubt and the fences; but the latter proved a great protection to the redoubt notwithstanding.

As Warren entered the redoubt, the troops loudly cheered him. He again declined the command tendered him by Prescott. The British, anticipating an easy victory, now prepared for a general attack. While General Howe was to advance with the right wing, and turn the American flank, cutting off their retreat, General Pigot was ordered to ascend and force the redoubt. The Americans reserved their fire till the enemy were within forty paces, and then poured upon them so deadly a volley, that it produced immense carnage. Another subsequent advance was met with a more destructive fire than before; and Pigot was compelled to retreat. Stark, Read, and Knowlton, forming the left wing, in the meantime were attacked in their positions by General Howe's troops. The Americans suffered little loss, and had orders not to fire till the enemy were within a very short distance. Some of them neglected this order; whereupon Putnam swore that he would cut down the first man who fired contrary to orders. At the proper time rifles, muskets, and fowling-pieces were discharged with deadly effect; the slaughter became terrible, and the British were put to confusion. The advancing enemy halted; Prescott praised his men, and exhorted them to restrain their next fire till the word of command was given.

The British ascended again to attack the redoubt. Charlestown was now in flames; and the thunder of artillery from the ships, the bursting of bombs, the report of musketry, and the shouts of those engaged in the deadly strife, were terrible. The Americans again reserved their fire till the enemy was near, and then poured in another volley with the most dreadful result. The continued and irregular stream of fire caused the enemy to stagger, as they advanced after the first shock. Whole ranks were then mowed down; many officers were slain or wounded; and the enemy again retreated. These achievements were performed in the presence of thousands of every age and sex, who beheld them from the roofs and towers of Boston. General Howe's officers remonstrated against a third attack in front; and it was then resolved to take the redoubt in flank, where a weak point was presented between the breastwork and the fortified fence.

The Americans were now found to be in want of ammunition, and the foe prepared to take advantage of this misfortune, and carry the works at the point of the bayonet. General Howe led the main body against the fortified fence, and a severe fire drove the Americans from the breastwork; while balls entered the sallyports, and great damage was effected. The works were again assaulted; the Americans fired with fatal precision, which carried death to several officers, and General Howe himself was wounded. But his soldiers now rushed forward with fixed bayonets, and Pigot and Clinton advanced, so that the redoubt was attacked on three sides simultaneously. Several mounted to the back of the redoubt. The first exclaimed: "The day is ours." He was instantly shot down. Their ammunition being exhausted, the Americans fought hand to hand with desperate courage, using their bayonets, the butt-ends of muskets, and even stones. Prescott then gave the order to retreat; two divisions cut their way through the enemy, and the patriotic Warren received a mortal wound.

While these events were being enacted, Stark, Read, and Knowlton, the brave defenders of the fortified fence, resisted till after Colonel Prescott had left the hill. Their purpose being effected, they abandoned the weak outpost, and retired slowly, with admirable order. Among the valuable officers who fell in this battle was Major Pitcairn. The heroic Warren, whom his friends had in vain dissuaded from the perils of this conflict, died, repeating the beautiful and patriotic words of the Roman poet: *Dulce et decorum est, pro patria mori.* His death was an incalculable loss to his country.

The British, in this memorable battle, had one thousand men slain and wounded, out of three thousand; while the American loss was four hundred and fifty, out of fifteen hundred. This conflict taught the patriots that they could cope successfully with the best troops of England, even when commanded by her most distinguished generals.

CHAPTER XVI.

WASHINGTON'S JOURNEY TO THE ARMY — ITS CONDITION AND DEFICIENCY IN POWDER, CLOTHING, AND INTRENCHING TOOLS — THE FORCES OF THE ENEMY, THEIR POSITION, SUPERIOR DISCIPLINE, AND EQUIPMENTS — GENERAL GREENE — THE COMMANDER-IN-CHIEF ENFORCES STRICT DISCIPLINE — HIS ESTABLISHNENT AT HEAD-QUARTERS — GREAT ANXIETY IN CONSEQUENCE OF THE WANT OF POWDER — WRITES FOR A SUPPLY TO TICONDEROGA, AND THE JERSEYS — BOLD PROJECT — CORRESPONDENCE WITH GENERAL GAGE — ITS EFFECTS — DESCRIPTION OF EVENTS TRANSPIRING AT A DISTANCE FROM HEAD-QUARTERS — RIVALRY OF ARNOLD AND ALLEN — PROJECTS FOR THE POSSESSION OF CANADA.

WHEN General Washington had advanced twenty miles from Philadelphia, on his way to the army posted at Boston, accompanied by Generals Schuyler and Lee, he met a courier, riding at full speed, carrying despatches to Congress, with tidings of the battle of Bunker Hill. In answer to his eager inquiry respecting the conduct of the militia, he was assured of their bravery, their reception of their enemy's fire, and their own effective fighting. He was satisfied, and exclaimed: "The liberties of the country are safe." On arriving at the camp at Boston, he found the army numbered fourteen thousand five hundred men. Several circumstances rendered them less efficient than might have been expected from their numbers. The time had not been well employed in discipline and preparation, as it was hoped that an open rupture between England and her colonies might have been avoided. On examining the magazines, soon after his arrival, Washington ascertained that only nine cartridges could be furnished to each soldier. The supply of powder was not to be obtained from Congress, but from committees and other sources, who, in different localities, had collected small quantities for their defence. There was also a deficiency in arms, and many were of a quality so inferior, as to render them nearly useless. The troops were almost destitute of clothing, and had no tents under which to be sheltered. The siege of Boston was to be conducted without engineers or intrenching tools, as there was so great a deficiency in these important requisites, that such as existed were scarcely deserving of notice. There was also a good deal of dissatisfaction with many, respecting the officers selected by Congress; the officers, in some of the colonies, having been chosen by the soldiers, and were therefore very inimical to the exercise of proper discipline. Yet the general, on viewing such a large number of able-bodied men, who were zealous in the cause of their country, and were no doubt possessed of courage, was pleased to find that he had "good materials for an army," and set himself about organizing and disciplining it, so as to bring it up to the necessary standard.

On making particular inquiries respecting the situation and resources of the enemy intrenched in Boston, Washington concluded that the works might be taken, though the effort was attended with difficulties.

In a council of officers, it was the general opinion that an assault should not be undertaken. Beside Gen. Gage, Washington was brought into competition, in this contest, with three other distinguished British commanders. The next in rank to Gage was General William Howe, who possessed a noble person, was six feet in height, and not unlike Washington in appearance. He was a brother of Lord Howe, who fell on the banks of Lake George, whose death the colonies had lamented. He had commanded the light-infantry under the gallant Wolfe, when he was slain on the Plains of Abraham. General Clinton was son of George Clinton, a former Governor of New York; and had seen service on the continent in the seven years' war. General Burgoyne was a natural son of Lord Bingley; he early entered the army; eloped with a daughter of Lord Derby; was lieutenant-colonel of dragoons in 1758; and in 1761 served against Spain. He was also a dramatist, and a man of wit; had been elected to a seat in Parliament; and in 1772 received the rank of major-general.

When Washington reconnoitred the camp of the British, he found everything in admirable order; the works being constructed on the principles of military science, and the troops well disciplined. The main force under General Howe, was intrenching itself on Bunker Hill, near the late battle-field. Their scarlet uniforms presented a bright and striking appearance as they gleamed in the sunlight. Washington observed that the British forces lay very compactly, and had command of the water; so that their main strength might be made to bear on a single point, and thus divide the Americans. One of the American encampments claimed his admiration. Tents and marquées were pitched; the soldiers were well disciplined, and their equipments were complete. Their leader was one who well deserved notice, on account of his importance in the war. The father of Brigadier-General Nathaniel Greene was an anchor-smith and Quaker preacher. His heroic son was born in May, 1742. He had received only a limited education, but was endowed with great natural talents. His spirit had been roused by the late warlike demonstrations. He delighted to study the military art; perused Cæsar's Commentaries and Plutarch's Lives with interest; and having gone to Boston, observed the order and discipline of the British troops. In June, 1775, he brought three regiments before Boston, which proved to be the best appointed in the army. Greene made an address to the general, welcoming him to the camp. He seems to have gained Washington's confidence at once. He continued always one of his most faithful aids, and never lost his esteem.

Washington, observing the perilous situation of the American army, on account of the length and weakness of their lines, summoned a council of war. The difficulty was considered with due attention; and it was thought that an abandonment of the line of works, after so much time and labor had been expended in their construction, would be impolitic, disheartening to the soldiers, and leaving a large tract of country open to the ravages of the enemy. It was therefore concluded best to strengthen the works, occupy them, and augment the army to twenty thousand men. In carrying out this purpose, General Putnam rendered great assistance; and, as Washington remarked, he "seemed to have the faculty of infusing his own spirit into all the workmen he employed."

The army was then divided into three parts. The right wing commanded the heights of Roxborough. It was under the command of Major-General Ward. The left wing had its position on Prospect Hill, and was placed under Major-General Lee. The centre, stationed at Cambridge, was commanded by General Putnam and Brigadier-General Heath. The most rigid discipline was enforced in the army. Every one was made to know his place, and to keep it; or if neglecting to do it, received thirty lashes. The greatest distinction was observed between officers and soldiers, and new orders were read to each regiment every morning after prayers. This usage was thought to be partly owing to General Lee, who daily inspected the lines with the commander, and, it is said, once threatened to cane an officer for unsoldierly conduct. The Legislature of Massachusetts, and the Governor of Connecticut, had earnestly solicited a detachment of troops for the defence of the sea-coast against armed vessels; but Washington, having consulted several of his officers and members of the Continental Congress previous to making his reply, respectfully declined to accede to the request, as tending to weaken the main army. This refusal produced dissatisfaction with some parties, until Congress sanctioned it; and the wisdom of the determination soon became apparent.

The head-quarters at Cambridge assigned to the general manifested liberality on the part of the Assembly of Massachusetts, who designated the house of the president as his residence. A committee was commissioned to procure "a steward, a housekeeper, and two or three women cooks." The wishes of the commander-in-chief were to be complied with respecting the supplies of his table; which, from his high station, required to be furnished in hospitable style; and every day some of the officers dined with him. He was social, but not convivial; and though courteous to his guests, grave matters pressed upon his mind too heavily to allow the indulgences of the table. He subsisted on very simple fare; and at times, only on baked apples, or berries with cream. He early left the table, and on retiring an aide-de-camp took his place. The great purpose of Washington now was, to draw the enemy out of Boston, and try the issue of a general battle. The commander had some time since caused all the live stock within reach to be driven back into the country, and fresh provisions could not be obtained. It was just then that the scarcity of powder was discovered; and Washington sent letters to Rhode Island, the Jerseys, and Ticonderoga, requesting immediate supplies, and stating that any quantity, however small, would be welcome. Writing to Governor Cooke, of Rhode Island, he suggested that an armed vessel should seize on a powder magazine in the island of Bermuda. Days passed by, but no supplies arrived. It did not seem possible to conceal the fatal deficiency much longer from the enemy; because in one camp they could perceive what was transpiring in the other. A secret intercourse sometimes took place between the men. It is thought that the enemy was informed of the deficiency of powder; but did not believe the report, on account of the bold front presented by the Americans. The camp remained during two whole weeks in this critical state, when the imminence of the danger was diminished by the reception of a small supply of powder from the Jerseys; which in some degree relieved the apprehensions of an attack, which were experienced by Washington.

A correspondence now took place between Washington and General Gage, in which the former put his army on a proper footing with respect to the king's troops; claiming perfect equality, and manifesting that the courtesies of civilized warfare were expected from them. He remarked on the ill treatment received by several American officers, who had been confined in the Boston jail; and that those who were of the most respectable rank, had obtained the least consideration. The claims of humanity were urged, and he concluded by remarking that his own conduct toward British prisoners would be regulated by the treatment received by captive Americans. The reply of General Gage contained much that might rouse the indignant feelings of Washington. The latter sent him a very spirited and dignified reply; and concluded with the remark, that if "your officers our prisoners receive a treatment from me different from that which I wished to show them, they and you will remember the occasion of it." This threat was followed by the committal to the common jail of North ampton of certain British officers then at large on parole; they being informed of the reason of it; to the effect that, as no difference in rank had been made in the treatment of American prisoners by General Gage, so none should be made in the treatment of the British. Circumstances subsequently occasioned a recall of this order, and the officers were allowed to remain at large on parole as before.

As Boston was the great centre against which the American commander-in-chief was directing his efforts, he had removed his camp near to it; but, to carry on the object the colonies had in view in resisting the encroachments of Great Britain, it was necessary that the generals of the continental army should lead their troops to battle both in the north and south. These being under the supervision and direction of Washington, we will follow them in their different encounters, which were so many links in the general chain of operations.

Letters received from General Schuyler in July, 1775, rendered Washington apprehensive of dangers from the interior. The Indians, it was said, were being stirred up by the Johnson family, who had great influence; and danger in the rear began to threaten the patriots who, on the seaboard, were fighting for liberty. The rivalry of Arnold and Ethan Allen respecting the command at Ticonderoga, caused the matter to be referred to the Albany Committee, who asked the opinion of that at New York. It was referred in turn by these to the Continental Congress, who accepted of the captured fortress, and committed it to the custody of New York, as it was in that province, with such aid from New England as might be necessary. The idea of the dismantling of Ticonderoga and Crown Point by the order of the Continental Congress, had been exclaimed against by both Arnold and Allen; but both were ambitious of leading an expedition into Canada, and these fortresses would open the way to it. Allen wrote to the New York Assembly to say that an army of two or three thousand men might subdue Canada, unless it were reinforced from England; and Arnold wrote on the same subject to the Continental Congress, stating that, from knowledge then in his possession, two thousand men would suffice to take the province; and proposing himself as the leader of the enterprise.

CHAPTER XVII.

BENEDICT ARNOLD — HIS AMBITION — THROWS UP HIS COMMISSION — GENERAL SCHUYLER ATTEMPTS THE CONQUEST OF CANADA—HIS CORRESPONDENCE WITH WASHINGTON — STATE OF CANADA — SCHUYLER MAKES A TREATY WITH THE SIX NATIONS AT ALBANY — GENERAL MONTGOMERY IN COMMAND — INDIANS IN CAMP AT CAMBRIDGE — MONTGOMERY AND SCHUYLER ON THE WAY TO ST. JOHNS — AFFAIRS IN BOSTON — OPERATIONS IN BOTH CAMPS — EXPEDITION INTRUSTED TO ARNOLD—ATTACK ON ST. JOHN'S ABANDONED—CAPTURE OF ETHAN ALLEN—MONTGOMERY IN COMMAND—GALLANT CONDUCT OF ARNOLD AND HIS MEN — TREASON IN THE CAMP — FALMOUTH BURNT — CAPTURE OF CHAMBLEE — ST. JOHN'S CAPITULATES — ARNOLD AND HIS TROOPS REACH QUEBEC — THEIR INTENSE SUFFERINGS.

ONE of the suggestions made by Arnold was, that no Green Mountain Boys should be received as volunteers; and these now returned home, their time of service being expired. Ethan Allen and Seth Warner proceeded to Congress to obtain the pay due to their men. They resolved to raise another company of Green Mountain Boys, consisting of five hundred men. In the meantime Arnold had had a difficulty with Colonel Hinman, in reference to the command of the fortresses; and was now at Crown Point with one hundred and fifty men. While he expected to achieve a triumph over his rival, his assumption of the command had been complained of to the Assembly of Massachusetts, who now sent a committee of three to inquire into everything relating to his spirit and conduct; and to order him, if expedient, to account for the moneys, arms, stores, and ammunition which he had received. The troops were placed, meanwhile, under the chief officer from Connecticut. Arnold was greatly enraged, and threw up his commission. The disbanded men clamored for their pay, and refused to serve under any other officer. Part of the men joined Arnold on the lake, and he meditated an attack on St. John's. The difficulty was eventually settled by promises of pay made to the men, and Arnold went to Cambridge to settle his accounts. The Congress had, about this period, directed General Schuyler to proceed on the 27th of June to Ticonderoga; and, if possible, to take possession of St. John's and Montreal, and pursue such a course respecting Canada as might seem to him most expedient. At this time political dissensions, and the late success on Lake Champlain, had rendered the Canadians disposed to assist the Americans. The regular troops of Carleton were much reduced. Now was the time, therefore, for the enterprise against Canada, before Carleton was reinforced from England, or had launched the vessels which he was building, on the lake. In a letter to General Trumbull, bearing date July 12th, 1775, Ethan Allen remarked, that but for the incorporation of the Green Mountain Boys into a battalion, by the Continental Congress, he would march with them into Canada, and would invest Montreal without any aid from the colonies. General Schuyler then resolved to stir himself, and he reached Ticonderoga on the 18th of July. Colonel

Hinman was in command of Ticonderoga at the time, or at least was the officer of highest rank.

The garrison of the fort consisted of twelve hundred men. General Schuyler, on assuming the command, sent an agent to Major John Brown in Canada, to gain information in reference to the British force and fortifications, and to feel the public pulse as to the probable result of an attack on St. John's. Meantime he prepared boats, should the enterprise be undertaken. A letter of General Schuyler to Washington about this time, furnishes a curious account of his approach to the fort. He found the men who were placed as sentinels soundly asleep. He declared: "With a penknife only I could have cut off both guards, and then have set fire to the block-house, destroyed the stores, and starved the people here." This occurred at a post where all the stores must be landed from Lake George, and which necessarily required the utmost vigilance. The insubordination of the soldiers, especially of the Connecticut troops, and the difficulties, dangers, and delays which were the consequence, greatly vexed General Schuyler. He complained of these misfortunes to Washington, who consoled and encouraged him by dwelling upon his own greater difficulties at Cambridge, and the persevering spirit with which he encountered them. He informed Schuyler that the difficulties he had incurred were only a miniature of what became a full-length portrait at head-quarters; and drew such a picture of the state of the army, as renders it evident that, at the time in question, an attack by the enemy might have been attended with the most unfavorable consequences.

Ethan Allen, who had been omitted in the nominations for officers of the regiment, from having quarrelled with Seth Warner, now offered himself as a volunteer to Schuyler; who received him as a pioneer to act on the frontiers of Canada. Schuyler was informed by Major Brown, that the Canadians were dissatisfied with British tyranny, and that the province might now be subdued at very small expense or risk. The province had but seven hundred royal troops within it; of which three hundred held St. John's, fifty, Quebec, and the rest, Montreal; that two batteries of nine guns each, and other works, were erected at St. John's, where two galleys were almost ready; and that Colonel Guy Johnson, with about three hundred men and some Indians, was at Montreal. Schuyler now professed himself ready to march against the foe, and only waited for orders from head-quarters. While thus waiting, he attended a conference held at Albany, to conclude a treaty with the Caughnawaga and the Six Nations, whom he had invited to meet him at that place. In his absence General Richard Montgomery commanded Ticonderoga. This person was an Irishman by birth; had entered the American service when eighteen years of age; had served in the French War; had obtained a lieutenancy for his brave conduct at Louisburg; had served under General Amherst on Lake Champlain; and for his services had been promoted to a captaincy in the West Indies. He resided in England after the peace of Versailles, but had sold out his commission, and emigrated to New York several years before the Revolution. There he married, and lived on his estate in Dutchess County, on the Hudson River. He had lately been made brigadier-general, and subsequently became one of the heroes of the Revolution.

Meanwhile, several Indian chiefs of the Caughnawaga and other tribes, appeared as ambassadors from their nations at Boston, and were received with great ceremony by the commander-in-chief at his head-quarters. They offered to take up the hatchet against the English; and Washington sent by express to General Schuyler to ascertain the state of affairs, and learn what intentions the British governor entertained in reference to the Indian tribes. This express arrived at the time when General Schuyler was holding his conference at Albany with the Six Nations; he had just heard of the ease with which Canada could now be taken; and having sent word to Montgomery to prepare for it, was about to proceed to Ticonderoga. He replied, therefore, to Washington: "I should not hesitate one moment to employ any savages that might be willing to join us." These despatches being sent, he hastened to Ticonderoga, but before his arrival, Montgomery had been informed of the completion of the armed vessels at St. John's, and their destination to Lake Champlain by the Sorel River. The entrance to that river it became important, therefore, to possess; Montgomery embarked one thousand men in haste, and two pieces of artillery, and sailed down the lake to seize the Isle aux Noix, by which the mouth of the stream was commanded. He left a letter for General Schuyler, explaining his sudden movements, and beseeching him to follow him as quickly as possible, leaving the remainder of the artillery to be transported when convenient Schuyler proceeded, suffering from sickness, on the 30th of August, 1775; and by travelling in a bed prepared in a covered batteau, overtook Montgomery at Isle La Motte; and assuming the command reached the Isle aux Noix, twelve miles from St. John's.

We return from following this expedition to the events transpiring at Boston, where the British were strengthening their lines, hemmed in by the besiegers who had received a supply of ammunition, and were now eager for action. Washington ordered his men to take an eminence on Charlestown Neck, in order to provoke the enemy to battle on the next day. It was silently done during the night, and presented to the astonished British, on the next morning, the aspect of a fortified position. Some firing then took place, but no sally was made; and Washington wondered that the British, who despised the Americans so intensely, did not issue forth and attempt to terminate the contest by an easy victory. Seeing that the enemy would not come forth, Washington employed himself in attending to the expedition which was to be sent into Canada by way of the Kennebec. For this purpose, a detachment of eleven hundred men was selected and encamped on Cambridge Common; and Arnold, who was then at Cambridge, adjusting his accounts, was intrusted by Washington with the command of the expedition. It was an important one, and required both skill and courage. Arnold was deficient in neither, and he had been treated honorably at head-quarters. He now received, beside his written orders, particular instructions from the general. The chief of these was, that he should be very careful in marching through the country, to consider the inhabitants not as enemies, but as friends, and, by every means to prevent the Canadians from suffering insult and plunder; that any American soldier who should injure a Canadian or Indian, in person or property, should be severely punished; and, in some cases, death itself should not be deemed too great a penalty. The right to worship according to one's conscience was to be insisted on; and all disrespect to religion and its ceremonies in the country, was to be avoided. It was stated particularly, in the letter of instructions, that should the son of Lord Chatham fall into the power of the Americans, he was to be treated with respect, on account of the eminence of his father. The Canadians were to be informed by handbills of the purposes contemplated by the expedition; and were to be assured that ample compensation would be given for the necessaries and accommodations which they furnished. Thus Arnold, more fortunate than his rival Allen, marched forth with great spirit and ardor on the 13th of September, 1775.

General Schuyler having proceeded along the Sorel River within two miles of St. John's, a cannonade from the fort was commenced. He landed his troops on a swamp half a mile in advance, and after considerable loss repulsed some tories and Indians, who had attacked him from an ambuscade. They cast up an intrenchment about nightfall; and Schuyler was informed in the night, that the works of the fort were completed, that cannon were mounted on them, and that a sixteen-gun vessel was ready to sail to its relief. A council of war declared the impossibility of a successful siege. They then returned and fortified the Isle aux Noix, and threw a boom across the river to intercept the passage to Ticonderoga. Ethan Allen afterward arrived, and stated his conviction that an attack on St. John's and an incursion into Canada would be successful. Preparations for an attack were completed, when General Schuyler felt too ill to assume the command, being confined to his bed. General Montgomery then received the charge of the expedition. Washington was much concerned at this misfortune, and preferred that General Wooster would take precedence and the command, as he considered Montgomery to be deficient in the energy which the difficult nature of the service required. He became, therefore, anxious about Arnold, whose forces he thought in danger, should the expedition of Schuyler be discontinued. General Wooster, however, was not superior to Montgomery in rank, but a degree lower, the grade of his commission being mistaken by Washington. The garrison of St. John's then contained a force of five or six hundred regulars, with two hundred militia. Its commander, Major Preston, being attacked, made a gallant defence. The necessary number of cannon was wanting to Montgomery; and he effected but little progress till the arrival of Captain Lamb from Saratoga, with a thirteen-inch mortar. This piece, however, produced but little injury to the fort, from being too far distant.

Ethan Allen was on his way to St. John's, when he

met Colonel Brown near Longueil, who informed him that the garrison at Montreal was very weak. An attack was then concerted. Allen was to pass over the St. Lawrence in canoes by night, from Longueil; Brown, with two hundred men, was to cross above; and the two forces were to make a simultaneous attack on Montreal. This adventure was arranged without the knowledge of Montgomery. Allen crossed the river, but Brown did not appear. He evidently had not made the passage. Day dawned, and yet no signal was given. Allen would then have returned, but it was too late. Canadians and Indians commenced an attack on him. In a brisk action which ensued, a number of Americans fell; Allen surrendered to Major Campbell, was marched into town, and delivered over to the commanding officer. Washington was concerned for this capture, and hoped it would serve as a lesson to demonstrate the evils of insubordination.

While these events were transpiring in the north, armed vessels were sent by the British from Boston to ravage the coasts of New England, and obtain a supply of cattle and forage. Stonington was commanded by Captain Wallace of the Rose, a man-of-war vessel. Newport was the place whence he issued; and a woman was sent from Cambridge with a letter to Major Kane of Boston, which she was to deliver to Captain Wallace, or to the collector. She intrusted it to a Mr. Wainwood for delivery; and as he entertained suspicions in reference to its contents, he opened it, and found it written in cypher, which he could not comprehend. From him it passed into the hands of Henry Ward, the secretary of the colony, by whom it was sent to General Greene. He conveyed it immediately to the commander-in-chief. The woman was arrested, and tradition informs us that Washington, looking from a window, beheld General Putnam approaching on horseback, with a fat woman, the prisoner, placed before him; that the figure thus presented was so strikingly ludicrous, that Washington burst into a hearty fit of laughter; the only time, it is said, in which he thus indulged during the whole campaign. The female was conducted to the presence of Washington, who informed her that unless she would make a full confession in reference to the transaction, she should be hanged. She pondered over this threat for some time. On the one hand she saw the gallows before her; on the other the consequences of an avowal. The terror of death prevailed, and to the astonishment of every one, she named Dr. Benjamin Church, a member of the Massachusetts House of Representatives, who was supposed to be a true patriot, and was surgeon-general of the hospitals, as the author of the letter. He was immediately arrested, and his papers secured. The latter had been previously inspected by a confidant. The doctor was greatly agitated, but acknowledged that he had written the letter. He was put into close confinement, but was afterward allowed to embark for the West Indies, on account of his health. It is supposed that he was subsequently lost at sea.

On the 11th of October, Falmouth was set on fire by Lieutenant Mowat, of the royal navy. Two hundred and twenty-eight stores, and one hundred and nine dwelling-houses were consumed; and all the vessels in the harbor were sunk or captured. It was his intention wholly to destroy Portsmouth. It was supposed that orders had arrived from England to burn all the towns which would not surrender their arms, and furnish hostages to the British. It was afterward ascertained that no such order had been received; but that these acts of violence had their origin with General Gage and Admiral Graves. Various ships were at this time dispatched for the protection of the coast; and an act of the General Court of Massachusetts granted letters of marque and reprisal to American cruisers, which were declared by John Adams "to be one of the most important documents in history."

General Gage, who had lost his laurels at the battle of Bunker Hill, was at length recalled; and he set sail for England on the 10th of October. Major-General Howe was appointed commander-in-chief of the colonies on the Atlantic in his place, and Major-General Carleton commander of the English troops in Canada.

A committee from Congress arrived at Boston on the 15th of October, 1775, to hold a conference with Washington and with the delegates from several of the colonies, and take into consideration the subject of putting the army on a new footing. After a session of four days, the report which they rendered caused a resolution to be passed in Congress, to the effect that an army of twenty thousand men should be raised, and composed as much as possible from the troops then in service. These had been enlisted for one year only; and this mistake led to the most serious embarrassments during the war; requiring that process to be repeated every year, which ought to have been effected for several years, or during the continuance of hostilities. In this committee was the celebrated Benjamin Franklin. The committee had uttered an intimation, that Congress desired Boston to be attacked, if it were possible; but in a council of war which was held, it was the opinion of the ablest generals, that that movement would be inexpedient. Washington asked the delegates how far, in case of a bombardment, it might be carried to the destruction of houses and property; but they would not take the responsibility on them to reply, without first referring the matter to Congress; though two of the committee expressed the wish to see Boston in flames.

General Howe now proceeded to fortify Bunker Hill and Boston Neck; and to strengthen the town by defences on the eminences within it. Several patriots were shocked at witnessing the desecration of Old South Church, in which some of the most eminent divines had ministered during a century. The pulpit and pews were taken out, and it was turned into a riding-school. The North Church was used for fuel. These places of worship the British commander had stigmatized as "meeting-houses." He now issued proclamations, forbidding any one to leave Boston without his permission; and each of those who obtained this permission was forbidden to carry more than five pounds' weight of baggage with him. All the inhabitants were commanded to arm for the preservation of order in the town. Washington, being aware that the bay would soon be frozen over which separated the camp from Boston, and that soldiers could easily cross on the ice; and that if General Howe received reinforcements, he would desire to free himself from the blockade, erected batteries at every assailable point; and being in want of artillery and ordnance stores, dispatched Henry Knox for a supply to the forts on Lake Champlain.

He now made the attempt to re-enlist the troops then in service, and found that half of the officers who held the rank of captain desired to leave the army. Their pernicious example, he well knew, would exert much influence with the men. Those who came from one colony were reluctant to join the same regiment with troops from another. Some stood apart, and some who had declined to serve again, sent in their names. It was difficult to induce the soldiers to remain, unless they knew the colonel under whom they were to serve; and the officers had to be appointed first. In short, a lamentable want of public spirit became prevalent, and instead of being anxious to benefit their country, they felt so strong a contrary impulse, that the general was fearful of the consequences; and apprehended that General Howe, who knew the state of affairs, as soon as he obtained reinforcements would take advantage of their condition. Washington at this period declared, in a letter to Colonel Joseph Reed: "I tremble at the prospect. We have been enlisting three thousand five hundred men. To engage them I have been obliged to allow furloughs to as far as fifty men to a regiment; and the officers, I am persuaded, indulge many more. The Connecticut troops will not be prevailed upon to stay longer than their term."

The mercenary spirit which characterized the troops was such as to give Washington great cause for uneasiness; and at the close of the letter just referred to, he remarked that had he known what had happened as having been likely to take place, no possible consideration could have induced him to accept the command. General Greene, who entertained great admiration for the character of Washington, and was happy to serve him, was one of his most valued friends in the embarrassing position in which he was now placed. While sympathizing with that great man in the immense difficulties and harassing perplexities which he was compelled to encounter, was of opinion that when Washington became better acquainted with the New England people, he would find them as brave and public-spirited as those of any other colony, and patriotic in the highest degree. That they were acquisitive, and accustomed to count the cost of every movement, was true; but sentiments of honor prevailed among them, and they would fight with admirable fortitude for their country's liberties.

Washington received dispatches from Schuyler, bearing date October 26th, which informed him of the capture of Chamblee and three hundred Canadians; in which place a large quantity of military stores, gunpowder, and arms, was obtained, that were indispensable in the siege of St. John's. That enterprise was now vigorously pressed by General Montgomery, who had then heard of the capture of Ethan Allen. He addressed a letter to Carleton in reference to the indignities inflicted on Allen and his men at the hands of their captors, who had thrown them into irons; and he threatened to retaliate upon the garrison of Chamblee, which was then in his power, if he persisted in such dishonorable treatment of the patriots. He demanded a reply, and allowed six days for its delivery; in the meantime besieging St. John's with vigor.

The firing on the fort had continued during some hours, when word was brought that General Carleton had embarked on the 31st of September, at Montreal, in thirty-four boats, to proceed to the relief of St. John's, with Maclean and his famous Highlanders. Colonel Seth Warner's Green Mountain Boys opened a sudden fire on these troops as they landed at Longueil; and after dispersing the boats, some of which were disabled, and others driven on shore, Carleton retreated to Montreal. Montgomery then ceased his fire, and sent to Major Preston, demanding a surrender. Preston doubted the truth of the report, but replied that he would surrender if assistance did not arrive within four days. This delay was not allowed; and he was then obliged at once to capitulate. The garrison was composed of five hundred regulars and one hundred Canadians. Montgomery sent his prisoners to Ticonderoga.

Maclean had reached the mouth of the Sorel, and was hastening onward to St. John's, when he was encountered by Majors Brown and Livingston, by whom he was forced to retreat to the mouth of the Sorel. From that point he sailed down the St. Lawrence to Quebec. The Americans took up a position at the mouth of the Sorel, and erected batteries to prevent ships from approaching Montreal. Montgomery had not yet been apprised of Arnold's proceedings. He had experienced the greatest difficulty in transporting his troops from the Kennebec to Dead River. They had subsisted on salmon, which there abounded; and having launched their boats on Dead River, they sailed to the foot of the great granite mountain chain which traverses this continent from south-west to north-east. His soldiers here became disheartened on seeing their boats upset, a large portion of their provisions destroyed, and sickness greatly increasing. They had a wilderness before them which it would require fifteen days to penetrate; and Arnold concluded to send back the sick, who only impeded his progress. He dispatched a message to the other commanders, desiring them to send as many men as they could provision for fifteen days, and directing the remainder to be sent back.

Washington was informed of these events by a letter from Arnold, who pushed forward through ice and snow on the bleak mountains, until, at the Chandière, he met an emissary whom he had sent in advance to ascertain the feelings of the Canadians. He received a favorable report; and after distributing among the different companies the provisions which he yet possessed, he ordered them to hasten forward to the settlements on the Chandière, toward which, without a guide, he set out. It was a perilous undertaking. Three of their boats were broken to pieces, and the crews were saved with difficulty. The cargoes were lost, and the party were at one time almost dashed over a cataract. They met a kind reception at the first French settlement which they reached, and from hence Arnold sent provisions to his famishing men. The distress of the invading troops was very great. They had even cooked their dogs, and boiled their moccasins and other leathern articles for food; and some of the men had not eaten for forty-eight hours. They remained to recruit in the valley of the Chandière for some days; and on the 9th of November appeared at Mount Levi on the St. Lawrence, not far distant from Quebec.

CHAPTER XVIII.

CAPTURE OF MONTREAL AND ESCAPE OF CARLETON — HOME SICKNESS AND INSUBORDINATION — MRS. WASHINGTON IN THE CAMP — ARNOLD PLANTS HIS FLAG ON THE HEIGHTS OF ABRAHAM — HIS JUNCTION WITH MONTGOMERY AT POINT-AUX-TREMBLES — THEIR ATTACK ON QUEBEC — GALLANT CONDUCT AND DEATH OF MONTGOMERY — BRAVERY OF ARNOLD — HE FORTIFIES HIS POSITION AND CONTINUES THE BLOCKADE OF QUEBEC — LORD DUNMORE IN VIRGINIA — LEE'S POLICY — TRIALS OF WASHINGTON — WANT OF PATRIOTISM IN THE SOLDIERS — GENERAL GREENE'S INFLUENCE.

THE letters received from General Schuyler informed Washington of the events transpiring in Canada. On the 12th of November Montgomery appeared before Montreal, which Carleton had evacuated, having embarked the garrison on board a dozen small vessels. Montgomery took possession of the place, and soon gained the good will of the inhabitants. Intercepted letters had informed him of Arnold's arrival at Quebec, and of the intense fear inspired by his presence. Montgomery's intention was to seize Carleton, by which decisive blow he thought the fate of Canada would be decided. He prepared to attack with batteaux and light artillery, in order to force the party down to the mouth of the Sorel, on the batteries there; but Carleton perceived his danger, escaped in disguise to Three Rivers, and thence embarked for Quebec. Garrisons were now

15 *

placed in Montreal, St. John's, and Chamblee; and Montgomery hastened to descend the river, and join Arnold in the attack against Quebec. But his troops had become disorderly, and even mutinous, their time of service having expired. They went to Ticonderoga, and being home-sick started, after being discharged by Schuyler, without even waiting for boats to convey them. Washington was greatly pleased with the capture of Montreal, and bestowed a high encomium on Arnold. He hoped a similarly favorable account would soon arrive from Quebec, and was assured that Arnold would do all in his power to take that city by an attempt which must be successful on the junction of Montgomery's troops with his own. By this means Washington anticipated the speedy subjugation of Canada.

Insubordination among the troops so disgusted Schuyler at this time, that he was about to retire from the army; and the same annoyance induced Montgomery to express a similar intention; but by the request of Congress, and through the influence of Washington, the Confederacy was spared the misfortune of losing the services of these able men, so essential, in the present crisis, to its interests. General Schuyler, throughout the whole campaign, was the victim of sectional prejudice; and his enemies were those mean and distrustful persons who were incapable of being influenced by generous sentiments.

The revolutionary zeal that had manifested itself at the outbreak of the war now began to diminish; and an ill-regulated commissariat had induced many soldiers to long for their homes on the expiration of their term of enlistment. Three thousand of the minute-men and militia of Massachusetts, and two thousand from New Hampshire, were ordered to be at Cambridge, to relieve the Connecticut troops, on the 10th of December; and till the arrival of these, the troops were ordered to remain. Their officers assured Washington that no defection of the troops need be feared; but, notwithstanding this declaration, they left on the 1st of December, 1775, and could not be prevented from carrying their arms and ammunition with them. Washington sent a list of their names to General Trumbull, and submitted the question to him, whether an example should not be made of these deserters of the cause of their country, in so critical a period. Trumbull, with many others, was extremely indignant at such conduct; and so were the people of Connecticut, as well as the persons living on the road, who would scarcely furnish them necessary food.

On the same day that these troops departed, a long train of wagons brought into the camp the cargo of a captured brigantine, consisting of munitions of war, two thousand stand of arms, one hundred thousand flints, thirty thousand round shot, and thirty-two tons of musket balls, beside ordnance. Washington thought nothing could have come more opportunely. Lord Dunmore had been exercising martial law in Virginia, and the favorite abode of Washington was in danger of pillage. John Augustine had entreated Mrs. Washton to leave it; and her friends earnestly advised her to take refuge beyond the Blue Ridge. But she did not think herself in danger; and the steward of the estate, Lund Washington, thought that Lord Dunmore would not venture up the river. Washington, in accepting the command, had promised to visit home in the autumn; and as it was likely he would remain all the winter before Boston, he sent his wife in November an invitation to join the camp. She complied, and travelled in her own carriage, drawn by the beautiful horses in which Washington so much delighted. Guards of honor attended her throughout the journey. Her arrival was a happy omen to the army, and her presence relieved the general from much perplexity. Invitations to dine with the commander were matters of solicitude to the officers. A disturbance which arose in the camp between some Virginians and troops from Marblehead was promptly suppressed by the general, who seized two athletic riflemen and held them apart at arm's length. "He was commanding in his serenest moments, but irresistible in his indignation." The ground was thus cleared of the rioters in three minutes.

Arnold still remained at Point Levi, opposite to Quebec. His intention was to cross at once; and such a step might have succeeded, had he not wanted boats; for his letters to Schuyler and Montgomery had been carried to the lieutenant-governor, who had thus become aware of the danger, and had the boats removed. Arnold was not easily discouraged. He collected together forty birch canoes; but the weather for some days continued too tempestuous to embark. Reinforcements in the meantime arrived from Nova Scotia. Maclean, who had been driven from the mouth of the Sorel, had now arrived; and the river was guarded by a frigate, a sloop-of-war, and two armed schooners, with guard-boats, which rendered an attempt on Quebec hazardous in the extreme. He heard of the capture of St. John's by Montgomery, was roused to valorous rivalry, and attempted to cross the river, whose wide and rapid current required unusual skill in the management of the canoes. By four o'clock in the morning he landed a considerable number of his men a little above Cape Diamond, at a spot which the gallant Wolfe had rendered memorable, and called from him "Wolfe's Cove." A boat belonging to the Lizard, the frigate already mentioned, discovered them; and not answering when they hailed it, it was fired into, and three men killed.

Arnold led those who had landed up a craggy defile, without waiting for the main body; and in imitation of Wolfe, had planted his flag at dawn of day on the Heights of Abraham. The strength of the fortifications presented an almost insuperable obstacle to his attempt, and a council of war was held, in which Arnold argued in favor of storming the gate of St. John's. This attempt might have been successful — it being open, and at that moment unguarded. Imprudent delay, however, rendered their operations abortive; for the lieutenant-governor thus obtained time to array his forces, and the din of arms proclaimed the startling fact that the enemy was on the Heights of Abraham. The gate of St. John's was secured, and the walls properly manned. Arnold summoned the commandant to surrender; but his flag was insulted during several days.

Arnold's threats were now derided, as the inhabitants had entirely recovered from their alarm. He was informed of the capture of Montreal, and ascertained that Carleton had escaped, and was hastening to Quebec. He retired, therefore, to Point-aux-Trembles, twenty miles distant from Quebec, and expected the arrival of General Montgomery with troops and cannon. A vessel at that crisis sailed by, after touching at the Point. It contained a precious cargo; for General Carleton was on board, on his way to Quebec. He fortified his position, and expelled all whom he either suspected, or who would not aid in the defence of the place.

Washington entertained hopes of the success of this enterprise, and reposed great confidence in Arnold. He did not doubt that he would render all the assistance in his power to General Montgomery after their junction; and he was kept informed of the progress of events by General Schuyler. On the day of the "crisis of the army," the 31st of December, 1775, General Greene wrote thus: "We never have been so weak as we shall be to-morrow, when we dismiss the old troops." Washington was not discouraged by the accounts which he received from Canada; and when all was gloomy and cheerless around him, a ray of light and hope beamed upon him from that distant horizon. The news of the junction of Montgomery with Arnold, at Point-aux-Trembles, now reached him. They mustered together an army of two thousand men, and were about to attack Quebec, which, it was supposed, would quickly surrender, if the inhabitants could obtain the same conditions as those accorded to

Montreal. The hopes of the general were not destined to be realized. Montgomery arrived before Quebec on the 5th of December, and thought the works could not long be defended by "Maclean's banditti." This force consisted of nine hundred men, six hundred of whom he found with Arnold. He described these as being in a superior state of discipline, and spoke of Arnold as an officer of great intelligence and activity. On his arrival, he sent a flag to the garrison, with a demand of capitulation. It was fired into; and he then wrote Carleton an indignant letter, renewed the requisition, and concluded with threats. After dispatching another messenger with no better effect, he prepared for the assault. The ground was frozen to a great depth, and was covered with snow. A breastwork was thrown up with extreme labor, made of gabions filled with ice. From this point, Captain Lamb opened a fire; but produced little effect, because his guns were too light. In the meantime, during five days and nights, he kept the garrison in a state of apprehension. On the fifth day Montgomery visited the battery. It had been shivered into fragments, and several guns were useless. It was abandoned during the following night. On this occasion Montgomery was attended by Aaron Burr, who was his aide-de-camp. Three weeks were thus consumed to little purpose; and the ill-clothed and ill-fed army feared the severity of a Canadian winter. A determination was made to take the place by *escalade*. One body was to fire the houses of the suburbs, and to force the barriers; while the main body was to scale the bastion of Cape Diamond. The ladders were provided; a council of war called; and three captains in Arnold's division, whose term was nearly expired, would not serve unless under another command. Montgomery overcame this adverse movement with difficulty; and transposed the arrangement previously made. Livingston was ordered to fire the gate of St. John's; Brown, to assail the bastion of Cape Diamond; and Arnold and Lamb to attack the batteries of St. Roque. Montgomery was to pass Cape Diamond, capture Drummond's Wharf, and enter the city at one end; while an entry was to be made at the other by Arnold. These movements were all to be simultaneous; the signal, a discharge of rockets. At two o'clock, on the last day of December, 1775, the troops, under cover of a snow-storm, set out to perform their several duties. The signal rockets were let off too soon, and thus gave the alarm; while Livingston failed to make the feigned attack on the gates of St. John's. The gallant Montgomery descended to Wolfe's Cove, and led his men along the shore round Cape Diamond. The guard fled from the first barrier. Montgomery rushed forward, pulled down the pickets with his own hand, and entered. Terror seems to have overwhelmed the Canadians, for the battery was silent; and Montgomery exclaimed: "Push on, my brave boys, Quebec is ours." When within forty paces of the battery, this heroic commander was slain, and two other valuable officers fell at the same time. The troops then retreated. The battle on the other side of the town was hotter still. Arnold, while gallantly leading on his men, was wounded in the leg, and the command devolved on Captain Morgan; who, attacking the first barrier, scaled the battery, and made the captain and thirty men prisoners. A fire from the walls thinned the ranks of the Americans as he led them on to the second barrier. This also was taken, after a brave defence. The way to victory now seemed open; but the death of Montgomery, and the retreat of Campbell, had drawn out a large detachment from Carleton; and Morgan and his men being surrounded, were compelled to surrender as prisoners of war. Arnold, wounded as he was, and dragging along his helpless limb, exposed to the fire of the enemy, assumed the command of the shattered forces; and put his troops in such a condition as to render them formidable. No pursuit was therefore attempted by General Carleton. The remains of the gallant Montgomery were interred by Carambé, the lieutenant-governor, who formerly knew him; and now honored him with a soldier's obsequies. The most eminent orators in the British Parliament displayed their eloquence in laudation of his virtues; and his death was universally lamented. Congress directed a monument to be erected to his memory. Four hundred men were lost in this engagement. The rest fortified themselves within three miles of Quebec, which Arnold continued to blockade during the winter, with not more than five hundred effective troops.

While these things were taking place in the north, a vessel was captured which Lord Dunmore had sent to the relief of Boston; and letters were intercepted to the British general, which invited him to make the south the seat of war, and aid his operations by the excitement of a servile insurrection.

The year 1775 was now closing. It was a period of intense anxiety to Washington, who saw his army gradually melting away, in spite of all his exertions. His appeals to their patriotism were unheeded; and their homes possessed greater attractions for the troops, than their country's glory and welfare. Washington was aided by none with more sympathy at that time, than by General Greene; who, in the darkest hours of this sad period, still indulged in cheering hopes, and anticipated the assembling of a full army within six weeks.

CHAPTER XIX.

CONDITION OF THE ARMY — KNOX BRINGS AMMUNITION — LEE SENT TO NEW YORK TO PREPARE DEFENCES AND FORTIFY THE HUDSON — TAKES THE COMMAND IN CANADA — BRITISH THEATRICALS — WASHINGTON'S ANXIETY—PREPARATION TO TAKE DORCHESTER HEIGHTS—THE HEIGHTS CAPTURED, AND SURPRISE OF THE BRITISH — THEIR PREPARATIONS FOR EMBARKATION FROM BOSTON — WASHINGTON ENTERS BOSTON IN TRIUMPH — CONGRESS PASSES A VOTE OF THANKS TO WASHINGTON, AND A GOLD MEDAL IS STRUCK REPRESENTING HIM AS THE DELIVERER OF THE CITY — DESTINATION OF THE BRITISH FLEET—THE SERVICE DIVIDED INTO TWO DEPARTMENTS BY CONGRESS — GENERAL LEE APPOINTED TO THE SOUTH — GENERAL THOMAS TO CANADA — PUTNAM COMMANDS NEW YORK — GENERAL GREENE IN COMMAND AT LONG ISLAND AND BROOKLYN.

THE American army did not amount, in January, 1776, to ten thousand effective men; and to raise even this force, which was distributed in half-filled regiments, it was necessary to grant the men a very large number of furloughs. The troops who returned home were required to leave their arms for those who were now enlisted, who either brought their own guns or paid a dollar a-piece for the use of arms during the campaign. Any one who brought a blanket received two dollars, and few were equipped in uniforms. The lines of the army were at times so extremely weak, that they could have been easily forced. Perhaps history does not present a similar instance of a post being maintained during six whole months without a supply of ammunition; while in the camp, one army was dismissed, and another organized in the presence of an observant and vigilant enemy. While the army was reposing at night, Washington kept his anxious vigils; and no commanding officer, in any great and perilous crisis of his country's fate, deliberated with more anxiety and assiduity than did Washington, as to the means by which he might overcome the enemy intrenched in Boston. He now regretted that he had not already made an attack on that city; and resolved so to do as soon as it became possible. He received information from Knox, whom he had sent to Ticonderoga for ammunition and ordinances. He had obtained forty-two strong sleds and fifty yoke of oxen, to convey stores to Springfield. This was a source of encouragement; and the energy with which the commission was executed, was enough to evince the ability of the officer.

Early in January a great commotion appeared in Boston harbor, and arrangements were made for embarking troops. An intercepted letter had been laid before Congress, revealing a secret plan for gaining over New York and Albany, through Governor Tryon. All those who did not join the king's forces were to be considered as rebels. The Hudson and East Rivers were to be filled with English ships of war, and Ticonderoga and Crown Point were to be recaptured from the Americans. This revelation rendered Congress anxious in reference to the Hudson, and its protection. Sir Henry Clinton was supposed to be about to lead an expedition against New York, and General Lee, in a letter to Washington, urged him to act at once, and without waiting for the sanction of Congress, to seize New York. Washington conferred with John Adams, one of the most influential members of Congress, in regard to the matter. He thought that town was within the limits of his command, as much as Boston. Lee was therefore directed to raise volunteers in Connecticut, and march at their head to New York; to put the posts on the Hudson in a state of defence; and to carry out the views of Congress in taking full possession of everything useful to the army. The people of New York having heard of Lee's intentions to take military possession of the city, some of them left it; and the committee of safety showed the impropriety of provoking hostilities, through a letter by their chairman, Van Cortlandt. Lee wrote in answer that he did not intend to commence hostilities with the ships of war then riding in the harbor, but that he merely wished to carry into effect the commands of the general, and exclude the enemy from the city and from Long Island. He promised to take only such troops with him as might be necessary to secure the city against the designs of the enemy.

Washington was much disturbed when a letter from General Schuyler informed him of the disastrous events which had transpired in Canada. He could not spare any soldiers from Boston; but three regiments were granted from New England, and more reinforcements were promised. Schuyler afterward forced Sir John Johnson to capitulate, and to surrender all the arms and military stores which he possessed; and after the capitulation took place, behaved with great generosity to the fallen foe. As the province of New York was the central link which bound the Colonial Confederacy together, Washington became very anxious respecting it; and looked to Gen. Lee to adopt such measures as were necessary to make headway against the enemy, as well as to conciliate the inhabitants. Clinton entered New York on the same day on which Lee arrived; but only, as he said, on a visit to his friend Tryon. Lee had proceeded to erect a strong redoubt, which would contain three hundred men, at a point commanding the pass at Hell Gate, in such a manner as to exclude the enemy's ships from Long Island. A regiment was preparing to make an intrenched camp, so as to prevent the foe from obtaining a foothold; and in order to keep the fire of the ships of the enemy at due distance, batteries were erected behind Trinity Church. Heavy cannon were to be sent to defend the forts in the highlands. While Lee was busied in effecting these changes, he received orders to take the command in Canada.

The monotony in Boston during this period was such, that private theatricals were enacted by the British officers; and a farce was played called the "Blockade of Boston," in which Washington was exhibited in a big wig, and a long, rusty sword. The play was put an end to by General Howe, who said: "Officers, to your alarm posts!" It was then that Putnam ordered Major Knowlton to surprise and capture a British guard stationed at Charlestown. The public now began to consider Washington as slow in his operations, and it required much self-denial on his part to refrain from putting everything on the cast of one adventurous die. Even before his own officers, he was compelled to conceal his situation; which, at that time, must have been extremely irksome and disagreeable.

Washington now summoned a council of war, and proposed a general assault upon the British works, but it was declined almost unanimously, on account of the scarcity of ammunition. A cannonade and bombardment were deemed more advisable, when a sufficient supply of powder should be obtained. Preparations were now made for taking Dorchester Heights and Noddle's Island. Colonel Knox at length arrived in the camp with cannons, mortars, flints, and lead in abundance. There came also ammunition from the royal arsenal in New York, and ten regiments of militia. Thus matters were assuming a more cheering aspect. Everything depended on the success of the attempt now about to be made. All games of hazard were banished from the camp; for the troops were about to contend for the glorious cause of liberty, which was a sacred and holy enterprise. A proclamation was made, that should any one attempt to desert he would be shot down.

The evening of Monday, the 4th of March, 1776, was fixed upon for the taking of the heights. The ground was frozen eighteen inches deep, and was difficult to be intrenched. Materials had been collected some time previously, consisting of bundles of screwed hay, fascines, and gabions. The enemy's batteries were cannonaded and bombarded to call off the attention from the real purpose in view, and the spirited reply made such an overwhelming din, that the rumbling of wagons and ordinance carriages was entirely unheard, and the enemy had no suspicion of the purpose of the Americans. Eight hundred men, with intrenching tools and carts, advanced to their task; and General Thomas, with the working party of twelve hundred men, and three hundred wagons, with the fascines, gabions, and screwed-hay bundles, eight tons in weight, made such a disposition of materials as to protect the troops from being raked by the enemy's shot. The whole of the detachment escaped observation, and reached the heights at eight o'clock, when they formed in two divisions; one going to the point nearest to Boston, the other to that nearest to Castle Williams. Washington inspected the works in person; as the men, under the eye of the commander, exerted themselves with greater diligence. They commenced fortifying by digging the frozen ground, under the direction of Gridley, who had superintended the defences on Bunker Hill. So rapidly did the work progress, that on the arrival of a relief party at four o'clock in the morning, two forts had been erected capable of resisting grapeshot and small arms; and the fortress exhibited such a formidable appearance as to inspire astonishment in the British camp as soon as day dawned, resembling in the celerity of its creation, the castle which was constructed in a night by the slave of the wonderful lamp. Howe looked up, and declared "the rebels had done more in one night, than his army would have accomplished in a month." Two thousand men reinforced General Thomas; and Putnam, with four thousand picked troops, was now ready for the attack. Washington, as he rode through the lines, reminded the men that it was the 5th of March, the anniversary of the Boston massacre; and he stirred up their warlike enthusiasm to such a pitch, that they panted for action. The Americans now held the heights which commanded Boston; their shells could reach the houses and the ships; and the enemy must either be dislodged, or Boston be evacuated.

Such was the situation of the British. Howe, therefore, determined on a night attack; but when twenty-five hundred men were ready to embark at Castle Williams, the surf was so heavy that they could not reach the place, and a succession of stormy days prevented their subsequent embarkation. Meanwhile the works of the Americans grew so strong that Howe despaired of success, and was necessitated to abandon Boston. He operated on the fears of the inhabitants by saying, that if his troops should be harassed in the evacuation of the city, he would be compelled to set fire to it in order to cover his retreat.

The people did not relish this dilemma; and a paper, signed by the chief inhabitants, setting forth that General Howe had promised not to injure the city if his troops were permitted to retire unmolested, was sent into the camp on the 8th, with a flag of truce, and taken to head-quarters. As it was not authenticated by Howe, it received no answer from Washington; and while the flag returned, the Americans fortified themselves yet more strongly. On the night of the 9th the Americans attempted to erect a battery on Nook's Hill, but were discovered; and a fierce cannonading again terrified the Bostonians. Putnam's mortar, the "Congress," burst on this occasion, and the Americans were compelled to abandon the undertaking for the present.

The enemy, in preparing to depart, had ordered that all linen and woollen goods, and such as might aid the rebels in carrying on the war, should be given up. Under this commission such depredations were carried on, that it was declared that the first soldier who was found stealing should be hanged. Yet the plunder continued unchecked. Adverse winds delayed the embarkation of the British, and the Americans threw up a breastwork on Nook's Hill, though the enemy cannonaded them. A report that a general assault was now intended, hastened the embarkation; and at four o'clock in the morning a scene of great tumult and confusion was exhibited. Seventy-eight ships and transports, with eleven thousand men, were preparing to depart; and their preparations being at length completed, the discomfited fleet set sail. The movements of the enemy had been watched by land and water; and the scouts sent to reconnoitre found sentinels posted, who remained motionless. They turned out, upon examination, to be mere effigies. Putnam's troops were then ordered to occupy Boston; General Ward's corps of five hundred men advanced from Roxbury; and by ten o'clock the flag of thirteen stripes waved above the forts and steeples of Boston.

On the next day Washington entered the evacuated city, and was received with great joy. There were traces of the bombardment all around, and evidences of the confusion and distress that had prevailed in the enemy's camp. It is said that in sailing out of the harbor, General Howe had the vexation to receive despatches from the ministry, approving of his resolution to keep his post until he was reinforced. The fleet lingered for some time in Nantucket Roads, and Washington threw up defences on Fort Hill, lest the British should attempt something there. The fleet, however, soon vanished, and the applause of the nation was at length given to Washington, who had, with undisciplined troops, expelled an army of veterans, marshalled under one of the most distinguished of British generals. On the motion of John Adams, Congress passed a unanimous vote of thanks to Washington; and ordered a gold medal to be struck, in which the deliverance of Boston was ascribed to him. The destination of the British fleet was supposed to be New York; but Howe steered for Halifax, to await reinforcements from England, and the fleet of his brother, Lord Howe.

As the middle and southern colonies were supposed to be the scene of the future operations of the enemy, Congress divided these colonies into two parts; the first consisting of New York, New Jersey, Pennsylvania, Delaware, and Maryland; the other embracing Virginia, the Carolinas, and Georgia. A major-general and four brigadier-generals were to command the northern, and a major-general and four brigadiers, the southern division. General Lee was appointed to the southern department, to watch the motions of Sir Henry Clinton; and the command in Canada was entrusted to General Thomas, lately promoted to the rank of major-general. General

Schuyler was ordered to superintend the defences of New York, the Hudson, and all the affairs of the middle department.

Brigadier-General Lord Sterling had taken temporary command of New York when Lee departed. As that city seemed to be the future destination of the British fleet, Washington sent detachments thither under Generals Heath and Sullivan, and wrote for three thousand men from Connecticut. General Putnam was put in command of the whole force, with orders to complete the defences of the city and of the Hudson, as Lee had planned and commenced them. After sending on divisions of the main body, Washington intended to follow. Meanwhile, the greatest strictness of discipline prevailed in the city, and under the command of Putnam. No one could pass a sentry without the countersign, and the ships in the harbor were forbidden to obtain any additional provisions. All communication between the ships and the shore was prohibited, and any person found holding such intercourse was to be treated as an enemy. Most of the works which General Lee had begun were finished; and as Long Island and Brooklyn were presumed to be the scene of the chief operations of the enemy, Washington, who was now on his way to New York, appointed General Greene, with a division of the army, to that important post. The whole American force then in New York and its environs, and on Long Island and Staten Island, amounted to ten thousand men; but on account of sickness and furloughs, there were not above eight thousand effective troops, who were without pay, and many of them even without arms.

CHAPTER XX.

THE DEFENCE OF NEW YORK AND THE HUDSON — DISASTROUS NEWS FROM CANADA — WASHINGTON'S APPEARANCE IN CONGRESS — ITS IMPORTANT CONSEQUENCES — THE AMERICAN FORCES COMPELLED TO RETIRE FROM CANADA — A CONSPIRACY, AND ITS SUPPRESSION — THE DECLARATION OF INDEPENDENCE — THE BRITISH FORCES IN THE VICINITY OF NEW YORK — ON STATEN ISLAND — IN THE HUDSON — DISPUTED QUESTION OF COMMAND BETWEEN GATES AND SCHUYLER — THE BRITISH FORCED TO GIVE UP THEIR ATTEMPT ON CHARLESTON — THE SUCCESS OF GENERAL LEE AND COLONEL MOULTRIE — WASHINGTON COMMENDS THE BEHAVIOR OF THE AMERICAN TROOPS.

THE defence of New York and of the Hudson was of the utmost importance to the Americans; for the British commanders opened the campaign of 1776 with a force, including army and navy, of fifty-five thousand men. New York was to be the centre of operations, and the navy was prepared to supply the army with provisions from the islands. A very great advantage which the royal troops possessed over the Americans, during the whole conflict, was the facility with which soldiers and the munitions of war could be transported from one place and one department of the service to another. But important as was New York, Canada also demanded attention, and the army there received a reinforcement of four regiments under Brigadier-General Thompson, and six regiments under Brigadier-General Sullivan. These were sent to join General Thomas, and were all the assistance which could then be spared. Arnold kept up the blockade of Quebec during the whole winter; and in consideration of his gallantry, he was raised by Congress to the rank of brigadier-general. He had every possible disadvantage to contend against, from want of money, necessaries, and troops. The army which he commanded numbered only a few hundred, and sickness had much reduced them.

General Thomas arrived at the camp during April; and when the river became clear of ice, he resolved to make a bold effort to take Quebec. His plan was to scale the walls while the enemy's vessels were enveloped in flames from a fire-ship which he intended to send among them. The plan failed; and General Carleton in return made a sortie with nearly a thou sand men. As the Americans could not resist so large a force, being able to muster only three hundred men at any given point, they lost their artillery, baggage, and almost all beside, and left even the sick behind them. General Thomas halted at Point Dechambault, and in a council of war they resolved to proceed farther up the river. The despatches of General Thomas had greatly discouraged General Schuyler, but Washington hoped that the losses incurred were not irretrievable. The news of these disasters, however, produced such an effect in the New Hampshire Grants, that it operated disadvantageously against Schuyler; and much ill-will was already manifested. Bold imputations against his conduct and character were now made, of which he took no notice at the time. At length, however, he insisted on an examination being made into them, and the scrutiny ended in his honorable acquittal. As the events transpiring in Canada were highly important, Washington sent General Gates to Congress with the despatches; and that body conferred on the bearer the rank of major-general.

Washington was now summoned to Philadelphia, to confer with Congress in reference to the campaign. He set out accompanied by Mrs. Washington, leaving Putnam to command the troops in New York in his absence. Several important consequences followed this conference with the Congress. It was resolved that soldiers should be enlisted for three years, and a bounty of ten dollars be given to each soldier. Thirteen thousand eight hundred militia were to reinforce New York till December 1st, 1776, and a flying camp of ten thousand militia was to be stationed in Jersey. Washington was empowered to call on the neighboring colonies for aid from their militia, if he deemed it necessary. A regular war-office was also established, which was an important improvement, inasmuch as Congress had previously been referred to in every case, by which process much time was frequently lost.

The despatches received from Canada at this period were ladened with news of disasters. General Arnold had left Colonel Bedell in command of a post called the "Cedars;" and Bedell, having heard of a large force setting out to attack him, placed Major Butterfield in command, and hastened to Montreal for reinforcements. Arnold sent a hundred men under Major

Sherbourne to the relief of the post, and prepared to follow in person with a larger force. The whole affair turned out most unfortunately. In the meantime the "Cedars" were besieged, and the troops were compelled to surrender; the party of Sherbourne was attacked and captured by Indians; and Arnold, who set out in the pursuit, could effect nothing except an agreement with Captain Foster, that the captives should be exchanged for a like number of equal rank. Washington, on hearing of these events, became anxious about Montreal, the loss of which would now be in substance the loss of Canada. General Thomas, having retreated to the mouth of the Sorel, found General Thompson preparing for its defence; and being taken ill with the small-pox, went to Chamblee, where he died of that disease on the 2d of June. General Wooster having been recalled, General Sullivan took the command, and soon joined General Thompson, whom he detached to aid St. Clair. The latter had been sent to the Three Rivers, to check the operations of Colonel Maclean. His orders were, not to attack Three Rivers, unless with a certain prospect of victory. The accounts sent by Sullivan to General Washington were full of encouragement and hope. The commander-in-chief had correctly estimated the merits of that officer in a letter to the President of Congress; but in the meantime, that body had appointed Major-General Gates to the command of the troops in Canada. The aspect of affairs was now changed. The enemy was reinforced with thirteen thousand men; and General Thompson, who was not aware of this fact, and intended to effect a surprise at Three Rivers, was led by treacherous guides into a morass; was cannonaded in passing through it; and on arriving at Three Rivers, was attacked by General Frazer, repulsed, and he and Colonel Irvine were captured. Two hundred prisoners were made, and twenty-five persons killed. The remainder were driven through the swamp, and after enduring great suffering, found their way back to the Sorel. General Sullivan contended manfully against every misfortune. A council of war being summoned, he was induced to leave the Sorel; after having dismantled the fortifications, and taken his guns along with him, he was joined by Arnold and the garrison of Montreal; and having destroyed everything at Chamblee and St. John's, continued his retreat to the Isle aux Noix, where he waited for further orders. Having obtained these, he embarked for Crown Point; and thus terminated the memorable but fruitless invasion of Canada.

A conspiracy was organized at this time, by the Tories in the city of New York and on Long Island, for the purpose of assisting the enemy in their approach to New York; and it was resolved that Washington should either be captured or slain by the conspirators. The plot was detected, and one of the general's body-guard hanged as an accomplice. While the public were yet pondering upon this event, four ships-of-war anchored in the bay. The troops which had lately been expelled from Boston, and six transports filled with Highland troops, were now in sight. Washington knew that General Howe was waiting for his brother to commence hostile demonstrations.

He ordered all the troops, on the 2d of July, to prepare for a conflict which was to be decisive in its effects; promising that acts of bravery would be rewarded, and those of cowardice would meet with punishment. While the city was thus threatened, the Congress at Philadelphia was engaged in deliberating on the momentous question of American independence; and on the 2d of July, 1776, resolutions were unanimously passed, that these united colonies were, and ought of right to be, free and independent States. This declaration was hailed with joy by Washington, on the 9th of July; and he ordered it to be read at six o'clock in the evening, at the head of every brigade. The populace of New York pulled down the statue of George III. in the Bowling Green. It was afterward broken up, and being made of lead — a very appropriate and significant material, — it was melted into bullets. Washington censured this display of enthusiasm, or at least the part which some of the soldiers had taken in the transaction, as exhibiting a want of discipline. Several other ships appeared on the 12th of July in the bay, and joined the hostile fleet. The Phœnix and Rose, emboldened by this accession of strength, sailed up the Hudson. The batteries of the city, and on Paulus Hook, fired upon them as they passed; and the city was full of consternation. Washington suspected that their purpose might be to command the passes of the highlands; and as Forts Montgomery and Mifflin were not completed, he sent an express to General Mifflin, advising him to be on his guard, and he dispatched orders to others in command, in important places, to the same effect. George

Clinton had been appointed brigadier-general of the militia in Ulster and Orange Counties. Washington wrote to him to protect the highlands against the enemy with all the forces he could obtain. But he had already anticipated the order. Three regiments had been sent to Fort Montgomery, Forts Constitution and Newburgh; and all the other regiments were placed in readiness for immediate action. Clinton directed also that all the boats should be drawn off, so as to keep them from grounding; and after having visited Fort Constitution, fixed his headquarters at Fort Montgomery. Here he received Washington's letter, and in his reply bore witness to the patriotism of the yeomanry in leaving their fields in the defence of their country.

While these events were passing in the highlands, the danger had become imminent at the mouth of the Hudson; every one admired the great size of a noble man-of-war vessel which now hove in sight in the bay; and each ship of the enemy's fleet complimented her with a thundering salute as she sailed by. She bore the flag of St. George, and it soon became rumored that it was the Admiral's ship, and that Lord Howe had arrived. Such indeed was the fact. A formidable British force had now assembled; and a contest with it, at fearful odds, was soon to task to the utmost the capacities of Washington and the American troops.

The Assembly of the colony of New York, located at White Plains, had a secret committee. To them Washington now wrote, suggesting the policy of removing from New York and the vicinity, all who were known to be enemies to the patriotic cause. Thirteen persons then in confinement, were taken to Litchfield jail in Connecticut; among them was a certain major, who had been suspected of treachery; but on being seized, and his papers examined, nothing was discovered that criminated him. Lord Howe was opposed to the continuance of hostilities. One of his first movements after his arrival, was to proclaim the extensive powers which were invested in his brother and in himself, to make peace; to urge upon any who had left their allegiance, to return to it; and promised a free pardon to all who did so. He added that all those who rendered any service to the British domination would, when the war was ended, meet with due consideration. The Declaration of Independence had preceded him; but it was hoped by the British that the royal cause would find partisans by the proffer of these inducements.

In a few days Lieutenant Brown, of the British Navy, was sent with a flag of truce from Lord Howe, and a letter addressed to "George Washington, Esq." He expressed the desire to hold a conference with *Mr*. Washington. Colonel Reed replied to the bearer that he knew of no such person in the American army as Mr. Washington; and said that a letter thus addressed could not be received. The lieutenant regretted that fact, as the letter was of an amicable spirit and import; adding, that Lord Howe had lamented the lateness of his arrival, and had very extensive powers intrusted to him by the British monarch. As Colonel Reed would not receive the letter, the lieutenant inquired by what name *General*-

then, correcting himself—*Mr.* Washington, should be addressed. Colonel Reed replied that his station in the American army was such, that his proper title was universally known. The adjutant-general of the British commander, Colonel Patterson, was afterward sent by General Howe to Washington; and was received with ceremonial courtesy—the reception being held by the American commander in the midst of his guards. The colonel addressed him as his *Excellency*, during the conversation which ensued, and produced a letter addressed to "George Washington, Esq., &c., &c.," the writer doubtless expecting that the *et ceteras*, which were ambiguous, and implied everything, would remove all obstacles of military etiquette. Washington replied that the "et ceteras" signified everything, but they also might mean anything; that a letter written to a person of an official character should be designated by a definite title, whereby it could be properly distinguished; and on this account he declined receiving a communication addressed to him as a private person. Colonel Patterson then explained the power which Lord Howe and his brother possessed for effecting an accommodation between the two countries. Washington replied, their power seemed to be only to grant pardons; but those who had committed no offence required no pardon. The applause of Congress was subsequently received by Washington; and the public admired the dignity with which he maintained his position on this occasion.

The Phœnix and Rose had roused a spirit of resistance as they proceeded along the Hudson; and the mountain passes of this river were deemed so important, that the New York Convention urged the militia to protect the military stores collected at Peekskill, and to guard every avenue to the highlands. The Tappaan Sea and Haverstraw Bay were watched with vigilance by Colonel Pierre Van Cortlandt, along their eastern shore; Colonel Hay observed the western as far as the Donderberg. The two ships cast anchor both in the Tappaan Sea and Haverstraw Bay, keeping up communication with the shore. As the vessels approached Fort Montgomery, a guard was prepared to light a blazing fire in case of any alarm. By this means, it was expected the fort would obtain an opportunity to fire at the ships by the assistance of the light. Five rafts also were to be brought, and an iron chain to be cast across the river, from Fort Montgomery to the foot of Anthony's Nose. Whaleboats were prepared to reconnoitre; and galleys, with nine pounders at the bows, were made ready for action.

Washington was anxious, during this period, in reference to the prevention of an irruption from Canada; and the question of superior command, disputed between Generals Gates and Schuyler, gave him much uneasiness. Gates considered the army in Canada under his authority, after that province had been evacuated; while Schuyler contended that the command of the army of the north was his alone. The two generals agreed to refer the dispute to Congress for adjustment; and in the meantime to co-operate. They set out together, and reached Crown Point, after suffering much on Lake Champlain from leaky boats, without awnings, under a burning sun, the army suffering from small-pox; with scarcely any medical stores, and with little food except rancid pork and hard biscuit. About six thousand men reached Crown Point, half of whom were sick; and two thousand eight hundred were sent to a hospital at the south end of Lake George. A council of war agreed that Crown Point was no longer tenable, and that it was more advisable to strengthen the defences at Ticonderoga. General Sullivan had taken great offence at the appointment of General Gates over him, and he now obtained leave of absence. Preparations were made for strengthening Ticonderoga, and for encamping the troops with all possible dispatch. Arnold joined Gates and Schuyler on the 9th of July, 1776; and Colonel Trumbull, who had been making observations, had fixed on a location for a fortress, where Fort Independence was subsequently built. At the place where Lake George separates from Lake Champlain, he advised another fort to be built; but, unfortunately, his advice was not taken, and Fort Defiance was afterward erected on the same spot,—an eminence that commanded both lakes, at the narrowest part of each. Carpenters from the Eastern States were employed to construct hulls and boats to be sent to Ticonderoga, under the command of Arnold. Congress decided the disputed question of command by informing Gates, that his commission was independent of General Schuyler only when the army operated in Canada. Gates professed to be satisfied with this decision, but his jealousy was much inflamed by his friend, the commissary Trumbull. General Sullivan, who had proceeded to Philadelphia for the purpose of resigning his commission, received such an explanation as induced him to retain it, and remain in the service. The sectional jealousy also, which sprang up at this period among the troops, was a source of great anxiety to the commander. The Southern soldiers entertained very unfriendly feelings toward those of New England. The troops of Connecticut, in particular, were laughed at by their fellow-soldiers, on account of some peculiarities which they possessed. The Connecticut light-horse refused to descend from their horses, and became very turbulent when required to mount guard. Colonel Seymour, their commanding officer, sent a note to Washington informing him that, by the laws of Connecticut, their light-horse were exempted from garrison duty, and in fact from every service which separated them from their horses; and that, therefore, they had not expected to be called upon to perform such service. They were dismissed, according to their request; and Washington told them, in a reply that proved that his feelings were deeply hurt, that if they would not do service separate from their horses under circumstances in which they could not possibly be used, he did not regret their departure.

Washington now received from General Lee an account of Clinton's southern cruise, who had been outwitted at all points by that general; in New York, in the first instance, and afterward when he stopped at Norfolk, Virginia, and in a bold attempt which he had made on Charleston. Fort Johnson, on James' Island, three miles distant from Charleston, which had full command of the channel, was defended by

Colonel Gadsden, and a regiment of regulars. Fort Moultrie, on Sullivan's Island, was defended by three hundred and seventy-five men, beside militia, under Colonel Moultrie. It contained twenty-six guns; was called after the name of its gallant commander; and, together with James' Fort, commanded the entrance to the harbor. Haddrell's Point, northwest of Sullivan's Island, had also mounted cannon. General Lee found the town defenceless. The British troops were landed on Long Island, and Sir Henry Clinton attacked Fort Moultrie with all his forces, in the belief that its capture would lead to that of Charleston. Works were thrown up by the Americans on the northeastern part of Sullivan's Island; and Colonel Thompson, with the regulars and militia, was stationed there to defend the passage over the Breach—a creek that separates Long Island from Sullivan's Island. Lee encamped on Haddrell's Point. The fleet advanced under Sir Peter Parker on the 28th of June, 1776, and threw shells into the fort. The ships anchored opposite the batteries at eleven o'clock. General Lee was very apprehensive of the result, from the little confidence which he reposed in the troops; but on sending to ascertain the spirit of the garrison, he found that they intended to fight with unflinching resolution. Having passed over in the boat to encourage them, he found that after twelve hours of incessant firing, the defence was so gallant that he had never witnessed a better display of fortitude. The fortifications were partly constructed of palmetto wood, which is yielding in its nature, does not splinter, but closes on the ball. In the hottest moment of the attack, the powder failed the Americans; but more being supplied, they kept up a spirited firing, during which the ship Actæon ran aground, and the others, that had borne the brunt of the conflict, were much injured. One hundred and seventy-five men were killed, and as many were wounded. Captain Morris, of the Actæon, and Lord Campbell, a volunteer, and late governor of the province, were among the slain. Colonel Thompson, with his men and cannon, prevented Sir Henry Clinton from crossing to attack the fort, and the combat terminated before ten o'clock. Sir Peter Parker had been injured by a contusion, and at length drew off his ships to Five Fathom Hole. Sir Henry Clinton, who again attempted to cross to Sullivan's Island, was beaten back. Sir Peter Parker at length became convinced that, in the present condition of his ships, he could accomplish nothing. He therefore gave orders to abandon the Actæon, after having set her on fire. After this command was obeyed, and her crew had left her, the Americans pulled her colors down, and kept them as a trophy; fired off her guns at the ships of the enemy, and carried off three boat-loads of her stores. The attempt of the British on Charleston became abortive, and was thus abandoned, and the fleet put out again to sea. The American loss on this occasion was thirty-five men killed and wounded; and for his gallantry in this, which was one of the severest actions of the whole war, Colonel Moultrie deserved and received much applause.

This repulse of the enemy caused great satisfaction to Washington; and in a letter written to Schuyler at this date, he remarked that "Sir Peter Parker and his fleet got a severe drubbing." On July 21st, 1776, in an address made to the continental army, the commander-in-chief expressed a hope, that the heroic example thus set them might stimulate the troops to outdo the brave efforts of the noble defenders of their country's liberties, whenever the enemy should make a similar attack upon them. Said he: "This generous example of our troops under the like circumstances with us, the general hopes, will animate every officer and soldier to imitate, and even outdo them, when the enemy shall make the same attempt on us. With such a bright example before us, of what can be done by brave men fighting in defence of their country, we shall be loaded with a double share of shame and infamy, if we do not acquit ourselves with courage; and manifest a determined resolution to conquer or die."

CHAPTER XXI.

ADVICE OF COLONEL REED — ARRIVAL OF FOREIGN TROOPS TO AID THE BRITISH — SECTIONAL DIFFERENCES OF THE AMERICANS, AND HOW WASHINGTON TREATED THEM—ILLNESS OF GENERAL GREENE—PREPARATIONS FOR ACTION ON BOTH SIDES — THE UNGUARDED PASS — THE MIDNIGHT MARCH — THE BATTLE OF LONG ISLAND — DEFEAT OF THE AMERICANS — WASHINGTON'S DISTRESS — THE RETREAT FROM LONG ISLAND — LORD HOWE AND THE AMERICAN COMMISSIONERS

A *chevaux-de-frise* was erected by General Putnam to prevent the enemy's ships from passing the fort; for some of them had already sailed up the Hudson, notwithstanding the batteries of Fort Washington. A number of galleys and fire-ships also were prepared; but they were too late to be of service. In a few days a very large fleet of ships arrived, bringing British troops, and with them were one thousand Hessians. Their disembarkation was effected on Staten Island, and the highest hills were fortified, so that the projected attempts at an attack were now useless. It was the advice of Colonel Reed, that after the interruption of communication by the Hudson had taken place, there was nothing to retain the American troops at New York, which should therefore be evacuated, burned, and a retreat be made to Manhattan Island; that a general action should be avoided, and the policy be adopted, of making the conflict one of outposts. At the end of July, or early in

August, 1776, other ships of war arrived, and disembarked a body of Scotch Highlanders, Hessians, and other forces on Staten Island. About the same time the troops of Clinton arrived from the south, and were accompanied by Lord Cornwallis and his army. The enemy's force about New York now included thirty thousand effective men. The American army destined to oppose them numbered about seventeen thousand; of whom one-fourth were on the sick list, and while many were absent on furloughs, the rest were distributed at stations fifteen miles distant from each other. Their sectional jealousies also gave much uneasiness to Washington. The army being collected from different parts of the country, and filled with partialities of a local nature, disrespectful language was often used by the officers toward each other. Discord arose on this account; and the soldiers imitated in this respect the conduct of their superiors. Washington at this crisis made a patriotic appeal to the army in these words: "The general most earnestly entreats the officers and soldiers to consider the consequences; that they can in no way assist our enemies more effectually, than by making divisions among ourselves; that the honor and success of the army and the safety of our bleeding country, depend upon harmony and good agreement with each other; that the provinces are all united to oppose the common enemy, and all distinctions sunk in the name of an American. To make this name honorable, and to preserve the liberty of our country, ought to be our only emulation; and he will be the best soldier, and the best patriot, who contributes most to this glorious work, whatever his station, or from whatever part of the continent he may come. Let all distinctions of nations, countries, and provinces, therefore, be lost in the generous contest, who shall behave with the most courage against the enemy, and the most kindness and good-humor to each other. If there be any officers or soldiers so lost to virtue and a love of their country as to continue such practices after this order, the general assures them, and is authorized by Congress to declare to the whole army, that such persons shall be severely punished, and dismissed from the service with disgrace."

This earnest appeal was not without its effect; but the troops from each State were kept together as much as possible, and were commanded by officers from their own State. The enemy's attack was constantly expected, and every point required to be guarded with vigilance, as New York was accessible to small boats, which might be detached in a variety of places. Mrs. Washington had repaired to Philadelphia, and the other wives of officers who had been in New York, left that city when danger approached. Important State papers were placed in a large case, to be sent to Congress; and all persons who were objects of suspicion, were removed. Indications became very clear that affairs now approached a crisis; and as the inhabitants became greatly alarmed on the approach of the ships-of-war, it was proclaimed by the general's orders, that as many as possible should remove from the city, which was soon expected to be the scene of a deadly combat. Signs of a meditated attack now began to appear, and as its precise point was doubtful, Washington retained most of his troops in the city for its defence. It was rumored that the enemy would in all probability attempt to get possession of the heights of Brooklyn, which overlook New York; but General Heath was of opinion, that Lord Howe would prefer to make an attack on Kingsbridge, in preference to an assault on the strong works erected in the city; in which case the inexperienced recruits composing the continental troops would be compelled to contend with a well-disciplined army which had the facilities for action both by land and water.

General Greene had command of a considerable force in Brooklyn. He was perfectly familiar with every part of the island, and he fortified and disposed of his troops in the most advantageous manner. The rapid tides of the Sound, or East River as it is there called, separates New York from Brooklyn, at a distance of three-fourths of a mile. The deep inlets of Wallabout Bay and Gowanus Cove form the peninsula on which Brooklyn is situated, and strong redoubts and intrenchments ran along from the bay to near the cove; while a battery at Red Hook, and a fort on Governor's Island, almost opposite to it, defended the rear portion of the works from the ships of the enemy. Two miles in front of the defences, a barrier of a range of hills ran across the island, from southwest to northeast. Three roads traversed the island — one passing easterly to Bedford, and then through the Bedford hills to the village of Jamaica; another went to Flatbush; and the third, by Gowanus Cove to the Narrows.

A knowledge of these roads was important; and it so happened that General Greene, who was particularly well acquainted with them, was confined to bed by a fever, and the command was held by General Sullivan, who had returned from Lake Champlain. It was ascertained, on the 21st, that twenty thousand men had embarked, to attack Long Island and other places along the Hudson; that fifteen thousand men who were to assault Elizabethtown, Bergen Point, and Amboy, remained on Staten Island; and that the British commander had ordered no quarter to be given.

On the 22d of August the inhabitants of the city were alarmed by the report of cannon, and it was reported that several thousand troops had landed at Gravesend, with artillery and cavalry. This information gave Washington reason to think that the force was intended to surprise the lines, and he sent over six battalions, and five others were held in readiness, if they should be required. Washington exhorted them to "be cool but determined; to reserve their fire; and in case any one attempted to skulk, or lie down, or retreat, without orders, he was instantly to be shot down as an example." The possession of the heights of Brooklyn would give the enemy command of New York; and many of the inhabitants were distracted with fear. A report became current that the intention of Washington was to burn the city, should the American army retreat from it; but the general assured the New York Convention that there was no foundation for the report; that he appreciated the value of such a city; and that nothing but the last necessity, and the most cogent reasons, could induce him to issue such an order.

Nine thousand British, with forty cannon, now landed under Sir Henry Clinton, who was first in command, Earls Cornwallis and Percy, General Grant, General Sir William Erskine. Colonel Hand, on their approach, fell back on a wooded hill commanding the Flatbush road; and while the army was divided through Utrecht and Flatland, Lord Cornwallis, being detached with two battalions of light-infantry, a corps of Hessians, and six field-pieces, advanced to seize the hills. Being opposed by Hand and his riflemen, he took up his position at Flatbush. General Washington, in crossing over on the 24th to Brooklyn, observed the lines, scrutinized the locality, and felt the want of General Greene. While the forces of the enemy extended beyond the hilly chains, the advance of the Americans lay along the wooded hills, under Colonel Hand. A road from Flatbush to Bedford, by which the left of the Brooklyn works would be accessible to the enemy, was guarded on the north side by a regiment under Colonel Williams, and on the south side by Colonel Miles, with another regiment of Pennsylvania riflemen.

Firing had already taken place between the outposts, and Washington saw with concern the want of system that prevailed among the officers, and the independent action of each corps, which fired upon the enemy in an irregular manner, and advanced in groups or singly, as impulse dictated. Putnam was therefore put in command of Long Island, with orders to restrain the irregularities of the troops; to form intrenchments and defences in places best suited for them; and to station guards on the lines, to be under the inspection of a brigadier. The strictest orders were given; the field-officers were required to go the rounds, and observe the situation of the guards, while no one could pass the lines without written permission. The interior works were to be manned by militia, the most reliable troops were to defend the passes, and prevent the approach of the enemy.

The watchful eyes of Washington observed the augmentation of the enemy's forces on the 25th; and he sent as reinforcements, in addition to those already in position, the well-disciplined Delaware regiment, under Colonel Hazlett. These were joined by the Southern troops which formed Lord Stirling's brigade. These reinforcements were among the best troops in the American army. Washington, on crossing over on the 25th, observed a general movement on the part of the enemy's forces; for General de Heister occupied Flatbush with his Hessians, and commanded the centre; while diagonally, to his right, Sir Henry Clinton led the right wing to the Flatlands, and General Grant extended the left to Gravesend Bay. After aiding Putnam with his counsels during the day, the General returned to New York, and passed an anxious night, in expectation of a general attack on the morrow. On the evening of the 26th, about nine o'clock, Sir Henry Clinton began to march with the vanguard of light-horse. The centre was formed by Lord Percy with grenadiers, light dragoons, and artillery; while Lord Cornwallis with the heavy ordnance formed the rear. General Howe attended the last division, and a silent march brought the troops to the Jamaica road. They then halted, to prepare for an attack on the pass through the Bedford hills, and learned with wonder that it had been left unguarded, as indeed was the road between Bedford and Jamaica, to a great extent. Orders had been issued to patrol the road occasionally, but the pass was left undefended. Whether this point was included in General Greene's plan is uncertain; or whether it was deemed too distant, and not needing attention, it is difficult to determine; but the neglect was an unfortunate circumstance, and destined to produce a disastrous result. A detachment from Sir Henry Clinton soon secured the pass, and he held the heights at the dawn of day. He pursued his unperceived way on till near to Bedford, and refreshed his troops before leading them to the encounter.

In the silence of midnight the left wing, under General Grant, marched from Gravesend Bay along the road by the Narrows and Gowanus Cove to the right of the American works. His force consisted of two brigades, a regiment of regular troops, a battalion of New York royalists, and ten cannon. Lord Stirling was ordered to hold the advancing enemy in check with Hazlett's Delaware regiment, and Smallwood's Delaware troops. He marched in haste toward the Narrows. At Gowanus Cove they were informed of the approach of the enemy, and Atlee was stationed in ambush with the militia of Pennsylvania and New York; while Stirling formed his troops on a ridge leading to the summit of a wooded hill. Lord Stirling was reinforced by a party of riflemen, whom he arranged in the wood near, and at the foot of, the hill; while General Grant posted his light troops in the advance, behind the hedges.

The British and American riflemen fired during the space of two hours; and Stirling obtained an accession of force by the arrival of Captain Gardiner and two pieces of artillery, which were placed to command the road. A cannonading commenced as soon as General Grant brought his artillery within three hundred yards. An attack had been commenced by De Heister, by the discharge of artillery from Flatbush, the redoubt in which Hand had stationed the riflemen; and General Sullivan rode forward to make observations, while a brisk firing took place between the redoubt and De Heister's artillery. The left of the Americans was soon turned by Sir Henry Clinton; and Sullivan, who now realized the fatal truth that he was in danger of being surrounded, remained no longer to defend the redoubt, which Count Donop, with his Hessians, and De Heister, with his entire division, were attacking. Sullivan could not retire to the lines; for the British drove the troops back, and a wholesale slaughter was commenced by the Hessians, against whom the Americans fought with desperate valor. Some of them cut their way to the lines; others retreated to the woods; many were killed or captured, and General Sullivan was taken prisoner.

Washington had now crossed over to Brooklyn, and urged his horse up to the works at full speed. He had seen the final catastrophe approach, and was unable to prevent it. Lord Stirling and his corps were the chief objects of his anxiety. He saw the danger which threatened some of his choicest troops; and with his telescope he surveyed the hill on which he beheld the reserves of Cornwallis. Stirling knew, from the cannonading of the foe, that he was cut off from the lines. He attempted to reach them by a circuitous road, by crossing Yellow Mills, a creek which falls into Gowanus Cove. But just as he left some of his troops to face Colonel Grant, Cornwallis and his grenadiers arrested his further progress. He was under the eye of Washington, who apprehended that he and his men would be compelled to surrender; but with the half of Smallwood's battalion he attacked Cornwallis, while the rest succeeded in crossing the creek. At this moment Washington wrung his hands in agony, exclaiming: "Good God! what brave troops I must this day lose." The encounter which ensued was terrible. But, when on the point of repelling Cornwallis, he received reinforcements; and then the order was given that the remains of Lord Stirling's troops should force their way to the camp, and a party which attempted to intercept them received so hot a reception, that they were compelled to retire. A long and desperate struggle ensued; but at length Lord Stirling was overpowered, and surrendered to De Heister. Two hundred and fifty brave men of Smallwood's regiment, perished in this deadly encounter; and the entire loss of the Americans in the battle was nearly two thousand, in killed, wounded, and captured. Within a short distance of the redoubts, the enemy's victorious forces were concentrated. It was supposed that the works would be stormed, but the British general avoided the further effusion of blood; and drawing off his troops, encamped for the night. Had the works been stormed, a desperate defence by the Americans had been determined upon.

The night after the battle was one of sadness and gloom to Washington and his army. The camp of an enemy, of great force and numerical strength, abounding in all the appliances of warfare, was seen at no great distance; and the sentries of the triumphant foe approached the lines of the disheartened Americans. Skirmishes took place during the following day; but the main body remained in their tents till the afternoon, when they appeared to be throwing up works at five hundred yards' distance. A heavy fog which prevailed during the 29th covered their movements, and when it was at length removed by the breezes, it revealed the British shipping in the Bay of New York, opposite Staten Island. Great apprehension was then entertained in reference to the future operations of the British; and Washington having called a council of war, it was resolved to cross the East River during the same night. An army of nine thousand men, with warlike stores, were to be drawn off, under circumstances requiring the greatest secrecy and address. The least noise might arouse the foe; and it was impossible to compute the dangers which would attend the transfer of the troops across a river three-fourths of a mile wide, whose tides were rapid and not unlikely to prove dangerous. All the craft that plied between Spyt den Duivel and Hurl-gate, were ordered by Washington to be im pressed, and to be ready in the evening at the east side of the river. Colonel Hughes received the order at twelve o'clock; and with such diligence was it executed, that the vessels were all collected in the evening at eight o'clock, at Brooklyn. To conceal these proceedings from the enemy, and to obtain a simultaneous movement, a night attack was ordered; and the plan adopted was to post Mifflin and the Pennsylvania troops, with the remains of other gallant companies, as sentinels, till the rest of the troops could be embarked. The withdrawal of one regiment after another took place late in the evening. Washington stood by, watching the embarkation; and in his haste to depart, he sent an aide-de-camp, Colonel Scammel, to deliver a message, which being misunderstood and erroneously given, might have defeated the movement. He told him to hasten the troops that were on their march; but the Colonel, instead of reporting this order, directed General Mifflin and his party of defence to hurry on, thus drawing off the very sentinels who were stationed to guard the embarkation. Washington was surprised when he saw Mifflin approach, and after an explanation he returned to his post, remaining there till ordered to cross the ferry.

While the fog still hung over Long Island, by which the operations of the troops were involved in doubt and secrecy, the air was clear on the New York side, and everything favored the embarkation. The artillery, ammunition, and everything of importance were conveyed in safety to the other side; and Washington was the last, or among the last, to cross the river. The British were astonished at the celerity of the movement; and while the mist was clearing away the last boat had left the ferry. The plan, execution, and success of this retreat have been justly considered one of the most remarkable master-pieces in military history; and as covering Washington with renown for prudence, capacity, and skill. He experienced so much anxiety in accomplishing this design, that for forty-eight hours he did not sleep a moment, and was during most of the time in the saddle.

Long Island was now in possession of the British, and the continental troops were greatly discouraged. The situation of the Americans was indeed distressing. Both in numbers and in efficiency their troops were found to be deficient; and in a letter addressed to the President of Congress, Washington was compelled to admit his want of confidence in the fortitude of the majority of his soldiers. Lord Howe did not at that time press hostilities. He was sincerely desirous of peace, and sent General Sullivan to Congress with overtures; and although he was unable to treat with them as with a legally organized body, he was desirous of making some arrangement with the principal members of it. Congress agreed to send a committee to ascertain what authority he had to treat for peace with duly authorized persons, and to learn what were the proposals which he had to make. Accordingly, on the 6th of September, 1776, John Adams, Edward Rutledge, and Benjamin Franklin were appointed as a committee to wait on his lordship; but nothing of importance resulted from the interview which took place between them.

CHAPTER XXII.

NEED OF A STANDING ARMY — NEW YORK EVACUATED BY THE AMERICANS — THE BRITISH IN NEW YORK — SUCCESSFUL SKIRMISH, AND ITS EFFECTS — THE ARMY PUT ON A NEW FOOTING — BATTLE OF CHATTERTON'S HILL — THE BRITISH TAKE FORT WASHINGTON — INTELLIGENCE FROM THE NORTH — FORT LEE ABANDONED — WASHINGTON AT HACKENSACK — GENERAL LEE'S TARDINESS — THE MOVEMENTS OF WASHINGTON — HE REACHES TRENTON — PROCLAMATION OF LORD HOWE AND HIS BROTHER — WASHINGTON CROSSES THE DELAWARE — PHILADELPHIA IN DANGER — WASHINGTON'S APPEAL TO LEE — THE CAPTURE OF THAT GENERAL — WASHINGTON APPOINTED MILITARY DICTATOR.

THE gloom and depression which ensued after the retreat from Long Island, were so great as to place the American army in a very unpleasant predicament. The militia, instead of rallying to their country's standard, were eager as soon as possible to abandon the service, and return to their homes. Entire regiments began to desert in a mass, and this example produced on those who remained, and who were impatient of restraint, such a pernicious effect as to destroy the subordination so necessary in military affairs, and exhausted the patience and rendered nugatory all the efforts of the commander-in-chief. Washington therefore deemed a standing army during the war necessary to the defence of the liberties of the nation; which could scarcely be defended without one. He was of opinion that the expenses attendant on such a regulation would be diminished, while the prevalent confusion and disorder would yield to a more rigid discipline. Washington was determined to do all that could be accomplished to serve the cause which he represented; and no trials or disasters could depress his mind or diminish his energy.

When the British general had gained possession of Long Island, his plans were soon developed; and it was evident that he aimed at obtaining the control of New York. The taking of it by storm would have the effect of injuring it, and it would therefore be rendered of less service to his troops. His purpose, therefore, was to avoid a bombardment, but to compass the town on the land side. But to accomplish this the American army must be surrounded; and the evacuation of New York became, in consequence, the desire of its commander. The stores and luggage were partly removed beyond Kingsbridge; and in a general council of officers it was unanimously agreed that, if bombarded, the city was untenable; and as this might take place at any time, some advised to destroy the city to keep the enemy from gaining any advantage by it; while others thought it should be held till the army was driven out. Two-thirds of the inhabitants of the city were Tories. It was at length resolved to make such a disposition of the troops, that any attack on the upper part of the island could be repelled, and in the meantime the rest should be prepared to retreat when the occasion required it. The sick, in number about one-fourth of the army, were to be sent to the Jersey side of the Hudson; and while nine thousand men were to take their station at Mount Washington, Kingsbridge, and other places, five thousand were to remain in the city, the rest to occupy the intervening space, and render assistance wherever it was needed.

These arrangements were already progressing when Lord Howe met the committee from Congress on Staten Island; and when the object failed which he had in view, four ships anchored in the East River, and six others followed on the next day. Three men-of-war proceeded up the Hudson to Bloomingdale on the 15th of September, with the design of dividing the attention of the Americans; while a powerful division of the army, comprising British and Hessians, commanded by General Clinton, was embarked on Long Island, and landed in the East River at Rip's Bay, protected by the fire of two forty-gun ships and three frigates. The Americans were driven from the batteries erected there, by the firing from the ships. Washington was then at Harlem, but hastened to the landing-place as soon as he heard the report of the guns; and had the mortification to see troops which had been posted on the lines, flying before the enemy, without firing a shot, though only about seventy of the enemy had appeared. He also saw two brigades which had been sent to their aid retreating in all directions, in spite of the utmost efforts of their officers to rally them. Washington galloped up to the fugitives, and riding among them endeavored to stop the retreat, but without effect. The men still fled in terror; and so intensely was he excited by such dastardly conduct, that he was unable to repress his rage, and dashing his hat on the ground, exclaimed: "Are these the soldiers with whom I am to defend America?" In his fury and despair he snapped his pistols at some, and drew his sword at others; but an aide-de-camp at length persuaded him to retire, as the enemy were but eighty yards distant.

The self-possession and control for which Washington was so remarkable, soon returned; and as the enemy might seize the heights of Harlem, which was the central position of the island, he sent off orders for securing that position at once, and ordered Putnam to repair thither from the city. In his retreat from New York Putnam suffered the loss of fifteen men killed, and three hundred taken prisoners; while almost all the cannon, stores, baggage, and provisions, were left behind. The retreating division might have been cut off in the rear at Rip's Bay, had pursuit been made in that direction; but the Americans were not followed vigorously in their retreat. General Washington drew all the colonial forces within line on Harlem Heights, and encamped there all night. Morris House, situated about a mile and a half from Mount Washington, became the headquarters. The British general having, in the meantime, taken possession of New York, encamped within a short distance of the American lines, his right wing resting on the East River, and his left on the Hudson. In the course of his inspection of certain works of fortification and intrenchments at this time, Washington was on one occasion surprised at the skill and ability displayed in those which had been erected under the direction of a young officer.

This person proved to be Alexander Hamilton; and after having had some conversation with him, the general invited him to his marquée. This interview was the beginning of their long and celebrated intimacy. Lieutenant-Colonel Hamilton, on the 16th, when defending an advanced post, was attacked by a large force of the enemy. He had advanced boldly toward the lines of the British, and General Howe sent two battalions and a regiment of Highlanders to check him; and a battalion of Hessians, a company of chasseurs, and two field-pieces were likewise despatched afterward. When they appeared, Washington rode out to direct the engagement, and had not proceeded far before he heard the firing between the British and Knowlton. The rangers brought back a report that the enemy's force was about three hundred men. Three companies of Weeder's Virginia regiment were immediately sent to reinforce Knowlton, under the command of Major Leitch; who was ordered to gain their rear, while a feint was made to attack them in front. The party advanced, and the enemy rushed forward to fire from among some bushes. Knowlton attacked the other side, and advancing with great spirit a brisk engagement ensued, in which Major Leitch, who had been the leader in the attack, was mortally wounded by the passage of three balls through his body. Colonel Knowlton also soon fell, and the other officers and men maintained the conflict with great bravery till aided by reinforcements; after which the enemy was charged with such vigor, that they were driven into the plain. On this occasion General Washington experienced some difficulty in restraining the troops; which he did in order to avoid a general engagement, and also because a large reinforcement was then on the way from the camp of the enemy. In this action the British had fourteen men killed, and eight officers and seventy men wounded. The death of Colonel Knowlton was much lamented. He did not long survive the engagement, and his only inquiry amid his last agony was, whether he had driven in the enemy, and whether the honor of Connecticut had been maintained. He had the satisfaction of learning that his men had the advantage in the conflict. Major Leitch expired on the 1st of October; and his name was honored by being given as the watch-word the day after the battle.

The events of this day produced an encouraging effect on the American army. They had been dispirited with the discomfitures and disasters which had taken place since the enemy landed on Long Island; but now the tide of triumph was reversed. They gained confidence in themselves and in their officers; and it was evident that the heroic courage, so nobly displayed in the affair at Lexington, and the battle of Bunker Hill, yet remained in the hearts of the patriots. More than three weeks elapsed, and the British army still remained inactive; and the lines on Harlem Heights bade defiance to their assaults. During this interval Washington made vigorous preparations for defence, and his lines extended from Harlem to the Hudson; the Jersey side being commanded by General Greene, whose head-quarters were at Fort Lee; while Fort Independence, at Kingsbridge, was the post of General Heath. The king conferred the honor of knighthood on General Howe after the news of the battle of Long Island reached England. But his hopes of bringing the war to a speedy termination were not sanguine. He proposed an augmentation of the British forces by eight or ten line-of-battle-ships, and supernumerary seamen, as also by troops from Europe. Notwithstanding the remonstrances which were often made by the British generals, the actual number of European troops under arms fell far short of what was promised. This fact became a fruitful source of disappointment to British officers of every rank, and was the reason why Generals Howe and Clinton resigned their posts, long before their resignations were accepted by their superiors at home.

A fire was seen on the 20th of September, which seemed to proceed from the city of New York, and cast a lurid glare against the sky during the night. General Howe's aides-de-camp having arrived the next morning at the American camp to confer in reference to an exchange of prisoners, gave information that a great part of New York had been consumed, and that much more of it would have been burned, had not the British officers and men exerted themselves to prevent it. The conflagration was attributed to an American, but on no satisfactory grounds. While the enemy were bringing troops and heavy cannon and ships against the American forces, the time for which most of the troops had enlisted was about expiring; and their re-enlistment had not met with encouragement from Congress. A new dissolution of the army was expected, and the cause of liberty incurred great peril of ruin, unless Congress soon adopted prompt and efficient measures to avert so great a calamity. On the 24th of September, 1776, Washington addressed a letter to the President of Congress, portraying the cares and anxieties which harassed him; the inefficient state of the military system which existed; and, after complaining of the insubordination, confusion, and discontent which it generated in the men, proceeded to state the only effectual means by which all these disadvantages could be remedied. To this letter is unquestionably due the great improvements in the army which were made, and the fortunate aspect which affairs soon after assumed in the American camp. The whole army was reorganized; and, being put on a permanent footing, it was decreed that eighty-eight battalions should be furnished according to the respective ability of the several States. The men were to be enlisted during the war; and while the pay of the officers was increased, the men were to obtain a bounty of twenty dollars, a suit of clothes yearly during service, and one hundred acres of land. No bounty in land was to be received by those who served only three years. Officers obtained bounty at a higher rate. Arrangements were to be made with the commander-in-chief by the commissioners from the different States, in reference to the proportions of the States; and all vacancies were to be filled by the general, in case the States were slow in making their own appointments.

The President of Congress at this crisis addressed a circular letter to all the colonies, urging the immediate completion of their quotas; and though the reorganization had removed a heavy burden from the mind of Washington, yet the evils that crept into the service were often a great source of vexation to him. Thus, for example, in order to collect troops quickly, some of the States offered larger bounties than Congress had proposed; and many State governments raised it yet higher, and in varying amounts; extraordinary rewards were promised the militia for service in emergencies; the States were lavish in incurring heavy debts, for which the Continental Congress was responsible; and no power but that of Congress could control these evils. In addition to the duties of the chief command, Washington was compelled to organize a new army; to meet the commissioners of different States; to confer with them in reference to the appointment of officers, when the campaign was already in progress, the enemy superior in force and discipline, with all the anxieties and vicissitudes of the war pressing on him; and yet the mind and energy of this extraordinary man were equal to all these exigencies.

The plans of Sir William Howe being now matured, by which he hoped either to cut off the Americans from communication with the country, or bring on a general engagement, two ships, a frigate, and tenders, were sent up the Hudson, passed the batteries without injury, secured a free passage to the highlands, and prevented supplies from being sent to the Americans by water. On the 12th of October, he embarked his troops on board the boats, sloops, and other craft, passed through Hurl-gate into the Sound, and landed at Throg's Point. Five thousand men, British and Hessians, were left to cover New York, under Lord Percy, at Harlem. General Howe landed at Pell's Point; and having advanced to the high grounds between New Rochelle and East Chester, the second division of Hessians and a regiment of Waldeckers recently arrived, joined him under General Knyphausen. The American commander was on the alert, and marshalled his army to meet the foe in four divisions, under Generals Lee, Heath, Sullivan, and Lincoln. Lee was stationed on Valentine's Hill, opposite Kingsbridge; and the other divisions formed a chain of posts along the hills west of the Broux, from Lee's camp to White Plains. Washington was almost continually on horseback, in a broken, woody country forming posts and breastworks, and took his position so as to protect his army by means of the river Broux. They outflanked the enemy's lines, and covered the roads over which baggage had to be transported. Washington fixed his head-quarters at Valentine's Hill on the 21st, and removed to White Plains on the 23d, where he erected a fortified camp. It was placed on high ground, and two lines of almost parallel intrenchments defended it. The right wing rested on the Broux, the left on a small lake, by which it was well protected. If pushed by the enemy, Washington resolved to risk a general engagement at this place. Skirmishing had previously occurred; and on the 28th of October, 1776, the British army appeared on the hills only two miles distant from the American camp. About half a mile from the American right flank stood a commanding height, called Chatterton's Hill, on which Washington had stationed a militia regiment. He now detached Colonel Hazlett, with his Delaware regiment to their aid; and soon after added the brigade of General McDougall, consisting of Smallwood's Maryland troops, the New York troops, and two other regiments. These *corps* were so reduced by sickness as to amount only to sixteen hundred men. The enemy advanced in two columns; Sir Henry Clinton commanded the right, and De Heister the left. There was also with them a troop of horse, which shone in all the glittering panoply of war, and made an imposing appearance. Colonel Rahl was ordered to cross the Broux; and General Leslie, with a large force of British and Hessians, to advance in front, and endeavor to dislodge the Americans from Chatterton's Hill. The British commenced a furious cannonade, and under its cover Leslie hastened to construct a bridge over the Broux. He was severely galled by two field-pieces posted on Chatterton's Hill, under the skilful direction of Alexander Hamilton, the young officer of artillery. When the bridge was finished, the British made an attempt to take Hamilton's field-pieces; and three times they were discharged, ploughing through the enemy's columns. Rahl and the Hessian brigade having forded the Broux, attempted to turn McDougall's right flank. The militia were of little service: he posted them very prudently behind a stone wall, and there they did some service until they observed some British cavalry brandishing their sabres; after which, overcome with terror, they incontinently fled. Hazlett and Smallwood made a valiant resistance at the top of the hill, and twice repulsed the British and Hessians, both horse and foot. Being too closely confined, however, and inferior in number to their assailants, they retreated to a bridge over the Broux. Here they fell in with General Putnam, who was hastening with Beall's brigade to their assistance. The loss in this action on both sides was about equal; that of the Americans was four hundred men, killed, wounded, and prisoners.

The British now rested on the hill with their left wing, and with their right extended to the left of the American lines, forming a semicircle, with the evident design of outflanking the latter. On the next day it was expected that a deadly conflict would occur. The two armies lay within cannon-shot of each other. Washington passed an anxious night, and busied himself in placing his right wing on stronger ground. He doubled his intrenchments, and erected three redoubts. When Howe saw how strong these works were, he abandoned the purpose of a battle, and had no hope of being able to dislodge the Americans. Washington remained a few days in camp, till he observed what course the British general would pursue; for it appeared as if he intended to withdraw his army toward the Hudson and Kingsbridge. It soon became quite evident that his first purpose was to attack Fort Washington, and next to pass the Hudson and carry the war into New Jersey; then, if possible, to advance to Philadelphia. In order to oppose this plan, and as British vessels obstructed all other convenient places, Washington ordered five thousand troops to cross at King's Ferry. The rest of the army was separated into two divisions; while General Heath was to defend the passes of the highlands, General Lee, with four thousand men, was to remain at White Plains, or follow the general into New Jersey, as should be deemed most expedient after a full development was made of the enemy's plans. These orders being issued, Washington proceeded to inspect the forts of the highlands, and met at Hackensack the troops that had crossed the river, after a sixty miles' march in a circuitous direction; for the Phœnix, Roebuck, and Tartar having anchored in the broad waters of Haverstraw Bay and the Tappaan Sea, the army was compelled to wind its way through the mountain passes secured by Lord Stirling.

The British general now moved all his forces to the vicinity of Kingsbridge; and when he appeared, the Americans retired to the lines near Fort Washington. The British crossed in boats, which had been procured from the East River during the preceding night, and by these means landed on New York Island. The fort was to be attacked at four different points. The commencement of the action was made known by a heavy cannonade and by volleys of musketry. Knyphausen advanced in two columns from the north; Colonel Rahl led the right, and General Howe commanded the left. General Matthew crossed the Harlem River in flat-bottomed boats; Colonel Stirling, with the forty-second regiment, sailed down the Harlem River facing New York; while Lord Percy, with the Hessians, attacked the American intrenchments on the right flank. The fort was summoned to surrender, but Colonel Mayan returned a defiant answer, and said that he would defend himself to the last extremity. The attack was begun on the 16th by

General Knyphausen on the north, and by Lord Percy on the south, at the same time. Both parties landed at some distance from each other, and having crossed the Harlem River, forced their way up the steep ascent. The fort was defended during five hours with extraordinary bravery; but at length Colonel Mayan was overpowered and compelled to surrender, and the whole garrison became prisoners of war. The Americans lost about fifty men killed during the attack. Two thousand eight hundred men, including officers and privates, fell into the hands of the enemy. The only terms which they could obtain, were, that the soldiers should retain the baggage, and the officers should preserve their swords.

Washington beheld this battle from the opposite side of the Hudson. At one time he entertained the hope that the fort would be able to hold out. When he saw his men cruelly bayoneted by the Hessians, he is said to have burst into tears. This defeat was a severe blow to the Americans, and a grievous mortification to the General. There were mismanagement and want of skill somewhere; but with whom the fault lay is very uncertain. The fort not having proved efficient in preventing the vessels of the enemy from navigating the Hudson, had been left to General Greene to be defended or not, according to his discretion; but no positive command had been given to abandon it. General Washington, in a letter written at this time, giving an account of the battle, expresses the depressing and gloomy forebodings which he entertained from the fact that in ten days more he would not have above two thousand men, of the fixed established regiments, on this side the Hudson River, to oppose the entire British armament; and very few more with which to secure the Eastern Colonies, and the important passes leading through the highlands to Albany, and to the country in the vicinity of the lakes. Having then alluded to the evils which, with a prophetic spirit, he foresaw would arise from short enlistments, he ends as follows: "I am wearied almost to death by the retrograde motion of things; and I solemnly protest, that a pecuniary reward of twenty thousand pounds a year would not induce me to undergo what I do, and after all, perhaps, to lose my character; as it is impossible, under such a variety of distressing circumstances, to conduct matters agreeably to public expectation."

When posted at Peekskill, Washington had received intelligence from the Northern army on Lake Champlain, under General Gates, where he had made preparations for the defence of Ticonderoga. He completed a small flotilla, and gave the command to Arnold. In the meantime an armament was completed by Carleton, who, by October, 1776, had assembled between twenty and thirty vessels ready for action. Arnold displayed great bravery in an engagement which was fought on the lake; and during a whole day the contest continued with undiminished fury. The British squadron was then anchored as near as possible to the American, inasmuch as Carleton hoped to capture them; but during a cloudy night which ensued, Arnold slipped through the line of the enemy, without being perceived. When the wind lifted the fog in the morning, the British pursued them with full sail, and the Americans stood for Crown Point. The Inflexible, the Carleton, and the Maria, a schooner of fourteen guns, poured a tremendous fire upon them; the Washington galley was captured, most of her crew being lost, and General Waterbury and the rest were taken prisoners. To prevent the other vessels from being seized by the enemy, Arnold ran his gondolas on shore, set fire to them, and the men with their muskets kept the enemy at bay until they were burned. He now set off through the forests for Crown Point; escaped an Indian ambuscade; and reached his destination in safety. Several sloops, schooners, and a gondola were in the place; and Waterbury having arrived the next day on parole, with most of his men, they sailed for Ticonderoga. The American loss in the action was eighty men, the British forty. Arnold reaped fresh renown from these achievements, on account of the skill and courage which he displayed. Carleton was joined at the ruins of Crown Point by his army, and then meditated an attack on Ticonderoga, which General Gates prepared to defend with desperation. Carleton concluded that he could not capture a fortress of such strength with the force which he then commanded, and therefore returned to St. John's, and led his troops into winter quarters.

The American troops would not, therefore, be required to defend Ticonderoga, and many of them returned to Albany. Washington very reasonably hoped to be reinforced from their numbers. The British general now pursued the advantages he had gained, and detached six thousand men under Cornwallis, who, landing on the Jersey side above Fort Lee, and having taken possession of the high grounds, continued his march between the Hackensack and the Hudson. As the entire body of troops commanded by Washington was inferior in numbers to those under Cornwallis, he abandoned Fort Lee, and the garrison joined the main army at Hackensack. Washington was convinced that the intention of the enemy was to form a line of communication, and hem the garrison in between the two rivers. A great quantity of stores, baggage, and provisions was abandoned; and in such haste was the retreat made, that the tents were left standing, and the enemy's troops occupied them during the same night. Nothing now remained but a general retreat; and an aide-de-camp, by the orders of Washington, wrote to General Lee, directing him to occupy with his troops the Hackensack side of the North River.

The troops then at Hackensack numbered three thousand, were much dispirited, and without intrench ing tools; and the country being flat, Washington resolved, rather than incur the risk of being shut in between two rivers, to abandon the fertile lands to the depredations of the enemy. He therefore advanced on the west bank of the Passaic, not far from Newark. The Jersey shore was exposed to the enemy's vessels from New York to Brunswick; and a march near the Raritan River was necessary to prevent General Howe from intercepting him on his approach to Philadelphia. He now sent Colonel Reed to Burlington to Governor Livingston, and General Mifflin to Congress, then in session in Philadelphia.

to obtain immediate aid; inasmuch as the term of service of Mercer's militia of ten thousand men was almost expired, and they would not be likely to leave their homes to endure the deprivations of a miserable campaign in that inclement season of the year, disheartened as they were by defeats, and by gloomy forebodings of the future.

Washington afterward directed General Lee to cross the Hudson at once; and he then supposed him to be at Peekskill. Various other communications passed between them; and the diminished forces of the Americans being in a perilous situation, Washington again wrote to Lee in a pressing manner, and repeated his orders, informing him that the enemy had now passed the Passaic, and that probably Philadelphia was their ultimate object. A council of war was now summoned, and several officers recommended that a movement should be made to Morristown, where the troops of Lee's army could join them; but the General was of opinion that he would make a stand at Brunswick on the Raritan, or dispute the passage of the Delaware. He therefore retreated; and so closely was Cornwallis on his rear, that as he left Newark on the one side, the British troops entered it at the other. Washington wrote from Brunswick to Governor Livingston on the 29th, desiring him to remove to the western bank of the Delaware, and put under guard all boats on the river for seventy miles. The force assembled at Brunswick, united with the New Jersey militia, was not over four thousand men; and no assistance had been obtained from the Legislature of New Jersey. The term of the Maryland and New Jersey troops had expired, and they resolutely deserted the cause. Such great numbers of the Pennsylvania levies also departed, that they were intercepted at the ferries by guards placed there for that purpose, and were even stopped on the public roads.

Perfidy in the camp was now added to cowardice. A letter written by General Lee to Colonel Reed at this time, was brought to head-quarters; and as Washington supposed that it referred to official business, he opened it and read as follows: "I received your most obliging, flattering letter; and lament with you that fatal indecision of mind, which in war is a much greater disqualification than stupidity, or even want of personal courage. Accident may put a decisive blunderer in the right; but eternal defeat and miscarriage must attend the man of the best parts, if cursed with indecision." The surprise of Washington at detecting such treachery on the part of one of his most eminent and trusted officers, may readily be imagined; but with that self-possession and coolness which so remarkably characterized him, he enclosed this letter to Colonel Reed, accompanying it with a note, stating by what accident he had happened to open it. Colonel Reed was greatly mortified at this incident; and though Washington consulted him subsequently on military affairs, he lost much of the confidence of the commander-in-chief, who afterward confined his communications with him to mere matters of business.

While Washington was waiting to no purpose at Brunswick, as late as the 1st of December, 1776, in hopes of being reinforced by General Lee, the British troops made their appearance on the opposite side of the Raritan. Washington retreated, after having broken down the bridge over that stream; while Alexander Hamilton opened a spirited fire to check the attempts of the British to ford it. Two brigades, consisting of twelve hundred men, were left at Princeton under Lord Stirling and General Adam Stephens. The American army reached Trenton on the 2d of December, and their stores and baggage were removed across the Delaware. Washington expressed his fears in reference to the army to the President of Congress, and complained of want of exertion on the part of the gentlemen of the country, and of indifference in the militia. While the most gloomy period of the war now intervened, and the whole effective force of Washington was scarcely worthy of the name of an army, a joint proclamation was made by Lord Howe and the general, his brother, by which pardon was offered in the name of the British monarch to all who should, within sixty days, take the oath of allegiance to him. Many persons of wealth and importance accepted the offer and took this oath, and the whole Confederacy was filled with despondency. But these things could not intimidate the resolute heart of Washington: he determined to persevere; and asking General Mercer, who had shared his perils in the expeditions and adventures of his earlier days: "What is your opinion; would the Pennsylvanians help us if we should retreat to the back parts of Pennsylvania?" Mercer answered, that "if the lower counties gave up, the back counties would do the same." Washington replied: "We must retire to Augusta County in Virginia. Numbers will repair to us for safety, and we will try a predatory war. If overpowered, we must cross the Alleghenies." Such was the unconquerable perseverance and intrepidity which Washington exhibited, at one of the darkest moments of the Revolution.

The tardy Lee was still at Peekskill on the last day of November, and he promised soon to join Washington with four thousand men. He expected no less than two thousand from General Heath; and taking him aside he alluded to a former refusal of his to resign any of his troops, as being contrary to the orders of the commander-in-chief. Lee now asked for two thousand men, whom Heath could not spare; and the latter declared that not a man should leave with his consent. Lee then affirmed that he would order them himself; to which Heath replied, that *that* made a wide difference, and that though General Lee was his superior officer, he had received positive orders from Washington on the subject. These he then showed to Lee, who replied that the commander was now at a distance, and did not know what to do as well as he. Having obtained the return book of the division, Lee selected two regiments to march with him on the next morning. In the end Heath induced Lee to give a written order, by which, as senior officer, the troops were to be taken on his own responsibility. On the next day, however, Lee had altered his purpose, departed without the additional regiments, and crossed the Hudson on the 4th of December.

Washington, in the meantime, was posted at Trenton; and reinforced by fifteen hundred militia from Pennsylvania, was ready to march to Princeton. He sent twelve hundred men to strengthen Lord Stirling, on the 5th, and with the remainder, followed on the next day. While on the march he received a communication from General Greene, in which he stated that "Lee was at the heels of the enemy." Cornwallis, in the meantime, being strongly reinforced, marched from Brunswick to within two miles of Princeton; and Washington having heard of his movements, ordered all the troops and stores to be conveyed over the Delaware. He himself crossed on Sunday morning, and took up his quarters about a mile from the river; causing the fords to be protected, and all the boats to be destroyed, which before were collected together. The last of the troops had scarcely been transported, when Cornwallis came up, in expectation of seizing the boats; but not one was to be obtained on that side of the river for seventy miles. Washington had ordered them all to be removed to the right bank. Cornwallis, seeing he could not gain any advantage, led his main force back to Brunswick, intending to cross on the ice, and placed his German auxiliaries into cantonments. Washington again sent an appeal to General Lee: "Do come; your arrival may be fortunate; and, if it can be effected without delay, it may be the means of preserving a city, whose loss must prove of the most fatal consequence to the cause of America." Philadelphia was now under the command of General Putnam, who, with the aid of General Mifflin, placed it in a state of defence.

On account of the impending danger, Congress, on the 12th of December, adjourned to Baltimore. It was understood that General Gates was advancing with seven regiments from the north; and these, with five thousand five hundred men which he then had, together with those under Lee, would enable Washington to strike a blow at the enemy which he hoped would be decisive in its results. Lee had advanced as far as Morristown, when, in a letter of the 8th of December to a committee of Congress, he declared that he would immediately join the army of Washington, but that he was assured that it was already very strong. Nevertheless, on the 12th of December, he advanced to Vealtown, where he posted General Sullivan; while he took up his quarters at a tavern at Buskingridge, three miles distant from his troops. The enemy became acquainted with his situation by means of a Tory, who communicated the fact; and a party of light-horse, under Captain Harcourt, surrounded the house, and bore him off in triumph to their camp at Brunswick. General Sullivan then took the command, and hastened to join Washington. The loss of Lee was a heavy blow at that time to the interests of the patriots. Some doubted whether he had not purposely thrown himself in the enemy's way; but his subsequent treatment by the British disproved this suspicion. He was true to the American cause, but he was such more from hatred of the British, than through attachment to the cause of liberty. He was a man of military reputation, but violent in temper, of boundless ambition; and after the first year of the war, during which he had rendered important services, he became arrogant, presumptuous, and impatient of control.

Washington knew, at this crisis, the disposition of the people, and the resources of the Confederacy: he was well aware that the pressure of misfortunes would eventually be removed by perseverance; and that, as long as the Americans could keep an army in the field, England must carry on the war at an expense too enormous to be sustained even by the most opulent and lavish of nations. He therefore set himself about the renewed establishment of the army; wrote to Congress in the most pressing manner, and with such effect that, from the very force of circumstances, that body looked no longer with jealousy on the strengthening of the army; but confident in the ability and rectitude of Washington, constituted him *military dictator*, with greatly enlarged powers, which were to continue during six months. By a decree they directed that, "until they should otherwise order, General Washington should be possessed of all power to order and direct all things relative to the department and operations of war." Beside those troops already voted, amounting to eighty-eight companies, he had power to raise sixteen battalions of infantry, three thousand light-horse, three regiments of artillery, and a corps of engineers, and to summon what aid he might deem necessary from the militia in any State; to form magazines of provisions; appoint all officers under brigadiers, or displace them; to fill up the army; to take at a fair price, whatever provisions the army should need; to confine those persons who would not receive the continental currency, and to imprison all disaffected persons.

CHAPTER XXIII.

WASHINGTON REINFORCED—GATES REFUSES TO CO-OPERATE—PLAN OF ATTACK ON TRENTON — PASSAGE OF THE DELAWARE — BATTLE OF TRENTON — CAPTURE OF THE HESSIANS — THE TROOPS RECEIVE A BOUNTY, AND REMAIN — GENERAL HOWE SURPRISED — HE SENDS CORNWALLIS TO NEW JERSEY — CORNWALLIS AT THE ASSUNPINK — HIS CONFIDENCE OF SUCCESS — MASTERLY MOVEMENTS OF WASHINGTON — CORNWALLIS OUT-GENERALLED — BATTLE OF PRINCETON — DEATH OF GENERAL MERCER—EFFECTS OF THE BATTLE—INCREASING REPUTATION OF WASHINGTON IN CONSEQUENCE OF THESE VICTORIES.

THE troops recently commanded by General Lee were conducted into the American camp on the 20th of December, 1776, by General Sullivan. They were in a very destitute condition. General Gates also arrived with four regiments from the north. The enemy had now relapsed into a state of confident apathy, and Washington resolved to put in execution a skilfully planned *coup-de-main*, against the apparently invincible British. The Hessians were posted along the Delaware, opposite the American lines. The forces of the latter now numbered nearly six thousand men. It was the intention of Washington to attack the Hessian posts by several simultaneous movements at different points. The Hessians had become the terror of the Jerseys; and the reduced condition of the Americans had induced them to relax their diligence. Three Hessian regiments under

Rahl, Lossing, and Knyphausen, were then stationed at Trenton. Rahl, who had distinguished himself at White Plains and Fort Washington, commanded the post. He was a young man, very fond of music, light-hearted, and had taken but little pains with the fortifications. Now therefore was the time to strike. The river was frozen; and an intercepted letter informed Washington that General Howe purposed to cross over on the ice to Philadelphia.

Washington directed Gates to proceed to Bristol, and take the command of that place. But he declined the trust on account of ill-health; and though he wished to visit Philadelphia, Washington desired him to remain a few days at Bristol, and aid the counsels of Reed and Cadwallader. The secret was that he wished to obtain a separate command, and was going to Congress to make interest for this purpose. The 25th of December was the time appointed for the purposed assault on the British. The troops, two thousand four hundred in number, with twenty pieces of artillery, under Washington, began to cross the Delaware nine miles above Trenton, at McKonkey's Ferry. It was supposed that the passage of the river would be effected before twelve o'clock; but floating ice in the channel retarded the boats so effectually, that it was four o'clock in the morning before all had crossed, with the artillery, to the opposite bank. The passage was very dangerous on account of the ice; and Washington, who had accompanied the men, patiently waited on the eastern bank until the whole of the artillery was landed. Trenton was nine miles distant. It was not possible to reach it without discovery, or to retreat; and Washington therefore formed the troops into two divisions. Two roads at different points led to the town at nearly equal distances; and a simultaneous attack was ordered to be made by both. The first division, led by Washington, was to approach the north of Trenton by the Pennington road; Greene, Stirling, Mercer, and Stephen accompanied him in this direction. The other division, under Sullivan, took the road by the river, leading to the western end. The plan adopted was to force the outer guards, and then take possession of the town.

The two divisions reached Trenton about the same time; and encountered no opposition, except from two pieces of artillery, which they captured. The Hessians were driven from the town, and endeavored to retreat toward Princeton; but they were intercepted, driven back, surrounded, and made prisoners. Twenty-three officers, eight hundred privates, and others afterward found in concealment, were compelled to surrender. The whole number of the enemy placed *hors du combat*, amounted to one thousand men. A thousand stand of arms, and six brass cannon, also fell into the possession of the victors. The killed were six officers and thirty men. Colonel Rahl, the commander, received a mortal wound, of which he expired soon afterward. Four or five hundred Hessians, and the British light-horse, escaped to Bordentown. The American loss was only two privates killed; Captain William Washington, a cavalry officer, and Lieutenant Monroe, afterward President of the United States, wounded. Two men were frozen to death—an event which was a suffiicent proof of the intensity of the cold. Heavy snow and hail fell during the march. So rapidly had the ice formed below Trenton, that it was impossible for the troops of Cadwallader and Ewing to pass the river at the time appointed, in order to participate in the attack on Trenton; though Cadwallader succeeded in conducting one battalion over. But such was the condition of the ice, that he failed to transport the artillery. Had Ewing crossed, according to the orders and intention of Washington, and taken the bridge at the southern extremity of Trenton, the party that escaped would have been captured; and Cadwallader would probably have been equally successful with the detachment below, or would at least have driven them back so as to be taken by the victorious Americans.

As this portion of his plans had not been carried out; as the enemy was strongly posted at Brunswick and Trenton; and as his own troops were now much fatigued, General Washington wisely declined to pursue his victory any further; but again crossed the Delaware with his prisoners, and reached his camp. By this unexpected triumph the cantonments of the enemy on the Delaware were broken up, and the British and Hessian troops posted at Bordentown retreated to Princeton. The troops being at length refreshed, Washington again crossed the river tc Trenton, with an intention of following up his advantage. The main army at Trenton received an augmentation of eighteen hundred Pennsylvania militia, under General Cadwallader, and as many more under General Mifflin.

The service of several regiments expired on the last day of the year, and the men seemed anxious to return to their homes, being wearied with the labors and perils of the campaign; but the half of them, through the earnest persuasion of the commander, and a bounty of ten dollars, consented to remain six weeks longer. General Howe was patiently waiting until the Delaware should be frozen over, to conduct his troops to Philadelphia; and the news of the capture of the Hessians at Trenton having reached him in his pleasant winter quarters in New York, he was astonished that veteran forces which made war their trade should be beaten by a raw and undisciplined militia. He retained Cornwallis when about to embark for England; sent him back to the Jerseys, and the broken cantonments of the British were collected in a body at Trenton. A party of Philadelphia light-horse captured twelve British dragoons, from whom it was ascertained that the forces of Cornwallis amounted to eight thousand men; and news arrived soon afterward of the landing of General Howe at Amboy, with one thousand troops.

Washington was now in a critical position. Indications appeared which made an attack by the British probable; and while his force was too small to encounter the foe, a retreat would be discouraging. He therefore collected together the combined troops of Cadwallader and Mifflin, amounting to three thousand men, and placed the main body on the east of the Assunpink. The water was very deep; the bridge over it was commanded by the artillery placed on it; and the advance-guard was stationed in a wood three miles distant, with Skabbakong Creek in front of them. On the 2d of January, 1777, General Greene skirmished with the advanced guard of Cornwallis; and it was nearly sunset when the British forces entered Trenton. The British commander formed his troops into columns, and attempted to cross the bridge over the Assunpink; but he was repulsed with a heavy loss by the artillery. Washington superintended the operations, stationed by the bridge, mounted on a white horse. Cornwallis now felt assured that he held the American troops and commander in his grasp: he gave his forces a night's rest, to render them the more efficient in the approaching service. The cannonading continued till dark; and the two armies lay near each other, expecting on the morrow a decisive and bloody action. The danger to the Americans was imminent. A general engagement might be disastrous. A raw and inexperienced army was separated only by a shallow stream from a powerful and well-disciplined force. The Delaware, with its floating ice, lay behind; and even a retreat across it, if such could be effected, would leave Philadelphia in the power of the enemy, and depress the hopes of the Americans to desperation.

The following night was one of the most anxious of the many harassing seasons passed by Washington during this memorable war; but he possessed a mind fertile in expedients, and adequate to every emergency. Cornwallis had left but a small number of men behind him, and his baggage and stores were but weakly guarded at Brunswick. Very few of the enemy's force remained in Trenton. Would it not be possible to surprise those posted at Trenton, and after capturing or destroying the stores, to proceed to Brunswick? Success in such a venture would aid the American cause; and even in the event of the loss of Philadelphia, a blow struck in New Jersey would be advantageous. This scheme was approved by all the members of the council of war held in the evening; and there was but one opposing consideration. The mildness of the weather and the depth of the thaw, might render the miry roads impassable; but it so happened that a north wind dried them in several hours, when they became frost-bound. The baggage was then removed to Burlington, and the army prepared to effect a rapid march. Trenches were dug near the British sentries during the night; men kept bustling about and making the usual rounds; the guards at the fords and the bridge were relieved; while the camp-fires burned with more than their ordinary effulgence, and all seemed to denote the permanency and order of an encamped army. Those who were thus engaged were ordered to hasten after the troops in the morning.

The American army withdrew from its encampment at midnight. General Mercer led the van; Washington brought up the rear, and passing by a circuitous route along the Quaker road, reached Princeton by daybreak. Three British regiments under Colonel Mawood were then in Princeton, and two of them were already commencing to march to reinforce Cornwallis in the morning. They were the seventeenth, fortieth, and forty-fifth regiments. Mawood was advancing with the seventeenth regiment, when he saw Mercer's troops approaching along the Quaker road to secure the bridge. He imagined that they were fugitive Americans escaping from the pursuit of Cornwallis; and wheeling about, sent orders to the other regiments at Princeton to surround them, and cut off their retreat. He soon became aware of his error. After a severe action the disordered British regiment fled; or, according to other accounts, they broke through the American ranks. They made good their escape, however, by the Trenton road. The fifty-fifth regiment fought resolutely during a brief interval, and then retreated toward Brunswick: the fortieth also, which had been less engaged during the action, fell back to the same place. By this defeat the British lost one hundred killed, and three hundred prisoners. The Americans lost thirty men, and Colonels Hazlett, Potter, and others of subordinate rank; General Mercer was mortally wounded. That valiant officer was a Scotchman by birth, and had fought in the memorable battle of Culloden. He had served in the Old French War, and was an attached and devoted friend of the American commander. During this battle Washington exposed himself to the hottest fire of the enemy, and continued to order and animate his troops, regardless of the most imminent personal danger.

When Cornwallis discovered that the Americans had left their camp, the report of distant firing assured him that they were in Princeton. He entertained fears for Brunswick; retreated, and reached Princeton as the Americans left it. The two defeated regiments were pursued by Washington as far as Kingston; and he ordered the bridge there to be destroyed to hinder the enemy's march. He arrived at Pluckamin the same evening. The troops were now much fatigued, and had been thirty-eight hours without rest. As Cornwallis and his troops were advancing, he gave up his purposed attack on Brunswick, and remained at Pluckamin long enough to refresh his troops. He then led them to Morristown, where he established his winter quarters. This situation possessed the advantage of being in a mountainous district, in the heart of a fertile country; and was both furnished with supplies, and difficult to be approached by the foe.

Meanwhile, detachments of Americans assailed the troops of Howe with vigor, and harassed them so effectually that, except at Brunswick and at Amboy, the British and Hessian troops had entirely abandoned the Jerseys. The recent triumph had effectually turned the scale of public opinion, and transformed a campaign which had been begun amid gloom and despondency, into one of victorious exultation and confident hope. The poor, ill-clad, ill-disciplined troops of the patriots had been conducted to victory under the most unfavorable circumstances, and had overcome a well-disciplined and veteran army. The British general, who imagined that he had secured his enemy, had been outwitted; and while the British forces were nearly driven from New Jersey, the prudent policy of Washington, which had been censured by many, was shown to be a principle of practical greatness and of profound wisdom, which triumphed by awaiting its time; while the talents of the commander shone forth in their force and splendor, demonstrating him to be fitted for every emergency. This campaign was the ordeal by which he was to be estimated; and the *American Fabius* was the epithet applied to him by the generals and statesmen of Europe, in consequence of the nature and success of the operations conducted by him in it.

CHAPTER XXIV.

WASHINGTON'S PROCLAMATION — CORRESPONDENCE WITH GENERAL HOWE — ILL TREATMENT OF AMERICAN PRISONERS — WASHINGTON'S PERPLEXITY RESPECTING THE BRITISH FLEET — LAFAYETTE'S FIRST MEETING WITH WASHINGTON — MARCH OF THE AMERICAN ARMY THROUGH PHILADELPHIA — THE BRITISH AT THE HEAD OF THE ELK — WASHINGTON ON THE HEIGHTS AT CHADD'S FORD — BATTLE OF THE BRANDYWINE — ITS INCIDENTS — THE BRITISH IN PHILADELPHIA — BOLD SCHEME OF WASHINGTON — HE ATTACKS THE BRITISH AT GERMANTOWN — BATTLE OF GERMANTOWN — ITS RESULTS.

THE American head-quarters at Morristown consisted of huts made in a very frail and temporary manner. Cantonments were placed in various places from Princeton to the highlands, and partial engagements took place occasionally between British foraging parties and the advanced troops, though neither army performed any action of importance during the ensuing six months. The hopes of those were bitterly disappointed, who, after the proclamation of General Howe and his brother, had returned to their allegiance to the British monarch; not only because the Hessian troops, in scouring the country, had plundered indifferently both friend and foe, and had committed outrages more appropriate to savages than to the troops of a civilized nation; but on account of the victories of the Americans which had recently taken place, and had completely altered the general aspect of affairs. The patriots gained some advantages by the cruelty of the Hessians, in consequence of the indignation excited against them; by which means many were now induced to take up arms, urged on by a spirit of revenge. Many substantial farmers and men of wealth entertained conscientious scruples in reference to the oaths they had taken; but the matter was cut short by Washington, who issued a counter-proclamation, in which he stated that those who had formerly accepted British protection should hasten to head-quarters, and take the oath of allegiance to the United Colonies. He gave permission, at the same time, to those who preferred the British jurisdiction to the interests of their country, to betake themselves speedily within the British lines; and all who would not comply with these orders within thirty days, would be regarded and treated as the enemies of their country.

There were some who thought this proceeding an undue exercise of power on the part of Washington, and a few members of Congress took the same view; but Washington was firm and determined in his attitude, and gave stringent instructions to his officers, in accordance with the spirit of the proclamation. One of the disadvantages under which he had labored, was the principle of innocent deception which he was compelled to practise, in exaggerating the number of his troops; and this was necessary, in order to conceal his real situation, the knowledge of which would often have been detrimental to the best interests of the cause. This deception, which often had the tendency of keeping the enemy at a respectful distance, was injurious in several respects in its influence on the conduct of the different States; who inferred that there was less necessity for furnishing their respective quotas, and only thought of danger in the midst of a campaign. Washington now wrote to them in the most urgent terms, desiring them to recruit and fill up their regiments with promptness and energy. He made appeals to every possible motive of interest, patriotism, and pride, to accomplish this result, and that the supplies might be furnished; while even the Congress was slow in these matters, except when directly incited by the commander-in-chief. To his urgent representation on the necessity of an increase of officers, five additional major-generals and ten brigadiers were appointed. The selections for promotion made by Congress were often influenced by local partialities; and this cause had the disadvantage, that the influence of parties often bestowed honors on the less worthy, to the rejection of those whose claims, if less obtrusive, were more real and indisputable.

A correspondence now took place between Washington and General Howe, respecting an exchange of prisoners; in which an agreement was made that officers, soldiers, and citizens should be exchanged; the officers for officers of the same rank, and that soldiers and citizens should be transferred for each other, respectively. The British general affected to regard General Lee as a deserter, and under this view of the case he was rigorously confined. When Congress were informed of this fact, and also that he was to be tried by a court-martial, they decided on retaliatory measures; and decreed that such treatment as General Lee received should be extended to Colonel Campbell, and five of the Hessian officers who had been recently captured. Colonel Campbell was accordingly confined in the common jail, and the Hessians, who were sent to Virginia, were deprived of the usual privileges accorded to prisoners of war. The imprudence of this retaliatory course was seen, and it was disapproved of by Washington. Against it he used such arguments as were suggested by humanity and policy; and observed, that as yet the number of prisoners of rank taken by the Americans was only fifty, while that captured by the British amounted to three hundred. Yet, the American prisoners taken at Fort Washington were treated with great cruelty, being closely confined in New York during the winter. A large number of them was crowded together in prison-ships, in churches, and in other places; and many perished from hunger, cold, and loathsome diseases. Others, who were sent in exchange, were so enfeebled in health, that Washington refused to return for them an equal number of British or Hessians. Sir William Howe thought this conduct violated the rules of exchange; and being unable to deny the facts of the case, declared that he had treated his prisoners as well as circumstances had allowed.

The act of Congress respecting the captive officers did not produce any effect on Sir William Howe; yet a want of humanity was never supposed to be a characteristic of that general. The sufferings of the prisoners in his power probably arose from inattention on his part, rather than from any other cause. He now addressed despatches to the British ministers in reference to the case of General Lee, who was still retained as a prisoner of war; though it had been his intention previously to send him for trial to England. Policy induced this change in his purpose; because the Hessian officers might meet with less desirable treatment from the Americans, and this would in turn produce a bad effect on the Hessian troops serving in the war.

The spring of 1777 had considerably advanced before any indications of the plan for the ensuing campaign were given by the British commander; and such as they were, they seemed less extensive than were expected, in consequence of the lateness of the arrival, and the inferiority in the numbers, of his reinforcements. Howe sent two thousand men up the Sound under Governor Tryon, who, landing in Connecticut, advanced and took the town of Danbury, destroying the stores that were in it. The local militia, and a few continental troops, bravely opposed them, harassed them on their march, and followed them in pursuit to their boats. These movements were made under Generals Sullivan, Arnold, and Wooster. Before the British regained their shipping, they lost three hundred men. Generals Wooster and Arnold were wounded; the former mortally. General Washington assembled the Eastern troops at Peekskill, while those enlisted in the new army from Virginia and the Middle States, were collected at head-quarters. Twenty-four thousand muskets, lately received from France, proved a valuable acquisition at this time, as the want of arms had already been severely felt.

Meantime General Howe, with an augmented force, began the erection of a bridge at Brunswick. It was constructed in such a manner as to be capable of being laid on flat-bottomed boats. His intention was supposed to be to cross the Delaware on it, and advance to Philadelphia. At the end of May, Washington took up his position at Middlebrook, nine miles from Brunswick, and prepared to prevent the enemy from crossing the Delaware. Sir William Howe led the British army from Brunswick, on the 13th of June, and took up a strong position, secured by the Raritan in front, fortified on the right at Brunswick, and on the left by the Millstone. He made this arrangement to provoke a general action; but Washington would not risk it, or be allured from his prudent reserve. Howe then returned with his entire army to Brunswick, and soon departed for Amboy. Three regiments under Greene pursued him to Piscataway, and Washington advanced against the enemy to Quibbletown. Being thus drawn from his strong post, Howe attempted to turn the American left, and with this intention made a sudden march to Westfield. Washington defeated this movement by marching again to Middlebrook, and skirmishes between the two armies were all that took place.

Sir William Howe being thus foiled in drawing on a general engagement, abandoned the Jerseys, and passed over to Staten Island on the bridge he had constructed at Brunswick. News of the approach of

Burgoyne to Ticonderoga with a large force now reached Washington; and he had been informed that preparations to the same effect were being made in the harbor of New York. He was in great perplexity in reference to the destination of this fleet, which he thought, in the first instance, was Philadelphia. But afterward it seemed as if Burgoyne and Howe were meditating an attack in concert; and he entertained no doubt that, as the possession of the Hudson, and of the highway to the Canadas, was so important to the British, for the purpose of cutting off the Eastern from the Western States, this was the object of Burgoyne's expedition. The immediate danger, however, was on the Hudson; and thither Washington despatched two regiments, intending to follow them to Peekskill, as soon as possible, with the whole army. When he ascertained the real intention of the enemy, he advanced to the highlands by Morristown and Rampo, and at Cleve sent Lord Stirling on to Peekskill with a division. Just at that time the fleet, having sailed down the Hook, stood out to sea, and Washington commenced at once to return. He recalled the two divisions which had crossed the Hudson under Sullivan and Stirling; and marching toward the Delaware, resolved to watch the enemy, who might return and ascend the Hudson. It soon became known that the fleet was at the Capes of the Delaware. The American army proceeded to Germantown, and the general went on to Chester. It was still uncertain what course Howe intended to take, after the fleet had left the Capes. It was supposed to be destined for the Hudson, or perhaps to co-operate with Burgoyne in an invasion of New England.

Washington now visited Philadelphia to confer with committees of Congress; and there he met, for the first time, the Marquis Lafayette, a young French nobleman, who had left his country and espoused the American cause. This enthusiastic devotee of liberty, who sacrificed so much in the cause of America, and obtained such effectual aid from his government in behalf of the cause of the patriots during the Revolution, first waited after his arrival on Mr. Lowell, the Chairman of the Committee for Foreign Affairs. So many foreigners had already requested employment from Congress, that Mr. Lowell, to whom Lafayette had presented a letter, gave him little encouragement. But when it became known that the young nobleman offered both to serve at his own expense, and also as a volunteer, his tender was accepted: he was received, and promoted to the rank of major-general in the American army. The commander-in-chief was soon afterward expected to arrive in Philadelphia, and Lafayette thought he would delay, and have an interview with him previous to going to head-quarters. At a dinner-party, where several members of Congress were present, Lafayette first met Washington, who spoke to him in a complimentary manner, invited him to the camp, and wished him to consider himself as one of his own family. He could not offer him the luxuries of a court or capital such as he had left; but, as he had become an American soldier, he would no doubt adapt himself to the usages and privations of a republican army. Lafayette was pleased with the warmth of his reception; his equipage and horses were at once sent to the camp, and he became one of the family of the general, with whom he ever afterward maintained the most faithful and affectionate friendship. In a few days he accompanied Washington in his inspection of some defences on the Delaware.

It was supposed that the British fleet had sailed to Charleston, as no information was received respecting it during ten days. Intelligence soon arrived, however, that it was in the Chesapeake, and had ascended two hundred miles from its mouth. The design of Sir William Howe now became apparent. The American troops were therefore all recalled from New Jersey, and collected at Philadelphia. To encourage the friends and dishearten the enemies of the patriot cause, Washington marched his whole army through the city. Indifferently dressed as they were, in order to make a more uniform appearance, they affixed sprigs of green to their hats. Washington, accompanied by Lafayette, rode at the head of his troops. The long column of the army, with its various brigades, divisions, pioneers, officers, the cavalry and the artillery, presented a formidable appearance to eyes unused to scenes of martial splendor; while the thrilling fife and drum aroused the slumbering echoes of the peaceful city. The troops continued their march to Wilmington. Washington established his headquarters at the confluence of Christiana Creek and the Brandywine. His army was encamped on the adjacent heights. The British had landed at a spot below the head of the Elk, now called Elkton. The pickets of the American troops advanced as far as Christiana bridge, while the main body lay at Red Clay Creek. In some skirmishing which ensued, the Americans had the advantage, and took about sixty prisoners.

After the landing of his men and artillery, Sir William Howe attempted to outflank the American right. Washington therefore crossed the Brandywine, and took possession of the heights near Chadd's Ford. His right wing was so posted as to guard the fords above, and the left was two miles below. On the 11th of September, 1777, at daybreak, the British general divided his army into two columns. The first, under Knyphausen, advanced direct to Chadd's Ford; the other, under Cornwallis, with the general, advanced on the Lancaster road. On the approach of Knyphausen a sharp contest took place between General Maxwell, who commanded the light troops, and the enemy; after which the columns of the latter passed on, and Maxwell was compelled to retire. Knyphausen made no attempt to cross the ford, but his artillery kept up a heavy fire, which was vigorously returned. Skirmishing continued to take place; and Knyphausen desired to keep the Americans employed in front, until they should be attacked in the rear and right flank by Cornwallis. The crossings of the river had been guarded above Chadd's Ford for about seven miles; and Washington, who suspected the real design of Cornwallis, now waited in anxiety for the patrols whom he had sent to watch the road to the fords. About noon he learned by a messenger from Sullivan, that a large body of the enemy had been seen on their march in the direction of the upper crossings. Other information was obtained, before the order was carried into effect for Sullivan to cross and engage that column, while Washington proceeded to attack Knyphausen in front.

About two o'clock, however, it became evident that Cornwallis had made a compass of no less than seventeen miles, and had thus crossed two branches of the Brandywine above the fork; had reached Sullivan's right flank, or within two miles of it; and had obtained possession of the rising ground near Birmingham meeting-house. Sullivan, who had three divisions under him, Stephen's and Stirling's beside his own, now prepared for battle with all possible haste; but too little time was allowed to form in complete array, before Cornwallis assailed him with full force; and having broken the American line, threw the rest into disorder and put them to the rout. Those who afterward rallied, and made a gallant resistance, were again put to flight by the greatly superior numbers of the enemy. Knyphausen now crossed the river, and attacked the American intrenchments at Chadd's Ford, where he was opposed by Col. Wayne, who fought with unusual bravery. But although he made a heroic stand at the head of his division, he was not able to cope with the overwhelming weight and impetus of an entire army. General Greene covered Sullivan's retreat, and having seized a pass a mile from Dilworth, he resisted the advance of the enemy as long as day lasted, and thus checked their pursuit. He had taken up a central position between Chadd's Ford and the place at which Sullivan was engaged, so as to be able to render assistance in any direction that circumstances might require. The firing having ceased, and the British having become masters of the field, they remained on it; and the Americans kept up a disorderly retreat by different roads to Chester, where they arrived in the course of the night.

As no regular returns were ever sent to Congress of this battle, it is difficult to say what was the loss sustained by the Americans. The British general reported the American loss at three hundred killed, six hundred wounded, and four hundred prisoners; and his own loss ninety killed, four hundred and eighty-eight wounded, and six missing. The British force in this battle was eighteen thousand men, and the American eleven thousand. The wound which Lafayette had received, confined him to his couch for two months. Washington was obliged to fight this battle under many disadvantages. Knowing that Philadelphia must not be abandoned without a struggle, and being well aware of the expectations formed by the country and by Congress; he felt certain that a defeat would be less injurious, than to permit the enemy to take Philadelphia without an encounter. Mistakes are likely to happen in every engagement; and had there not been false information received by Washington, there can be little doubt that he would have struck a decisive and victorious blow, which would have given a different aspect to the state of affairs. He retreated to Philadelphia the day after the battle, and encamped near Germantown.

The American Congress, so far from feeling depressed by the loss on this occasion, resolved to increase the army as largely and as promptly as possible, and invested Washington with additional authority. Fifteen hundred troops were ordered from the Hudson, and the militia of Pennsylvania and other States were called out in all haste. Washington was authorized to fill up the vacancies in the army, and to suspend any officer whose conduct would require it. He was empowered to take provisions for the army within seventy miles of head-quarters, and either to pay for the same, or to give certificates. There were a good many of the disaffected in Philadelphia, who, in the event of the approach of an enemy to the city, would be ready to give the British control of their property. The General had authority, therefore, to remove such goods as might be useful to the enemy, or secure it for the owners. The enthusiasm of Washington and his troops was not damped by the result of the last battle; and when the men were refreshed by the rest of a day, he crossed the Schuylkill, and by the Lancaster road approached the left of the enemy. The two armies met within twenty miles of the city, and a battle would then have been fought; but a heavy fall of rain came on, which suspended hostilities.

Without being followed by the enemy, Washington proceeded to Yellow Springs, and at Parker's Ford passed the Schuylkill, for the purpose of giving the enemy battle. But they had obtained the advance of him; and it was impossible to overtake them, in the present wearied condition of his troops. They would in all probability be in Philadelphia on the same night. In the last partial engagement which occurred a few days before, Washington had advanced to give the enemy battle, as far as Warren's tavern on the Lancaster road, but the rain again prevented; and when the weather cleared, the Americans were so deficient in powder as not to have a round left. The forty rounds to a man which they had brought with them had been totally destroyed; and now a position was necessary by which they could be defended until their arms could be placed in order, and ammunition be procured. While this purpose was being accomplished, the enemy marched from their position near White Horse tavern to Swede's Ford; and the American general threw himself in their front, to oppose them either in the passage, or after they had crossed the river.

Congress now removed to Lancaster, in Pennsylvania, and thence to the town of York. Cornwallis marched into Philadelphia and took possession of it on the 26th. He was followed by the whole body of British and Hessian grenadiers, and by all the best troops of his army. The long trains of artillery and light dragoons, with martial music and glittering arms, made an imposing appearance; and formed a striking and painful contrast to the patriot army, which had passed through the city a short time before.

After the occupation of the city by the British, Lord Howe left the Chesapeake, intending to take the strong defences of the Delaware, and proceed to Philadelphia. To assist in this movement, a detachment of British troops was stationed in New Jersey, the main body was posted in Germantown, then a village consisting of one street; while the remainder of the troops held possession of Philadelphia. Washington now conceived the bold design of attacking the British by surprise. The Skippack or main road, was nearly parallel to the Monatawny or Ridge road, on its right. The largest portion of the British troops was almost equally divided by the Skippack. Their right wing was commanded by General Grant, and lay to the east of this road; the left wing extended to the west; while the head-quarters of General Howe were in the rear. Strong detachments with cavalry covered and defended the several wings. The second battalion of British light-infantry, with a train of artillery, was stationed two miles from the main body on the west of the road, and formed the advance. It had an outlying picket, and two six-pounders were posted at Allen's house on Mount Airy. Chew's house, which stood beyond the village, and was about a hundred yards east of the road, was then the country-seat of the Chief Justice of Pennsylvania. It was a large substantial stone edifice, with ornamented grounds around it. About three-quarters of a mile in the rear of the light-infantry, lay the fortieth regiment of infantry under Colonel Musgrave.

The American army had been weakened by a detachment having been sent to New Jersey, to attack the fortifications at Billingsport. The time, nevertheless, was propitious. General Sullivan, with the right wing, composed of his own division and that of General Wayne, and sustained by a body of North Carolina reserve under Lord Stirling, and Maxwell's Virginia brigades, flanked by the brigade of General

23 *

Conway, was ordered to march down the Skippack road, and attack the enemy's left wing. The Pennsylvania militia, under General Armstrong, was directed to pass along the Ridge Road, and attack the left and rear of the enemy. The left wing of the Americans, made up of Greene's and Stephen's divisions, flanked by McDougall's brigade, commanded by General Greene, were to enter the village at the market-house. The two divisions were to attack the right wing of the enemy in front. Smallwood's division, made up of Maryland militia, and Forman's Jersey brigade, were to march around the Old York road, and fall upon them in the rear. Thus two-thirds of the troops were to assail the right of the enemy, with the purpose of forcing it. If this should be accomplished, the enemy would be pushed into the Schuylkill, or be compelled to capitulate. The plan was skilfully laid, and took the enemy by surprise.

On the third of October, 1777, the American army left Matuchen Hills by four routes, it being expected that all would arrive at the scene of action in time. The right wing, accompanied by Washington, reached Chestnut Hill at break of day; and a detachment from it attacked Allen's house, and killed two sentries. But the roll of a drum gave the alarm; and the picket-guard, after discharging the six-pounders, fled to the light-infantry battalion, which was now preparing for battle. The sun rose in obscurity; the routed British light-infantry, supported by grenadiers, soon rallied; and Sullivan's division and Conway's brigade joined in the attack. The British infantry fought bravely, then took to flight, and abandoned their artillery. General Wayne pursued them; and his men inflicted fearful retribution on the foe with their bayonets, for their fallen comrades of the 20th of September. The fog, however, was so dense that, with the smoke of musketry and cannon, the Americans frequently exchanged shots with each other by mistake. The enemy were driven from their encampment, and abandoned their tents and baggage; and while the main body rushed in a disorderly retreat through the village, with Wayne in hot pursuit, Musgrave and six companies of the fortieth regiment of the British took possession of Chew's house, barricaded the doors and lower windows, and thus converted it into a post of defence. The British were then summoned to surrender, without effect; and a flag accompanying the bearer of the demand was fired on. During the action which ensued many of the assailants, and few of the defenders, were slain; but in consequence of this delay of half an hour, the divisions and brigades, which had been separated by the skirmishing around Chew's house, could not again be united to the main body. A regiment was left to check the garrison, while the rear division again pressed onward. The heavy fog still rendered objects dim at thirty yards' distance. Washington could not, therefore, take any observation, nor obtain any information in reference to what was passing. His original plan of operations was only partially carried out; and with effect merely in the centre.

Sullivan, at a mile distant from Chew's house, being reinforced by the North Carolina troops, and by General Conway's brigade, advanced against the enemy's left, which yielded to his onset. The left wing under Greene, came late into the action; and ne divisions of Greene and Stephen were separated, that of the latter being detained by receiving and returning a heavy fire from Chew's house. General Greene pressed on; drove a light-infantry regiment before him; took some prisoners, and reached the centre of the village, where he found the British right at the market-house, drawn up to resist him. The enemy, however, gave way. Forman and Smallwood now appeared on the right flank; and the American troops seemed on the point of taking the whole force of the enemy. But a mysterious panic seized the troops at that moment. Washington, in a letter to his brother, says: "If it had not been for a thick fog, which rendered it so dark at times that we were not able to distinguish friend from foe at the distance of thirty yards, we should, I believe, have made a decisive and glorious day of it. But Providence designed otherwise; for after we had driven the enemy a mile or two, and after they were in the utmost confusion, and flying before us in most places; after we were upon the point, as it appeared to everybody, of grasping a complete victory, our own troops fled with precipitation and disorder. How to account for this I know not; unless, as I before observed, the fog represented their own friends to them for a reinforcement of the enemy, as we attacked in different quarters at the same time, and were about closing the wings of our army when this happened."

The enemy having recovered from their surprise, and the left wing being brought up by General Grey, pressed the Americans as they retreated. Cornwallis then joined the pursuit with a squadron of light-horse from Philadelphia. The Americans withdrew in good order, caraying off all their cannon and wounded. General Greene kept up a fighting retreat for several miles; General Wayne turned his cannon frequently on the enemy, and brought his troops to a stand near White Marsh.

The loss of the British in this battle was seventy-one killed, four hundred and fifteen wounded, and fifteen missing. The American loss was one hundred and fifty killed, five hundred and twenty-one wounded, and about four hundred taken prisoners. During the engagement Washington exhibited the coolest courage, exposing himself to the hottest fire of the enemy in the most daring manner. Though the Americans lost the victory in this conflict, it is said that the impression which this bold attempt produced on the British, was greater than that of any event which transpired in the war since the battles of Lexington and Bunker Hill. The struggle had an effect even in France; procured a compliment for General Washington from the Count de Vergennes; and exerted no small influence in obtaining the valuable assistance rendered ultimately by France to the United States. This battle had also the effect of raising the spirits of the army, and of animating the hopes of the nation; inspiring the people with confidence in the valor of the troops, and in the ability of their commander. The British forces afterward compelled the Americans to evacuate all the fortified posts on the Delaware. The brave defence of Fort Mifflin and Red Bank on that river, continued for six weeks; was followed by the evacuation of these places; and the British fleet then sailed in triumph to Philadelphia.

CHAPTER XXV.

THE AMERICAN CAMP AT WHITE MARSH — WINTER ENCAMPMENT AT VALLEY FORGE — SPURIOUS LETTERS — ORIGIN, DEVELOPMENT, AND CONCLUSION OF THE CONWAY CABAL—THE LOYALTY OF LAFAYETTE—THE MAGNANIMITY OF WASHINGTON—RELIANCE OF THE GENERAL ON THE GOD OF ARMIES — AN AFFECTING INCIDENT.

After the battle of Germantown Washington established himself in a strong position at White Marsh; and dispatched General Greene with a body of troops to oppose Cornwallis, who was attempting to reduce Fort Mercer, at Red Bank. In a skirmish which took place at Gloucester Point, Lafayette highly distinguished himself. Greene joined the army at White Marsh, as the enemy had crossed over to the city. The surrender of Burgoyne, which had taken place in the meanwhile, had allowed reinforcements to be sent from the Northern army; and Morgan's riflemen, with some of the New Hampshire troops, joined Washington's camp. Sir William Howe advanced as far as Chestnut Hill on the 4th of December, 1777, within three miles of the American camp. His force consisted of twelve thousand men; and as he had been lately reinforced, he deemed this a propitious time to try the hazard of a battle. He thought that the American general would afford him some advantage for an attack; but Washington persisted in waiting for him to commence operations, and he retired at last to Philadelphia, having lost in skirmishing sixty-three men wounded, twenty killed, and twenty-three missing.

It now began to grow cold, and the increased rigor of the season rendered it necessary for the Americans to enter winter quarters. The men were not only poorly provided with clothes and shoes, but in many instances were destitute of provisions and forage; arising from the fact that many persons refused to sell provisions to the Americans, either through fear of the enemy, through disaffection, or from their want of confidence in the certificates issued by Congress. It grieved Washington to be obliged to exercise the authority vested in him, not only because he respected the cultivators of the soil, but also because he knew it to be bad policy to alarm the inhabitants of a peaceful country; as well as on account of the demoralizing influence which such a course would produce upon the army. In a letter addressed to the President of Congress he alluded to his embarrassed position, and his knowledge of the jealousy which existed against the exercise of military power. He promises that no exertions will be wanting on his part to provide his own troops with supplies, and at the same time to keep them from being used by the enemy; and that it was his wish that the different States, of their own accord, might see the importance of maintaining the troops and furnishing supplies.

In a council of war which was summoned, each member set forth his opinion in writing; and there were widely differing views taken by the officers as to the best method of disposing the army during the ensuing winter. The general therefore determined to act upon his own judgment, and to construct a fortified encampment. The spot selected for this purpose was Valley Forge, about twenty miles distant from Philadelphia. The place lay between ridges of hills and the Schuylkill, the ground being woody. Washington examined it himself, and his practised eye designated the localities appropriate to each division of the army. On the 18th of December the troops were marched thither, and preparations were made for their accommodation. The place which was then selected they retained till the succeeding June. Intrenchments on the land side surrounded the entire encampment; and its communication with the country beyond the river was effected by a bridge constructed across it. The main body of the army was ordered to remain there; but a detachment was sent to Wilmington to protect Delaware from the hostile incursions of the enemy.

This encampment presented a curious aspect, but was exceedingly simple. Huts, each sixteen feet by fourteen, were erected of timber, which was squared, the logs being laid one on the other. The huts were placed in parallel lines, and presented the appearance of a town in some places, in which the troops from one State occupied one street or avenue, and those from a different State another. A general officer occupied a hut exclusively; and in proportion to their rank, a number of officers had one hut. One of these structures was allowed to twelve privates. Although Washington was now denying himself the pleasures a temporary retirement from his harassing duties; while from his zeal for the public good, he undertook to lead the armies of his country, and fight her battles; a plan was laid by his open and secret enemies to blast his influence and destroy his character. The first attempt of this kind was made by means of certain spurious letters, said to have been written by General Washington, in the summer of 1776, to Mrs. Washington, Mr. Custis, and Lund Washington, his steward. It was asserted that, on the evacuation of Fort Lee, "Billy," a servant of Washington, was left behind in ill health; and that he gave a portmanteau belonging to his master into the keeping of an officer, who found these letters in it, and sent them to England, where they were published. They were reprinted in New York, and distributed largely in handbills; and one of them, published on the 14th of February, appeared in extracts in a Philadelphia paper. Except to his friends in private, Washington took no notice of these letters at the time; but he afterward, in a letter to the Secretary of State, declared they were false and fabricated. Their design and execution were remarkably ingenious, and they mingled truth with falsehood so adroitly as to give them an air of genuineness to those unacquainted with Washington's character. But, whatever effect they may have produced in England, they could do him no injury with Americans, who knew him too well to believe him capable of writing them. In fact, the letters carried with them their own refutation; for they insinuated that Washington was secretly opposed to independence, and to the separation of the colonies from Great Britain. The real author of these letters was never discovered; and the servant of Washington referred to had never been at Fort Lee; but the individual who wrote them, with so much skill, it is supposed extracted portions of genuine letters of Washington which had been intercepted, and mixed them with his own composition. While the design of the author was self-evident, Washington truly remarked: "It is no easy matter to decide whether the villany or the artifice of these letters is the greatest." The individual who became most prominently identified with this disgraceful affair, and who obtained the unenviable notoriety of having it pass under his name, was General Conway; and the cabal in question is now known, and has become historical, by the name of "Conway's cabal." Beside General Conway, who was an Irishman by birth, had been in the French service, and prided himself on his thirty years' experience, Generals Gates and Mifflin were also implicated in the conspiracy, as well as several members of Congress.

When General Gates obtained his victory over Burgoyne, he had not the civility to inform the commander-in-chief of that event; and this mark of disrespect to the general whom they had chosen to conduct their armies, was passed over without censure by Congress. This circumstance affords a proof that the cabal had some influence among its members. Another evidence of this fact was the institution of a new Board of War, of which General Gates was president, and Conway and Mifflin members. This board was invested with extensive powers; many of its most important functions were not only independent of Washington, but appointed with the evident purpose of sapping the foundations of his authority, and securing his downfall. Gates and Mifflin had both been professed friends of Washington; and through him the former had, in a great degree, obtained his appointment. At the organization of the first continental army, Gates had desired the command of a brigade, and Mifflin that of a regiment. Both were refused, because their offices required their whole time, which they were reluctant to give to the service. Cambridge was the spot where the first signs of their discontent began to be manifest. At that period Gates was adjutant-general, with the rank of brigadier; Mifflin was aide-de-camp to the general, who appointed him quartermaster-general, with the rank of colonel. When the army left Cambridge, Gates employed all his influence, but in vain, to obtain a separate and independent command.

Conway eventually obtained his just reward. In a duel fought subsequently with an American officer, he was wounded, and as he supposed mortally. He then wrote to General Washington as follows: "My career will soon be over; therefore justice and truth prompt me to declare my last sentiments. You are, in my eyes, the great and good man. May you long enjoy the love, veneration, and esteem of these States, whose liberties you have asserted by your virtues." He recovered of his wound, however, and then went to France, leaving an unenviable reputation behind him. An affecting incident is related of Washington at this gloomy period, which shows his pious trust in the Supreme Being. Though often narrated, it deserves again to be repeated. "Isaac Potts, at whose house Washington was quartered, relates that one day, while the Americans were encamped at Valley Forge, he strolled up the creek; when not far from his dam he heard a solemn voice. He walked quietly in the direction of it, and saw Washington's horse tied to a sapling. In a thicket near by was the beloved chief upon his knees in prayer, his cheeks suffused with tears. Like Moses at the bush, Isaac felt that he was upon holy ground, and withdrew unobserved. He was much agitated, and on entering the room where his wife was, he burst into tears. On her inquiring the cause, he informed her of what he had seen, and added: 'If there is any one on this earth whom the Lord will listen to, it is George Washington; and I feel a presentiment that under such a commander there can be no doubt of our eventually establishing our independence, and that God in his providence has willed it so.'"

CHAPTER XXVI.

SUFFERINGS OF THE ARMY AT VALLEY FORGE — BARON STEUBEN — TREATY WITH FRANCE — "CONCILIATORY BILLS" OF LORD NORTH — SIR WILLIAM HOWE SUCCEEDED BY SIR HENRY CLINTON — PEACE COMMISSIONERS — THEIR RECEPTION AND DEPARTURE — THE BRITISH EVACUATE PHILADELPHIA — THEIR MARCH THROUGH THE JERSEYS — BATTLE OF MONMOUTH — CONDUCT AND COURT-MARTIAL OF GENERAL LEE — ARRIVAL OF THE COUNT D'ESTAING — OPERATIONS OF THE ALLIES AGAINST NEWPORT — ITS FAILURE, AND THE RESULT — CAMPAIGN OF 1779 — THE MASSACRE OF WYOMING AVENGED — ARRIVAL OF THE FRENCH FLEET UNDER DE TERNAY, AND ARMY UNDER COUNT DE ROCHAMBEAU.

THE American army suffered severely during the winter spent at Valley Forge. The march to that place was attended with much difficulty to the soldiers, many of whom marked the frozen ground with the blood of their lacerated feet. Clothing was ill provided; and when it was announced that a foraging party of the British were about to ravage the country, and several regiments were ordered to be ready to attack them, it was found that they had no provisions, and a dangerous mutiny was on the point of breaking out. To remedy this evil, parties were sent out to collect provisions, and orders were given to procure them wherever they could be obtained, to supply the pressing wants of the army. The same exigency existed several times during the winter;

and Washington had occasion to observe that, "for some days there has been little less than a famine in the camp. A part of the army have been a week without any kind of flesh, and the rest three or four days. Naked and starving as they are, we cannot enough admire the incomparable patience and fidelity of the soldiery, that they have not been, ere this, excited by their sufferings to a general mutiny and dispersion. Strong symptoms, however, of discontent have appeared in particular instances; and nothing but the most active efforts everywhere can long avert so shocking a catastrophe."

At that time blankets were so scarce, that many of the soldiers were compelled to sit up all night at the fires. They were destitute of that covering which should have kept them comfortable while they slept. But this was not all. They wanted, in many cases, decent clothing to leave their huts. The officers also, though not so poorly provided, suffered great hardships. The whole number in the field, when the army came into the encampment, was eleven thousand and ninety-eight. Two thousand eight hundred and ninety-eight of these were unfit for duty, from want of shoes and clothing. Yet, in this deplorable condition of the army, there were some who thought there should have been a winter campaign, and looked upon the army and its commander as inactive. Washington, in a statement made to Congress, represented the real condition of the army, and administered a rebuke to those who had presumed to remark on the inactivity of the troops: "I can assure those gentlemen, that it is a much easier and less distressing thing to draw remonstrances in a comfortable room by a good fireside, than to occupy a cold, bleak hill, and sleep under frost and snow, without clothes or blankets. However, although they seem to have little feeling for the naked and distressed soldiers, I feel superabundantly for them; and from my soul I pity those miseries, which it is neither in my power to relieve nor prevent."

Washington's first care now was to supply the pressing wants of the army. The chief cause of the famine was not in the absolute scarcity, but in the mismanagement of the affairs of the commissariat department. Congress having interfered with the matter, Colonel Trumbull, a gentleman of ability, who had charge of the department, indignantly resigned; and things fell into still greater confusion. A new system of arrangement was now absolutely necessary; and at the earnest solicitation of Washington, a committee of five, who were termed the "committee of arrangement," was appointed to investigate the affairs of the army, and to assist the general in adopting the new system. The pay of the officers was found to be insufficient for their subsistence; and it was ascertained that, for want of straw or materials to protect them from the wet earth, many of the troops had lost their lives. The army was in a more critical condition than when it lay before Boston; and a night attack upon it might have been fatal.

While the Americans suffered greatly from want of food and clothing, the British troops passed the winter sumptuously in Philadelphia. An attempt was made to capture Henry Lee, where he was stationed at an advanced post. But he distinguished himself by his great valor, won the praises of the commander-in-chief, and on his recommendation to Congress he was appointed commander of two troops of horse, with the rank of major. Mrs. Washington now returned to Valley Forge, as also did Lady Stirling, Mrs. Knox, and the wives of other officers. Some misunderstanding having arisen in reference to the embarkation of the troops of General Burgoyne from Boston, Congress resolved not to permit the embarkation till it should receive the ratification of the convention from the court of Great Britain. Bryan Fairfax, the old friend of Washington, visited the American camp, when on his way to England. The general was glad to see him, though they differed fundamentally in their views respecting the war. Baron Steuben, who had served in the army of Frederick the Great, came to the camp to offer his services, and was soon appointed inspector-general of the army. He rendered valuable aid to the troops, though he often became enraged at them; and the rigid discipline to which he subjected them was exceedingly useful, though irksome.

General Putnam had made a survey of the highlands of the Hudson, and West Point had been selected as an eligible site for the erection of a fortification. Major-General McDougall, with Kosciuszko to assist him as engineer, was ordered to take the command of the different highland posts. Brigadier-General Parsons, who had been previously in command, was now directed to seize on the person of Sir Henry Clinton, who lived at the Kennedy house, near the Battery, and not far off the Hudson. The attempt was never made, in consequence of the wise suggestion of Alexander Hamilton, that they knew the feeble disposition and abilities of Clinton, but did not know those of his successor, who might be an abler and more formidable man. The idea was therefore abandoned.

The capture of Burgoyne and his army had a powerful effect in England and France. The former feared that France was about to take up arms in the American cause; in consequence of which apprehension Lord North's "conciliatory bills" were passed in Parliament. One of these regulated taxation in such a way as was thought might be acceptable to the colonies; the other clothed commissioners with full power to negotiate a peace. General Tryon hastened with these bills to Washington, who sent them to Congress, with the just remark, that the time for overtures was past. The bills were in favor of peace; but it was agreed there could be no peace till all the hostile fleets and armies were withdrawn, and an acknowledgment made, in express terms, of the independence of the United States. On the 2d of May, 1778, a messenger arrived from France, bearing two treaties, one of which stipulated that should war occur between France and England, it should be an agreement between the contracting parties, that neither of them should proclaim the war without the concurrence of the other; and that, should a war take place, neither should lay down their arms before the establishment of the independence of the United States. There was great rejoicing at Valley Forge at the receipt of this news, and shouts of "long live the King of France," "long live General Washington," reverberated around the tottering huts of the destitute but heroic troops. The enthusiasm was immense, and proclaimed Washington to be the idol of the soldiery. On the 8th a council of war decreed that they should remain on the defensive, and not attempt offensive measures without an opportunity of striking some decisive blow.

Sir William Howe had now finished his military career, and was superseded by Sir Henry Clinton, who took the command on the 18th of May. Howe was a man of amiable and engaging manners. He held an extraordinary pageant at Philadelphia, a kind of regatta and tournament, at which the unfortunate Major André performed a conspicuous part. The British force in Philadelphia at that period amounted to nineteen thousand five hundred and thirty men. When Clinton took the command, indications were exhibited of the evacuation of Philadelphia. To watch the movements of the enemy, Lafayette was sent with twenty-one hundred horse. Crossing the Schuylkill on the 18th of May, he proceeded to Barren Hill; and either by the carelessness or treachery of a picquet, was nearly surrounded by a force sent out to intercept him. He saw their purpose, and threw out small parties to show themselves at different portions of the wood, as if he meditated an attack. The enemy came to a halt, and Lafayette pushing on, crossed the Schuylkill at Mason's Ford, and took up a strong position on the other side. The alarm guns at sunrise had informed Washington of his danger. The general with his staff galloped to the summit of a hill, and by the aid of his glass, discovered that the marquis was safe, who, returning at length to Valley Forge, was hailed with loud acclamations. An exchange was effected at this time of General Lee for General Preston. Lee was now restored to his position of second in command. Colonel Ethan Allen was also liberated in exchange for Colonel Campbell.

Preparations were now made by the British for the evacuation of Philadelphia; and New York was understood as the place of their destination. Affairs remained in suspense during three weeks. The New Jersey militia, and a brigade of troops under Maxwell, were now on the alert to throw down bridges, and to harass the enemy if they attempted to march through that State; and Washington held the army in readiness to march to the Hudson the moment there should be any necessity for it. The British commissioners arrived in Philadelphia on the 6th of June, 1778; but they were left in the dark by their own ministry in reference to their mission. Orders had been given to evacuate Philadelphia three weeks before their arrival, and to fix the British head-quarters at New York. Yet they knew nothing of these orders. They were, therefore, surprised and indignant. The "conciliatory acts" and other documents with which they were intrusted, were forwarded to Congress; and in the first reading came near being rejected on account of some language disrespectful to France. In the reply made by Congress, they expressed a willingness to treat for peace when the

King of Great Britain should evince a sincere desire for it by the withdrawal of his troops, and by an explicit acknowledgment of the independence of the United States. The commissioners made several attempts to corrupt members of Congress; and when their transactions became known to that body, it was resolved that their honor would not permit them to have anything further to do with the commissioners. They then attempted to seduce the general public; and offered to treat with delegates of different colonies or provincial assemblies. But all these efforts proved to be futile, and they at length returned in disgust to England.

The sagacity of Washington had been unable to account for the delay of the British troops in evacuating Philadelphia. His own army now consisted of twelve thousand continentals, and thirteen hundred militia. That of the enemy was reduced by a detachment of five thousand sent to the West Indies, and three thousand despatched to Florida. Most of the cavalry had been ordered to New York. The aid of Baron Steuben had been found of great importance to the Americans. The commander thought the best route was through the Jerseys. General Lee opposed this opinion, and had relapsed into his former supercilious manner of criticizing generals and military affairs. Washington called a council of war on the 17th. The question to be decided was, whether the enemy should be attacked if their route lay through the Jerseys, or whether they should push on at once to the Hudson, and thus secure the means of communication between the Southern and Eastern States;

and also whether, in case an attack was made, it should be a general or a partial one. Lee strongly opposed a general attack. Greene, Lafayette, and others, thought the enemy should be made to pay for all the sufferings and privations endured at Valley Forge. Washington agreed with the latter opinion; but requested each officer to state his views in writing.

The British had evacuated Philadelphia before this was done; the army moving with great secrecy on the 18th, so that the rear-guard reached the Jersey shore at ten o'clock. The first impulse of Washington was to send General Maxwell and his brigade to aid the New Jersey militia in annoying the enemy on their march, and to despatch Arnold to take possession of Philadelphia. He prepared to take the command of the main body in person, and pursue the enemy with all the celerity possible. He was compelled to march up the right bank of the Delaware as far as Trenton, and to cross at the spot rendered famous as that at which he had crossed to attack the Hessians. On the 20th he had proceeded as far as Coryell's Ferry. He was de ained by heavy rains, and could not cross until the 24th. The enemy were then at Moorestown and Mount Holly; and their march was slow. Rain, heat, and the want of bridges, which the Americans had broken down, retarded the advance of Sir Henry Clinton. This slowness of movement on his part, induced Washington to think that he wished to draw him into an engagement. Washington determined to act upon the opinions of Greene, Wayne, and Lafayette, which coincided with nis own; and to have the main body in a condition to fight should this course be deemed advisable. Clinton marched first to Brunswick, but as he thought the passage of the Raritan would be disputed, he took the road through Freehold to Navesink and Sandy Hook, designing to embark from thence. No doubt was then entertained of the route of the British, and one thousand men under Wayne were ordered to join the advance.

Washington now moved the main body of the army to Cramberry. Lafayette set out on the 25th to join General Scott; but Lee had changed his purpose, and desired, as the corps was six thousand strong, to command it. Washington did not know how to adjust the matter without doing violence to the feelings of Lafayette. A change in the tactics of Sir Henry gave an opportunity to Washington to extricate himself from the dilemma. It became necessary to augment the advanced corps in sending Lee forward; and therefore, being the senior officer, he would necessarily take the command. In a letter the general explained the matter to Lafayette, and the marquis resigned the command.

On the evening of the 27th the enemy encamped at Monmouth Court House. General Lee was posted about five miles distant, at Englishtown. The main body of the Americans was three miles in the rear. The position of Sir Henry was carefully reconnoitred by Washington at sunset. Sir Henry was well protected in his present position; but if he were to advance to Middletown, he would be in a stronger position still. This he determined to prevent; and in order so to do, gave orders to Lee to have his troops ready, lying all night on their arms, and to attack the rear of the British in the morning. He then returned to his own place in the main body; but ordered Lee to send off a detachment of seven hundred men to watch the enemy's movements, and to check them on the route.

An express at length informed Washington that the British were in motion. He ordered Lee to attack them, promising that he would hasten to support him. Knyphausen descended the valley, and Sir Henry remained at Freehold Heights, though afterward he marched toward Middletown. As Washington advanced, he was astonished to meet the whole command under Lee in full retreat. This was an alarming disaster, and might have led to a general defeat. Washington advanced to General Lee, and peremptorily ordered him to re-form his troops, and bring them again into action. The command was obeyed, and order was again restored in the American lines. Lord Stirling commanded the left wing, and placed his cannon in such a position as to do effectual damage to the enemy. The right was placed under General Greene. Wayne brought up a body of infantry. After a desperate engagement, night and darkness put an end to the battle. Washington slept in his cloak to be ready for action, and the troops reposed on their arms. But Clinton withdrew his troops in silence, from the scene of his defeat.

This battle accomplished much to inspire the troops with new courage. The British lost four officers, and about three hundred men. The Americans lost sixty-nine killed. As Sir Henry hastened through Jersey, one hundred were taken prisoners, and six hundred deserters reached Philadelphia. The British army was thus reduced twelve hundred men. Lord Howe's fleet was ready to convey the troops from Sandy Hook; and Washington having crossed the Hudson, encamped at a short distance from White Plains. Two letters written by General Lee to the commander at this time, evinced disrespect; and he was subsequently tried by a court-martial on three charges: disobedience, misbehavior, and disrespect to the commander. He was pronounced guilty, and suspended for one year from all command. He then left the army; and after some wanderings, returned to Philadelphia four years after, in which city he subsequently died.

Before the army had crossed the Hudson, news came of the arrival of the Count d'Estaing with a French fleet, consisting of twelve ships of the line and four frigates. Arrived at the Capes of the Delaware, the count received information of the evacuation of Philadelphia; and after sending a frigate up the river, he sailed for Sandy Hook, where Washington congratulated him on his arrival, and planned with him a joint attack. Colonel Hamilton was afterward sent on board with four pilots, to explain the views of the commander to the count. The refusal of the pilots to take the responsibility of conducting the heavy ships over the bar, prevented an immediate attack on the enemy's fleet in Sandy Hook, with a simultaneous attack on land. There were then six thousand troops stationed chiefly at Newport in garrison; and the French proceeded to that place. To render the attack on them effectual, troops were sent thither to co-operate, under Generals Sullivan, Lafayette, and Greene. Several causes produced the failure of this expedition, which it is not here necessary to trace. An attack was concerted; and some works being abandoned, Sullivan thought he would profit by the circumstance, and cross the river in flat-bottomed boats to take them. This proceeding offended the count, as interfering with his prerogatives; and a coldness ensued which effectually prevented all vigorous measures. Several plans were now suggested for the campaign of 1779; but a purely defensive one was that adopted, as best suited to the exhausted resources of the country. Besides the comparative cheapness of this policy, Washington thought that no great need existed to multiply the calamities of war by any extraordinary exactions; as the alliance of France, and the indications of a war between England and Spain, rendered it certain that in the end the independence of the United States would be secured, whenever peace would be proclaimed between them.

During the winter of 1779 the enemy remained within their lines in New York, and nothing of any great moment was attempted on either side; spring likewise passed away, and yet no remarkable event happened. The massacres of Wyoming and Cherry Valley had caused universal indignation at the recital of their horrors. Washington therefore fitted out an expedition against the Six Nations of Indians, who, instigated by British agents and Sir John Johnston, had attacked and ravaged the frontiers, and carried desolation to the inhabitants. Several independent companies from New York and Pennsylvania joined the four thousand continental troops under General Sullivan, whose head-quarters were at Wyoming He advanced from this position into the Indian territory along the Susquehanna; there he met General Clinton, who came from the Mohawk River by way of Lake Otsego, and formed a junction with Sullivan at the fork of the Susquehanna. With him he advanced into the settlements of the savages; and with their combined force, amounting to five thousand men, they defeated a band of Tories and Indians, whom they drove back. They then continued their march in a circuit as far as the Genesee, and destroyed houses, villages, provisions, and property of every kind. They pursued the Indians as far as Niagara, where they were protected by the British garrison. The army then returned by the Susquehanna to Wyoming.

A detachment of two thousand five hundred British was sent to Virginia in the spring of 1779, under General Matthews, which sacked the town of Suffolk; and after destroying an immense amount of provisions and burning the village, they seized a large quantity of tobacco, sunk or destroyed many vessels, captured others, and then escaped with their plunder. The squadron, on its return, was joined by vessels on which a large body of troops were embarked; and the expedition then sailed up the Hudson, under Sir Henry Clinton, whose aim was to take Stony Point and Verplanck's Point on the Hudson, and thus make himself master of the highlands, their passes and fortifications. The American troops stationed in Jersey soon arrested the further progress of the enemy in that direction, but did not arrive in time to prevent the capture of the two posts already named; and these were unable to resist an army of six thousand men, assisted by a powerful naval armament. A strong garrison was left at each of these posts, and the fortifications were continued which had been already commenced at the time of their capture. Washington having left a sufficient force to hinder the advance of the enemy, placed his army in and about the highlands, and made New Windsor, near West Point, his head-quarters.

Thirty-five thousand two hundred and eleven men constituted the nominal force which Congress designated for the campaign of 1780. Several difficulties impeded the raising of this large army; one of these was the depreciated continental currency. Prior to March of that year two hundred million dollars had been issued by Congress; of which no portion had ever been redeemed. Forty paper dollars were worth only one in specie, and the effect of this disproportion was to derange every branch of business. Another difficulty was the bad system of procuring supplies, which left it with each of the States to furnish a certain quota. The large number of hands through which the business must necessarily pass, the want of authority to compel promptitude, the difficulty of transportation, and various other causes, operated in a most disastrous manner; and, till it was abandoned, greatly perplexed the commander-in-chief. Paper money was made a legal tender by the Congress, and all debts might be paid, at the nominal value, in this currency. Many persons took advantage of this decree to liquidate their liabilities; but the expedient was regarded as unjust by Washington, who was a sufferer himself by it, to a very large extent. Fresh enlistments were now to be made, and each State was ordered to furnish its quota of troops to oppose the enemy's force, which now amounted in New York to seventeen thousand effective men.

General Lafayette returned from France in April, 1780, and brought the joyful news that an armament of land and naval forces was prepared by the government of that country, and would soon arrive in the United States. They subsequently arrived on the 10th of July, and entered the harbor of Newport. The forces consisted of eight ships-of-the-line, two frigates, two bombs, and over five thousand troops. The Chevalier de Ternay commanded the fleet, while the army was under the Count de Rochambeau. Another division at Brest, detained for want of transports, was soon expected. The harmony between the French and American troops was promoted by the excellent arrangement, according to which all of them were to be under the orders of General Washington; and when the armies were together precedence was to be given the American troops by the French. French officers of equal rank were to be under the command of American officers, and in all military acts the American generals were to take the lead. Lafayette informed Washington of these instructions in detail; and the Count de Rochambeau sent him an official copy of them. This policy promoted harmony and friendship from the beginning to the conclusion of the service; and Washington, as a compliment to the French, who wore white in their cockades, recommended the continental officers to blend it with the black, as a symbol of friendship. A plan of co-operation was now adopted, which was afterward postponed in consequence of the arrival of Admiral Graves with six ships, which rendered the British force superior to the French.

CHAPTER XXVII.

FRENCH FLEET BLOCKADED — INTERVIEW BETWEEN THE COMMANDERS — ITS RESULT — REVOLT OF THE PENNSYLVANIA LINE — WISE CONDUCT OF WAYNE, AND PLAN OF WASHINGTON WITH THE JERSEY LINE —ARTICLES OF CONFEDERATION—BATTLE OF THE COWPENS—AFFAIR OF M'GOWAN'S FORD — PROCLAMATION OF CORNWALLIS — STATE OF GREENE'S ARMY—RETREAT OF CORNWALLIS—FRENCH FLEET IN THE CHESAPEAKE — WASHINGTON AT NEWPORT — OPERATIONS OF LAFAYETTE — THE ENEMY AT MOUNT VERNON — FRENCH AUXILIARIES — ATTACK ON NEW YORK ABANDONED — ROBERT MORRIS — THE MARCH OF THE ALLIES SOUTHWARD—SIEGE OF YORKTOWN—SURRENDER OF CORNWALLIS.

Sir Henry Clinton was duly apprised of the destination of the French fleet, and resolved to exert himself to counteract its operations in behalf of the cause of America. Six thousand troops were detailed to attack the French in Newport in conjunction with the fleet; but while he was making his preparations, Count Rochambeau and General Heath had so augmented their forces, that Sir Henry was compelled to return to New York without effecting his object. He feared also that, as Washington had crossed the Hudson, he might attack New York. The French fleet could not act without a superiority to the English, and was now blockaded in Newport by General Arbuthnot. The other division was detailed at Brest, and that under De Guichen never sailed for the United States at all. The French army was on board the fleet, which it remained to protect. An interview took place between the American general and the French admiral on the 21st of September, at Hartford; but as a naval superiority was the basis of any future enterprise, it was impossible at present to concert any scheme of co-operation, and any plan must rest on contingent circumstances.

The year 1781 opened with a formidable revolt of the Pennsylvania line stationed at Morristown; which might have been attended with serious consequences. Fifteen hundred of these men paraded under arms; refused to obey their officers; and when General Wayne pointed his pistols at them, their bayonets were at his breast. "We love you," they said, "we respect you; but you are a dead man if you fire. Do not mistake us; we are not going over to the enemy; were they to come out, you would see us fight under your orders with as much resolution and alacrity as ever." A bloody affray ensued, in which many were wounded on both sides, and one captain was killed. The mutineers compelled three regiments to join them, and were then thirteen hundred strong. They seized on six field-pieces, and under the command of sergeants marched to Philadelphia to demand redress of their grievances from Congress. They complained that their pay was in arrears; that they were paid in the paper currency which was so much depreciated; and that, in addition to the hardships which they suffered, many of them were detained beyond the time of their enlistment. They had been enlisted to serve three years or during the war, and when on the expiration of three years they had demanded their discharge, the officers interpreted the agreement to mean three years, or should the war continue any longer, until its close. The prudence of Wayne in procuring supplies for them on the march, prevented them from plundering the inhabitants, and an express sent to Washington informed him of the revolt. He advised Wayne to do all in his power to soothe their irritated feelings, and drawing out a statement of their grievances, promised to represent their case to Congress.

This course produced a good effect. The President of Pennsylvania met them at Trenton, and some of them who had served three years were discharged, certificates being given for the deficit in their pay. All their arrears were to be settled as soon as possible. The men were to be furnished with the articles of clothing necessary to their immediate wants. Those who were not discharged, obtained a furlough of forty days, and thus the whole revolting force were disbanded for a time. Two spies sent by Clinton to tamper with the troops, were given up and hanged. The revolters scorned the idea of deserting to the enemy, and said they had no intention of becoming *Arnolds*.

Washington, who questioned the policy pursued in this case, had an opportunity of acting in accordance with his own views; and doubting what results the example of the late revolt might produce, he ordered a thousand picked men from the highland regiments to be ready for action at a moment's notice. The New Jersey troops soon afterward revolted, and threatened to march to Trenton and obtain redress of grievances from the State Legislature at the point of the bayonet. Six hundred men, under the com mand of General Howe, were ordered to reduce the mutineers to unconditional submission. This was speedily accomplished. The mutineers were taken by surprise, ordered to parade without their arms, and to deliver up the ringleaders. They obeyed, and two of them were shot. The remainder returned to their duty, and thus the mutiny was suppressed.

Washington rejoiced to see the articles of confederation between the States ratified at this time; for though a set of articles had been submitted by Dr. Franklin in 1775, they were retarded by the disputes of some of the States. The confederation was now complete, and was expected to exert the happiest influence in this country and in Europe. The commander-in-chief, in a letter to the President of Congress, congratulated him in suitable terms on the long wished for and propitious event.

Washington now wrote to the Count de Rochambeau, who commanded the French fleet, suggesting that M. Destouches should at once sail with his whole fleet, and with a thousand French troops, to Virginia. An engagement between the French and English squadrons took place at the Capes of Virginia, in which the trophies of courage and victory were about equal. When Washington was informed that M. de Tilly had sailed to the south, he sent twelve hundred men, under the Marquis de Lafayette, to co-operate with the French against Arnold. Baron Steuben had operated in Virginia against that traitor before the arrival of Lafayette, who, as the senior officer, had now command of all the continental troops, and all the militia in that State. Washington

26

proceeded to confer with the French commanders at Newport. He set out on the 2d of March, and arrived after a journey of three weeks. The citizens of Newport presented an address to him in public, expressing the gratitude they felt for his services to his country. They dwelt on the joy it gave them to see him among them. He declared the lively satisfaction he experienced, and reciprocated their kindly sentiments, taking notice also of the magnanimity of the French allies, their zeal in the American cause, and their claims to the lasting gratitude of the nation.

No general arrangement could then be made for concerted action, on account of the uncertainty of the designs of the enemy. Though not then known, it became evident afterward that Sir Henry Clinton attempted to change the seat of war to the Chesapeake and Pennsylvania; to effect which two thousand men, under General Phillips, were sent to Virginia to coöperate with Arnold and Lord Cornwallis, who were expected to proceed through North Carolina and form a junction with these troops. As no part of the French fleet arrived in the Chesapeake, Lafayette, who was to act in concert with them, led his army to Annapolis; and having heard that the English, instead of the French fleet, was in the Chesapeake, he prepared to return to the Hudson. But when he had reached the head of the Elk, he received orders from Washington to march southward, and meet the British in Virginia, or join the Southern army. One of the enemy's vessels which ascended the chief rivers of the Chesapeake Bay, sailed up the Potomac to Mount Vernon. Lund Washington incurred the displeasure of the general by yielding to the demands which the enemy made, in order to save the mansion and estate from threatened ruin. Washington would rather have heard that Mount Vernon was in ruins, than that his steward, who was his representative, should have visited the vessels of the enemy, and furnished them with refreshments. These sentiments coincided with those which ever characterized the public and private life of Washington.

An entry made in Washington's diary of the 1st of May, 1781, shows the condition of the army to have been destitute of many necessaries; and the prospect of the coming campaign to have been gloomy in the extreme. He was soon cheered, however, by the arrival of Count de Barras in Boston harbor, with a French frigate, and with the news of a reinforcement of troops from France, and of another fleet from the West Indies, which would sail for the United States, under the Count de Grasse. A conference took place on the 22d of May, at Weathersfield, in Connecticut, between the American and French commanders. The Count de Barras was detained at Newport, as a British squadron had appeared. That nobleman had succeeded M. Destouches in the command. On the part of the French, the Marquis de Chastellux, who held the rank of major-general in the army, accompanied Count de Rochambeau; the commander-in-chief, with Generals Knox and Duportail, attended on the part of the Americans.

Two things claimed the chief attention of this conference: an expedition to Virginia, and an attack in concert on New York. These points were freely debated, and it was finally arranged that Count de Rochambeau should march from Newport, and join the American army on the Hudson. At this time Washington wrote to the governors of the Eastern States, requesting them to furnish their quotas; and if men could not be enlisted for three years or during the war, to enlist them for the campaign only, as the demand for their service was imperative. The militia were to defend Newport in the absence of the French fleet.

Washington was holding correspondence, during all this time, with the most distant portions of his command, and directing the operations under Gene rals Greene and Lafayette at the South; while the Canadian frontier, and the western posts beyond the Alleghenies, also claimed his attention. Robert Morris, then recently appointed Superintendent of Finance by Congress, procured on his personal credit two thousand barrels of flour for the army, of which it was in great need. The first position of the American army was at Peekskill, and it afterward encamped at Dobbs' Ferry on July the 4th. It was joined by Count de Rochambeau on the 6th, and the French occupied the left, extending to the Broux in a single line. An ineffectual attempt had been made by General Lincoln and the Duke de Lauzun previously, on the north side of New York Island. The two commanders reconnoitred the works; but so slow were the recruits in coming in, that the army was never capable of an attack, unless in the case of the superiority of the French fleet to that of the enemy. Count de Grasse was therefore advised to sail to Sandy

Hook. He sent a letter to the effect that he would soon sail from St. Domingo to the Chesapeake with his whole fleet, and three thousand two hundred troops. He could not, however, remain on the coast beyond October; and this circumstance changed the aspect of affairs. It was agreed, therefore, to give up the siege of New York; and, taking as many of the American forces as could be spared from the defences and highlands of the Hudson, proceed with the remainder and the French troops to Virginia. The advance of Cornwallis into the lower counties of Virginia, was checked by the valor and skill of the Marquis de Lafayette, whose prudence and good generalship merited and received the praises of Washington. The King of France, through the minister of war, expressed his approbation by the assurance given that, when the United States no longer required the services of the marquis, he should be raised to the rank of field-marshal in the French army. It should be mentioned to his honor that, when in Baltimore, he had clothed the troops at a cost of two thousand pounds, drawn from his own funds. The Hudson was now left in command of General Heath, and the two armies advanced through Philadelphia to the head of the Elk. Robert Morris obtained a loan of twenty thousand dollars for the use of the troops, as they marched through that city. On the way southward, Washington stopped at Mount Vernon. Six eventful years had elapsed since he had been sheltered under its peaceful roof; and now, with his suite, the Count de Chambeau, the Marquis de Chastellux, and other distinguished guests, he was once more received and entertained with the profuse hospitality of old Virginia. He joined Lafayette at Williamsburg on the 14th of September, 1781. Lord Cornwallis had hoped that the British would be superior to the French fleet, and had relied for aid on Sir Henry Clinton. He had taken possession of Yorktown, and of Gloucester, on the opposite side of the York River. These were places of considerable strength, especially the latter, into which he threw his main army, erected strong defences, and prepared for an obstinate siege.

Meantime the whole fleet of Count de Grasse, twenty-six ships-of-the-line and several frigates, had encountered Admiral Graves off the Capes, and had entered the Chesapeake Bay. The French squadron from Newport, under Count de Barras, had joined him. The army of Lafayette formed a union with the forces of the Marquis de St. Simon, consisting of three thousand men; and the French and American troops were brought down in transports sent up the Chesapeake. At Cape Henry the two commanders held a conference on board the *Ville de Paris*, with Count de Grasse; and the two generals marching all the troops from Williamsburg, the allied forces invested Yorktown on the 30th of September, 1781. The French were posted on the left, and formed a semi-circular line on the York River. The Americans were stationed on the right. Lauzun's legion, marines from the fleet, and Virginia militia, invested Gloucester. On the 6th of October, General Lincoln opened the first parallel, within six hundred yards of the enemy's works. Foundations for two redoubts were laid within it; its extent was nearly two miles;

and the American and French soldiers worked at it in harmony, under a severe fire from the enemy. When the parallel and several batteries were completed on the 9th, General Washington fired the first cannon. His operations were vigorous; he observed the siege progressing with a great display of gallantry on both sides; and though several times in imminent danger, he behaved with the utmost coolness and presence of mind.

The siege was conducted with the usual routine of operations, both defensive and offensive; but the chief event was the storming of two redoubts by a party of American light-infantry, headed by Lafayette; and by a body of French grenadiers and chasseurs, led on by the Baron de Viomenil. Both were successful under a destructive fire, and carried the redoubts at the point of the bayonet. Alexander Hamilton, who led the advance corps of the American party, manifested extraordinary bravery. Cornwallis soon saw that he could not hold the position. The defences were crumbling, and though his proud spirit recoiled from the thought of a surrender, he attempted to make his escape, though unsuccessfully. There was no other alternative, and on the 17th of October he dispatched a note, proposing a cessation of hostilities for twenty-four hours, and the appointment of commissioners to confer in reference to the surrender of Yorktown and Gloucester.

Washington desired Cornwallis to communicate the proposed terms in writing, and hostilities were suspended for that purpose. Some of the terms demanded were inadmissible; and Washington sketched and sent on the 19th the outlines of a capitulation, such as he was willing to accept. He expected that the terms would be signed by eleven o'clock, and the garrison would be ready to march out at two. Cornwallis eventually complied with these terms. They were as follows: The troops in the garrison were to be given up as prisoners of war; all the artillery arms, military chests, stores, shipping, and boats, were to be delivered; the officers were to retain their side-arms; and the private baggage of officers and soldiers was to be retained, except that which had been taken in the country.

The commissioners appointed on the part of the Americans and French were Colonel Laurens and Viscount de Noailles; and those on the part of the British were Colonel Dundas and Major Ross. The Bonetta sloop-of-war was left, at the request of Cornwallis, to convey despatches to Sir Henry Clinton. In it were taken all the traders within the lines; and it was afterward to be returned, and with the crew, guns, and stores, to be surrendered. The British lost, in this siege, six hundred men; the Americans and French three hundred in killed and wounded. The whole number of prisoners, exclusive of seamen, was seven thousand men. The allied army included seven thousand American regular troops, and four thousand militia; the French numbered five thousand. The land forces surrendered to General Washington, while the seamen, ships, and naval trophies, were received by the French admiral. General Washington obtained two stands of colors, Count de Rochambeau and Count de Grasse two field-pieces from the capture; and with these the commanders received the thanks of Congress.

CHAPTER XXVIII.

WASHINGTON URGES PREPARATIONS FOR ANOTHER CAMPAIGN — REASONS — THE NEWBURG ADDRESSES, AND CONCLUSION OF THE MATTER — VIEWS OF A PEACE ESTABLISHMENT, AND CIRCULAR LETTER TO GOVERNORS OF STATES — PEACE PROCLAIMED — WASHINGTON'S FAREWELL ADDRESS TO THE ARMY — AFFECTING SCENE IN PARTING WITH HIS OFFICERS — RESIGNATION OF HIS COMMISSION, AND RETIREMENT TO MOUNT VERNON — HE ENGAGES IN AGRICULTURAL PURSUITS — IS CHOSEN FIRST PRESIDENT OF THE UNITED STATES — ADOPTION OF THE CONSTITUTION — WASHINGTON'S DUTIES, AND HIS ILLNESS — HE RECOVERS — HIS RULES RESPECTING APPOINTMENTS — THE FUNDED DEBT — THE NATIONAL BANK ESTABLISHED — DUTY IMPOSED ON LIQUORS DISTILLED IN THE UNITED STATES.

THE Revolutionary struggle was now virtually terminated. The sword was to be turned into the ploughshare; and the desperate vicissitudes of strife and blood to be exchanged for the more attractive scenes of concord and peace. The chieftain whose wisdom and prowess had conducted the patriot army through the triumphs of the Revolution, was about to dismiss his valiant officers and his brave allies, and retire to the welcome retreat of Mount Vernon, and the cherished delights of home. He saw the armies of the despot vanquished, and the sceptre over the colonies broken; but he also knew the stern temper of the British Cabinet, and the resources which might yet be employed to prolong the conflict. It was his policy to be prepared for the future, and have the country defended by the presence of a powerful force. The pacific pretensions of such a wily foe could not be depended upon, and to prepare for another campaign was the proper policy to be adopted. Therefore Washington stirred up the people to vigorous action. Six millions of livres, to be paid monthly by France, were of great advantage; and in the departure of the Marquis de Lafayette to that country, America would possess an ardent friend, who would be mindful of her interests.

Nevertheless recruiting proceeded slowly, and Washington endeavored, by the strongest arguments, to induce the States to furnish their quotas. The officers who were in arrears of pay had become discontented, and serious consequences were apprehended from that source. But a still more dangerous influence was at work; a letter addressed to the commander-in-chief expressed the idea that a monarchy should be erected in the colonies; and suggested that the same abilities that had triumphed in the storms of war, would be no less likely to be useful in the calmer arena of peace. This idea was spurned by Washington with contempt; and he exhibited such marked manifestations of his displeasure as crushed the conspiracy in the bud. This he did at the zenith of his power, and when it was seriously proposed to make him king.

Sir Guy Carleton arrived in New York, bringing the tidings of peace. He wrote in August to say that negotiations were then progressing in Paris, the first condition of which would be the recognition of the independence of the United States. The French troops, after being two years and a half in the country, returned in December to France. The army at Newburg became full of malcontents, on account of the prospects of the officers and privates. The arrears of pay due them seemed to be insecure, and in order to obtain their rights, they sent three of their number with a memorial to Congress. While many in that body were found willing to commute half-pay for life into whole pay for five years, a sufficient number of States could not be induced to vote for it, and thus the matter was not adjusted. This gave rise to the famous *Newburg Addresses*, which were of a very inflammatory character, and summoned a meeting of the disaffected officers on the 10th of March, 1783. Washington, in his general orders, censured the anonymous address which had been published, and appointed a day for the meeting of the officers. This was held on the 15th of that month, at which time he addressed them, and promised to exert his utmost influence with Congress to have their grievances remedied, and their demands complied with. They thanked him, and by his prudence a state of tranquillity was restored, instead of one of insubordination and turbulence. Washington performed his promise; Congress voted the commutation of half-pay, and redressed the other grievances complained of by the officers in their memorial. Peace was proclaimed to the American army on the 19th of April, eight years after the first American blood had been shed at Lexington.

The time had now arrived when Washington was

to separate from his brave companions-in-arms, the officers who had been his associates in the dangers and trials of the war, and in whom he felt deeply interested. Their last interview took place on the 4th of December, at Francis' tavern, and the emotion which Washington exhibited on that occasion was intense. It was truly an impressive scene. He filled a glass, drank, and then added: "With a heart full of love and gratitude I now take leave of you; I most devoutly wish that your latter days may be as prosperous and happy, as your former ones have been glorious and honorable. I cannot come to each of you to take my leave, but shall be obliged if each of you will come and take me by the hand." A tear trembled in the eye of every officer present. The silence which ensued was profound; and after having bid adieu to each separately, Washington retired. As his barge lay at Whitehall, the company followed him thither in mute procession; and when he entered it, he took off and waved his hat to them as a final farewell. He now proceeded slowly to Annapolis, to which place Congress had adjourned; and on his way met with innumerable tokens of respect and affection from the people. Having arrived at Annapolis, he resigned his commission, on the 25th of December, 1783, in presence of a large concourse of spectators, in the hall of Congress; and thus withdrew from public life, and from official duties, to the repose and seclusion of a private citizen. He reached Mount Vernon on the same day — a spot which, except on his way to Yorktown, he had not seen for eight years and a half. His feelings on this occasion were expressed in a letter to Lafayette: "I have not only retired from all public employments, but am retiring within myself, and shall be able to view the solitary walk, and tread the paths of private life, with heartfelt satisfaction. Envious of none, I am determined to be pleased with all; and this, my dear friend, being the order of my march, I will move gently down the stream of life, until I sleep with my fathers."

One of the first duties which occupied the attention of Washington, on his return to Mount Vernon, was to look after his affairs; which, in consequence of his prolonged absence, had fallen into much confusion. As he would not accept any compensation for his military services, he felt it the more imperative to repair his losses, and not only to economize, but to add to the value of his possessions. On his retirement from public life, the Executive Council of Pennsylvania directed their delegates in Congress to say, that General Washington on his retirement, from the very fame of his illustrious achievements, would be put to expense by the admiration excited by his virtues; that in such a view of the case, though he would accept no pecuniary compensation for his services, and the matter required to be treated with great delicacy; yet, that the people of Pennsylvania would regret that his merits should be burdensome to him, and they relied on the good sense of Congress to give the matter an early attention. This step could not be taken without his previous knowledge, and he promptly expressed the wish that no movement of the kind should be made He now devoted his thoughts to improvements on his farm, and the entertainment of such company as were attracted to Mount Vernon from respect and admiration of its owner. He received with affability the friends who visited him, and entertained strangers with dignified politeness. In the reception of his guests, he was aided by the discretion and amiable courtesy of Mrs. Washington.

Washington made a tour to the West in September, 1784, in order to inspect some property which he owned beyond the Allegheny Mountains; and also to ascertain the practicability of opening a communication between the waters that flow into the Atlantic and those that flow to the West, and fall into the Ohio River. He travelled on horseback the whole distance of six hundred and eighty miles, following the route formerly taken by Braddock. When he reached the Monongahela, he spent a few days in surveying some lands which he possessed there, and which had been partly settled. He ascended the Monongahela, and then travelled across the country between the ridges of the Allegheny Mountains. It was his intention to ascertain whether a communication could be opened between the western waters and the Potomac and James' Rivers. On his return he wrote to the Governor of Virginia, communicating to him the information he had gained in reference to the matter; explaining the immense advantages that would accrue to the country from such an intercommunication; and setting forth how much commerce would thereby be facilitated. He urged the argument that the United States in that direction were possessed of formidable barriers; that the several States ought to be bound together by indissoluble bonds; he showed what injuries the Spaniards on the right, and Great Britain on the left, could effect by holding out inducements for the trade or alliance of those near them. He remarked, from what he saw, that the Western States stood on a pivot, which the weight of a feather would turn either way. "They have looked down the Mississippi until the Spaniards, very impolitically, I think, for themselves, threw difficulties in their way." He then showed how that was the most favorable time for Virginia to undertake the enterprise, which she could do with the utmost advantage; as the inhabitants of those territories were willing to meet her more than half way. The State of Virginia, at that time, was prosperous and powerful. Her area extended from the Atlantic to the western waters. She had two noble rivers, whose sources were in the Alleghenies; and he thought a commencement of this great work could best be made then.

On the departure of General Lafayette, who had accompanied Washington during his journey through the Eastern and Middle States, and had been enthusiastically received, and then spent two months in Mount Vernon, he wrote to his wife: "We restore the marquis to you in good health, crowned with wreaths of love and respect from every part of the Union." Lafayette was the attached friend of Washington, and these great men entertained the sincerest affection and esteem for each other. Washington entertained the conviction that this meeting would be their last; and such indeed proved to be the case.

The letter sent by Washington to the Governor of

Virginia impressed the Legislature with the truth of his views; surveyors were appointed, and two companies were organized, named the Potomac Company, and the James' River Company. The first offered Washington fifty shares of stock, valued at ten thousand dollars, and the other one hundred shares, which were worth five thousand pounds. To accept these tenders would have been contrary to his principles, while to decline them would be thought ungrateful, after the liberal manner in which they were offered to his acceptance. An answer was not needed till the next session of the Legislature. He apprehended that the non-acceptance of them might retard the operation of the companies, by the withdrawal of the subscriptions for the shares made on his account. He therefore wrote to the governor to say that, if permitted to receive the proffered shares as an appropriation for a public object, he would accept them. His proposal was agreed to; the shares of the James' River Company were transferred to Liberty Hall Academy, afterward called Washington College; and the Potomac Company's shares he left, at his death, to found a university in the District of Columbia. Washington was ever the friend of education, promoted its interests by contributions and donations, and accepted the office of chancellor of William and Mary College.

The famous Lady Huntingdon at that time entertained a scheme for the civilization of the Indians. It was her design to send out a settlement at her own expense to introduce knowledge and the influences of the true religion among them. She wrote to

Washington in reference to the matter, and he laid the affair before Congress; but social and political reasons operating at that time, prevented the enterprise from being carried into effect. Washington regularly appropriated fifty pounds a year, out of his own means, to educate the poor children of Alexandria; many benefactions were conferred by him which were never brought to light; and he even offered on several occasions to defray the college expenses of young men.

Washington's agricultural employments were much interrupted by his extensive correspondence; by the numerous applications of all kinds made to him; by the company he was compelled to receive; and also by the adjustment of his own accounts. Foreigners and his own countrymen resorted in large numbers to Mount Vernon. He rose early, and usually wrote or read until breakfast; after which he rode round his farm, "to inspect the outposts." He then returned, re-entered his study, and there remained till three o'clock, which was his hour for dining.

But whatever Washington's occupations and engagements may have been, his country always held a paramount claim upon his attention. Her Senators always consulted him in doubtful and important emergencies. The pressure of the war which had preserved the Union, now being taken off, the Federal Congress retained but a feeble organization, possessing little authority, and its power became in fact a mere shadow. The Confederacy was defective in many essential points, and Congress could neither regulate commerce, nor provide for the payment of the public debts. It had not the power to make treaties with foreign nations, or suppress discontents at home; and a crisis was approaching not less to be dreaded, perhaps, than the ordeal through which the nation had recently passed. The defects of the American Confederacy at that period are familiar matters of history; and need not now be pointed out more particularly. The thirteen States were in a condition of transition. The difficulties to be encountered were sufficiently great in themselves, but they were aggravated by designing men who endeavored to promote their own malicious and selfish ends; and demagogues diffused the rank venom of their baleful influence through the body politic. The States became jealous of the Federal Congress, and many thought that the less power possessed by that body, the better it would be for the several States. The condition of affairs was such, that between the sectional influences brought to bear, and the other defects under which the Confederacy labored, a speedy reform must take place, or the Union must be dissolved.

Washington clearly perceived the impending dangers. He possessed the same cool and steady courage, the same fertility of resources, the same bold yet prudent resolution, which had availed him on the battle-field. The flame of patriotism still burned within him, and all his private interests were nobly sacrificed on the altar of the Republic. It happened at that time, that the improvements suggested by him, and carried out by the Legislature of Virginia respecting the navigation of certain rivers, and the communication that would thus encircle the whole country, and bind the Republic together; caused the assembling of commissioners from several States to take place in reference thereto; and their delegates were to organize in a general convention, to which Washington was appointed delegate. He was thus placed in an embarrassing condition, inasmuch as, being President of the Cincinnati, — a society which had for its object the perpetuation of the friendship and intercourse of the officers of the army, and the aid of distressed members and their widows and orphans; — and now being about to resign the presidency of the same, assigning as a reason for so doing that he found it inconvenient to attend its meetings in Philadelphia; for him then to appear at the Convention seemed inconsistent, and might give cause to suspect his sincerity toward the members of the Society of the Cincinnati. The wisdom and prudence of Washington were imperatively required at the Convention; and Congress had appointed the second Monday in May as the time for its meeting in Philadelphia. This date possessed the advantage of allowing Washington also to be present at the meeting of the Cincinnati, if he wished so to do; and therefore he resolved to accept the appointment to the Convention as one of the delegates from Virginia. The result which he wished to effect by attending the Convention, was thus expressed by himself: "My wish is, that the Convention may adopt no temporizing expedients, but probe the defects of the Constitution to the bottom, and provide a radical-cure, whether they are agreed to or not. A conduct of this kind will stamp wisdom and dignity on their proceedings, and hold up a light, which sooner or later will have its influence." He was received on his approach to Philadelphia with public honors, and escorted by a troop of horse from Gray's Ferry. When the Convention was organized, all the States being represented but Rhode Island, its unanimous vote called Washington to the Presidential chair. This office he filled with dignity and wisdom during the four months of the sitting of the Convention; during which time the Constitution of the United States was adopted and substituted for the previously existing Articles of Confederation. All the members except three signed it on the 17th of September, 1787; copies of it were sent to Congress, and that body distributed them to the different States to be examined and approved by the several Legislatures.

This Constitution was not regarded as perfect by any of its framers. The opinion of Washington, Franklin, Hamilton, and others was, that, taken as a whole, it was the best that could then be devised; and the great marvel is, that the delegates of so many different and distant States, should, notwithstanding their local prejudices and conflicting interests, have framed and adopted such a Constitution. By a prevalent spirit of compromise and mutual concession, the Constitution was accepted by the Conventions of different States, and the ratification of nine of them gave it validity and effect. Under its provisions, Congress passed an act by which the people throughout the Union were, on a certain day, to appoint electors to choose a President of the United States, according to the Constitution, and another day for the electors to convene and vote for the person approved by the nation. The first of these elections was to be held on the first Wednesday in February, 1789; the other on the first Wednesday of the ensuing March.

Since the adoption of the Constitution, the public choice was centered upon Washington as the first President of the United States; and the conviction was universal that he was the only person in whom the country could place unlimited and harmonious confidence. His reluctance to mingle again in public life was well known, yet it was also believed that the call of his country would never be heard by him in vain. The day of election arrived; the electors assembled; the vote was taken; and George Washington was chosen President of the United States, and John Adams Vice-President.

A messenger was despatched to Mount Vernon bearing a letter from the President of the Senate, by which General Washington was officially informed of his election; and two days after, on the 16th of April, he departed for New York, at that time the seat of Congress. His feelings are thus portrayed by his own hand: "About ten o'clock I bade adieu to Mount Vernon, to private life, and to domestic felicity; and, with a mind oppressed with more anxious and painful sensations than I have words to express, set out for New York in company with Mr. Thompson and Colonel Humphreys, with the best disposition to render service to my country in obedience to its call, and with less hope of answering its expectations."* His

---

*** Immediately before his departure to New York to assume the duties of the Presidency, Washington hastened to Fredericksburg,**

whole journey to Congress was attended by every possible demonstration of popular respect and admiration; and he was met in New Jersey by three members of the Senate, and five of the House of Representatives, who, as a Committee from Congress, attended his public entry to New York. Processions, illuminations, and firing of guns, with the concourse of vast numbers of the inhabitants who poured forth on the occasion, hailed the public advent of the first President of the United States. On the 30th of April, 1789, amid the exercises of devotion, the ceremonial that attends the high station, the escort of troops, and the crowding of multitudes, the oath of office was publicly administered; and the man whose virtues had saved the country in war, was now to sustain its interests in the not less trying scenes of political conflict. With sentiments of sincere dependence on the Almighty; with the intimation that he would accept no compensation but the payment of his expenses; uttered in a speech which indicated at once his deep emotions, the ardor of his zeal in his country's cause, and his modest opinion of his own

---

where his venerable mother still resided, at an extremely advanced age, to bid her farewell. She was afflicted with a cancer in the breast; and it was probable that they would never meet again. The interview between them is described as having been affecting in the extreme. She bestowed her maternal blessing on her illustrious son; spoke of the pride and joy which she experienced in being the mother of one who had accomplished so much for his country's good; while he, on his part, promised to make her a speedy visit, expressed a hope for her recovery, and consoled her for the separation which his public duties required them to endure It proved to be their last interview.

abilities in the untried field before him; the first magistrate of the nation entered on the difficult duties of his office. No plan had as yet been organized by Congress for the various departments of government; and therefore for the present, business was transacted by the officers who had previously been chosen. From each of these the President requested a report respecting the matters appertaining to their duties; from which he diligently made extracts with his own hand. With reference to foreign affairs, which were the most difficult and intricate of all the departments of Government, he visited the public archives, examined the official correspondence which took place between the end of the war and his Presidency; and making copious notes, familiarized his mind with every important subject. His growing attachment to agriculture, when leaving Mount Vernon, incited him in the intervals of public duty to mature the systematic pursuit and study of that art; and he exacted from the superintendent of his estate a weekly account of all the transactions of each day upon each of his farms, the number of men employed, and every circumstance which occurred. Thus he became acquainted with the entire details, as minutely as if he had been present; and he made copies of his letters to his superintendent, which, with the reports received from him, he always put on file, and preserved. This practice he continued during the eight years of his Presidency; and he also corresponded with such persons in Europe and America as were distinguished for their eminence in the art of agriculture.

It soon became obvious to Washington that he must appoint certain hours in which to receive company, or he would never enjoy any leisure or privacy. He gave notice, therefore, that all persons who chose to call on him might do so on Tuesdays between three and four o'clock. Every Friday afternoon visits were received by Mrs. Washington, at which the general was generally present. He was always accessible on matters of business by appointment. He received no calls on Sunday; on which day he attended church in the morning, and retired in the afternoon to his private apartment. Promiscuous company was not admitted in the evening of that day, which he usually spent with his family; but an intimate friend was sometimes received. Washington was soon after seized by a dangerous illness, in which he was attended by Dr. Bard, an eminent physician of that day. The attack was very severe, confined him to bed six weeks, and it was six more before he regained his strength. He had scarcely recovered, when he was informed of the death of his mother, who expired at the advanced age of eighty-two.

Near the end of September, 1789, Congress adfourned for three months. They had been chiefly engaged in adopting such measures as were necessary to the organization of the Government, providing a suitable remedy for existing evils, and the establishment of the judiciary. Duties and tonnage on imported goods were imposed, and some amendments to the Constitution were suggested, and recommended for adoption by the States. A secretary was appointed to preside over each of the branches of the govern ment, including the department of foreign affairs, afterward termed the department of state, comprising both foreign and domestic affairs; the department of the treasury; and the war department. The navy, which was yet small, was placed under the secretary of war. Proper persons were appointed to fill the different offices; and from the great experience, the well-known disinterestedness, and the practical wisdom of Washington, it might be expected that Congress could rely with confidence on his nominations. Thomas Jefferson was appointed secretary of state; Alexander Hamilton secretary of the treasury; and the post of secretary of war, which he held under the Confederation, continued to be filled by General Knox. The office of attorney-general was conferred upon Edmund Randolph of Virginia. It was decided that the Supreme Court should consist of a chief-justice and five associate justices.

Washington regarded the Supreme Court as the firmest pillar of good government, and evinced his conviction of its importance by the appointment of John Jay as chief-justice, deeming him qualified, by his legal ability and attainments, to occupy the principal post in "that department, which must be considered the keystone of our political fabric." In all his appointments to offices, the President acted on the same uniform principle which regulated his conduct from first to last — a regard for the public good. With respect to qualifications for office, he considered three things as essential: the personal fitness of candidates, their comparative claims, and the distribu tion of appointments in equal proportions between persons from the different States.

In the recess of Congress the President made a tour of the Eastern States, for the promotion of his health, observation of the people's condition, their appreciation of the new government, and for the review of those military scenes in which he performed the duties of commander-in-chief. In company with his two secretaries, Mr. Lear and Mr. Jackson, he travelled in his own carriage through New Haven, Hartford, Worcester, Boston, Salem, Newburyport, as far as Portsmouth in New Hampshire. He was unable to advance a mile in any direction without attracting multitudes of enthusiastic admirers, who were gratified by a view of his person, and exhibited their affectionate delight and respectful veneration by greeting him with the most joyful acclamations. He was pleased to behold the improved state of the country, the agricultural prosperity, the abundant harvests, the flourishing manufactures, the extending commerce, and the increasing population. Order, peace, and contentment, evinced by the partiality of the people to the Constitution, and their attachment to the Government, gave a guarantee for its future security; and he returned to his duties improved in health, and greatly invigorated, mentally and physically.

In the first week in January, 1789, the President met the Congress in the Senate Chamber; and according to the custom during his administration, delivered a speech on the opening of the session. This custom was afterward changed, and it became usual for the President to communicate with Congress by messages. Washington also, at other times, addressed messages to that body; but at the commencement of a session he always delivered his views in person. After expressing a general congratulation on the prosperity of their affairs, he recommended to their attention, on that occasion, a better provision for the common defence; laws for the naturalization of citizens; uniformity in the currency, and in weights and measures; the promotion of commerce, agriculture, and manufactures; the diffusion of science and literature; and lastly, a system of finance for the support of the public credit.

A few days before the close of the last session, it was resolved to make adequate provision for the support of the public credit; and the Secretary of the Treasury was called on to prepare a plan for this purpose during the ensuing session. The Revolution was the chief source of the national debt, which was partly foreign, partly domestic; the first portion of it was due to France, Holland, and Spain, and amounted to twelve million dollars; the other was due to individuals in the United States, amounted to forty-two millions, and had been contracted by loans to Government, and supplies for the army. These debts had been incurred at the charge of the nation; but beside these, there were due twenty-five millions for the erection of works of defence in different States; for advanced pay to soldiers; and for supplies of clothing, provisions, and munitions of war. General Hamilton recommended the funding of all the debts together, and that the Confederacy should become responsible for the whole, and liquidate it. In an able and comprehensive report the Secretary clearly demonstrated that all the debts should be thus assumed; that in equity no distinction between these debts should be admitted; but that as a matter of policy, as well as of justice, these obligations should be paid; and that every form of government which aimed at securing public confidence, must honorably meet its engagements.

The plan proposed by the Secretary met with much opposition. Many persons contended that the debts contracted by Congress, of which the only evidences consisted in the paper currency, had greatly depreciated in amount, because the notes had passed through many hands for less than their nominal value; and that, by this depreciation, the first creditors and the intermediate owners had been heavy losers; to pay their full value, therefore, to the present holders would not be just. Mr. Madison suggested a plan by which the present holders should be paid a certain portion, the balance to go to the original holders. This proposition was rejected.

The disposal of the State debts produced a still greater sensation in Congress, and much more excitement out of it. The discussion respecting them revived the doctrine of State sovereignty and State rights, which had occasioned so much difficulty during the war; and now a host of new local prejudices were aroused, and invidious comparisons were instituted between different States. It was urged by some that each State was responsible for its own obligations; that to take the burden upon the nation, was an act which Congress had not the power to perform; and that such an assumption of authority would be hostile to the system and principles of republicanism. It was contended by another faction, that this prerogative was expressly invested in Congress by the Federal Constitution; that the sale of the public lands, and authority to raise revenues from imposts, belonged to Congress; that the public debts would be paid more promptly, if assumed by the nation; while they could be liquidated by the States only by means of excise duties, or by direct taxation, which would be objectionable in many respects. The strongest argument against the assumption of the State debts seemed to be, that the General Government would thereby gain an undue influence, and State sovereignty would be annihilated.

The resolution against the assumption was carried in a few days by a small majority. Subsequently the delegates from North Carolina took their seats in Congress; after which, upon a motion to reconsider the resolution, it was eventually negatived. The plan of the Secretary was ultimately approved by both Houses of Congress by a small majority; and its passage is known to have been aided by the consideration of the place in which Congress would permanently sit in future. The choice lay between a site on the Delaware, and another on the Potomac; and that question induced two members who had voted against the assumption, and who represented a district on the Potomac, to vote in favor of the bill. This law afterward became one of the chief grounds of accusation against the administration of President Washington.

The foreign relations of the United States at this period were in an unsettled condition. The understanding was good with France, though it soon became affected by the French Revolution. A treaty which was made with the Emperor of Morocco, did not prevent the seizure of American vessels by the Algerines. The British forts had not been abandoned, as was stipulated by the treaty of peace, on the pretence that the debts due to British subjects had not yet been paid. The navigation of the Mississippi was the great difficulty with Spain, though others also existed; and the expectation of the monarch of that country was, that the inhabitants of the West, wearied with obstructions to their commerce, would separate from the Confederacy, and establish a distinct republic under Spanish influence. The interests of the country also suffered, on account of certain influences growing out of the relations existing between England and Spain; and the Indians on the frontiers, though not at the instance of these governments, became incensed against the inhabitants of the United States. The efforts made to pacify the Indians did not succeed, and the nation was led into a long and expensive war with them, which continued during a large portion of the administration of Washington; which led to the defeat of Generals Harmer and St. Clair, and which was only terminated by General Wayne, first by a victory, and afterward by a treaty.

At the opening of the third session of Congress at Philadelphia, Washington returned from Mount Ver non, which he had visited during the recess. Two very important measures—the creation of a national bank, and the imposition of a tax on the ardent spirits distilled in the United States—formed the chief subjects of discussion during this session. The cabinet were divided in reference to a national bank. Jefferson and Randolph opposed its establishment, because they thought it unconstitutional; while Hamilton and Knox maintained the opposite position. The opinion of each member was given in writing; and the President at last affixed his signature to the act by which a bank was established, with a capital of ten millions, in which the Government held two millions. The tax on distilled spirits was intended to produce a fund for the payment of a portion of the domestic debt. It encountered much opposition at first, but afterward passed, and received the approbation and signature of Washington.

CHAPTER XXIX.

APPORTIONMENT BILL — DIFFERENCES IN THE CABINET — EFFECTS OF THE FRENCH REVOLUTION — DEVELOPMENT OF PARTIES — THE CITIZEN GENET — HIS INSOLENCE — WESTERN INSURRECTION QUELLED — TREATY WITH GREAT BRITAIN — THE EXCITEMENT IT PRODUCED — THE PRESIDENT REFUSES TO GIVE UP THE PAPERS OF INSTRUCTION — HIS FAREWELL ADDRESS — RETIREMENT FROM OFFICE — MOUNT VERNON — DANGER OF A WAR WITH FRANCE — WASHINGTON APPOINTED COMMANDER-IN-CHIEF — PACIFICATION — RURAL SCENES — LAST ILLNESS AND DEATH OF WASHINGTON.

During the recess of Congress in March, 1791, Washington made a tour through the Southern States, and was absent three months. The attention of the next session of the Federal Legislature was occupied in enacting laws for the apportionment of representatives in Congress, in establishing a uniform system of militia, and in augmenting the army. On the adoption of the Constitution, it had been enacted that the whole number of representatives should not exceed one for every thirty thousand inhabitants. When the new bill was proposed, it was found that a large fraction of the citizens would remain unrepresented by its operation. To remedy this injustice, a bill was introduced fixing the ratio at thirty thousand; making this the divisor, and the whole population the dividend, the quotient would give the entire number of representatives.

This bill was not in harmony with the Federal Constitution, in the opinion of the President; as the ratio was meant to apply to each of the States separately, and not to the whole aggregate. He returned the bill, therefore, unapproved; and a new one was framed and passed, in which the ratio was fixed at thirty-three thousand. Local jealousies prevailed to a great extent during the discussion on this bill. Many wished to have the representation as large as possible, in order to increase the influence of the several States, and hold in check the undue power of the Executive. The military force which was demanded for the protection of the frontiers against the Indians, met with opposition on the same grounds; for by increasing the executive power it was thought that it might become hostile to liberty, and thus the cure be worse than the disease!

About this time, very clear evidence was given of the existence of two hostile parties in Congress; one of which was opposed to, the other in favor of, the Administration. It is probable that in all free governments parties must exist, and that their operation is not injurious to the preservation of liberty; but in the present instance there were some who did not favor the Federal Constitution, and would have wholly condemned the state of things existing under it. This is not the place to discuss the origin from which these parties sprang, nor the principles on which they were based; but it is very certain that their existence greatly grieved, perplexed, and thwarted the patriotic purposes of Washington.

Differences also arose between Hamilton, the Secretary of the Treasury, and Jefferson, the Secretary of State. These eminent men differed on almost every subject which was discussed in the Cabinet; and they continued to remain diametrically opposite in policy and in feeling, till they began to cherish a personal hatred toward each other, which nothing could eradicate. This antagonism was deeply lamented by Washington, especially as he entertained a sincere attachment to both of these men, and believed both to be patriotic. Hamilton thought the powers of the Constitution were too weak; and that, in the Administration, the greatest possible authority should be placed in the hands of the executive. Jefferson contended that this policy gave too much power to one officer; and that the executive authority should be held in check, so that the States, in their separate rights, and the people in their liberties, might be free from the danger of encroachment. This was the reason why he opposed the funding system, the assumption of the State debts by the nation, the national bank, and the spirit-tax.

The conciliating temper of Washington was evinced in his letters to these two great men. We introduce here an abstract from a communication sent to each of them; and the feelings which they express confer as much honor upon their author, as any other portion of his memorable career. To Jefferson he wrote as follows, on the 22d of August, 1792: "How unfortunate, and how much to be regretted is it, that, while we are encompassed on all sides with avowed enemies and insidious friends, internal dissensions should be harrowing and tearing our vitals! The latter, to me, is the most serious, the most alarming, and the most afflicting of the two; and, without more charity for the opinions and acts of one another in governmental matters, or some more infallible criterion by which the truth of speculative opinions, before they have undergone the test of experience, are to be forejudged, than has yet fallen to the lot of fallibility, I believe it will be difficult, if not impracticable, to manage the reins of government, or to keep the parts of it together; for if, instead of laying our shoulders to the machine after measures are decided on, one pulls this way and another that, before the utility of the thing is fairly tried, it must inevitably be torn asunder; and, in my opinion, the fairest prospect of happiness and prosperity that ever was presented to man, will be lost perhaps for ever." To Hamilton he wrote about the same time, much to the same purpose, and then proceeds thus: "When matters get to such lengths, the natural inference is, that both sides have strained the cords beyond their bearing, and that a middle course would be found the best, until experience shall have decided on the right way, or (which is not to be expected, because it is denied to mortals) there shall be some infallible rule by which we could forejudge events."

The term of office prescribed by the Federal Constitution for the President of the United States, had now nearly expired, and great anxiety was felt as to whether Washington would be induced to accept a re-election. Three members of the cabinet, Jefferson, Hamilton, and Randolph, wrote to him, and made the urgent request that he should remain in office another term; adding, that his own reputation, and the present state of the country, required him to do so. Washington had indeed intended to retire at that time, but had not yet announced the fact; nevertheless, in consequence of the solicitations of his friends, and the unanimous vote of the electors, who declared him chosen President a second time, he accepted the appointment, and took the oath of office, on the 4th of March, 1793.

The United States and France had preserved the most friendly relations, which had extended to their commerce. After the downfall of Louis the Sixteenth, it was the opinion of the President and his Cabinet that the French nation possessed the right to adopt whatever form of government they pleased, and that other nations should recognize the existing authority. Mr. Morris, the minister from the United States to France, received instructions to that effect; and the prudence with which he avoided committing his nation, was a cause of dissatisfaction to a certain class of political leaders, who pretended that the United States exhibited no sympathy with France in the attainment of her liberties. War having been at that time declared by France with England, there was an apprehension that the country would be embroiled in it. But Washington determined to observe the most rigid neutrality. With this view he called a meeting of his Cabinet on the 18th of April, 1793, and proposed a series of questions to be answered by them. These involved the whole subject then in dispute. The Cabinet were of the opinion unanimously that the citizens of the United States should be forbidden by proclamation to take any part on the high seas against any of the belligerent powers; and warning them against any act not consistent with the conduct of a friendly nation. It was also agreed, that the ministers of the French Republic should be received. The President required each member of his Cabinet to put his opinion in writing, and he then gave it the most studious attention. The result was the issuing of a proclamation of neutrality, by which our intercourse with foreign nations was to be regulated. The United States being saved from the vortex into which a foreign war would have plunged them, were thus able, through the prudence and political sagacity of Washington, to lay the broad and deep foundations of the national prosperity.

This was one of the most important events connected with Washington's administration; and we cannot wonder at the excitement which it produced, and the hostility which it generated. It developed the principles then already at work, and brought into bold outline the two parties known as the Federal and the Democratic. The former of these were thought to be the partisans of England; while the latter were stigmatized as the abettors of the horrors of the French Revolution. The President was able to keep aloof from this rivalry for some time; but the opposers of his administration knew that, as long as his character remained superior to calumny, their labors would be vain. Attempts were therefore made at this time to asperse it.

From the extravagant attention which had been paid to the citizen Genet, who came to the United

States as minister of the French Republic, we may judge of the sympathy which the American people entertained for the French Revolution. This individual, with the greatest professions of amity for the United States on the part of his Government, had obtained private orders and blank commissions, by which he could appoint privateers who captured British vessels, and then brought them into American ports. The British minister complained of this abuse, and demanded restitution. There was but one opinion about the matter in the Cabinet of Washington, which condemned it as such a violation of neutrality as must be prevented by the American Government.

It was resolved, therefore, that no privateers thus fitted out should be harbored in American ports; and that the custom-house officers should keep a vigilant watch upon violators of the law. It was also agreed that in case the property seized was not restored by the captors to the owners, the Government should make indemnification. Genet was inflamed with indignation at these proceedings; he became extremely insolent, and continued to encourage armed vessels to sail from American ports under the French flag. He found, however, that the President would not permit him to proceed as he wished; and then his insolent rage exceeded all bounds. He became so infatuated and infuriated as to accuse Washington of having usurped the powers that belonged alone to Congress; and declared his intention of appealing to the people. His preposterous conduct, however, availed nothing, and on representation being made to the French Government, he was recalled. One of his projects was the establishment of Democratic clubs throughout the country. The first of these was instituted in Philadelphia after the model of the Jacobin clubs in France.

That the American people suffered so little injury from the baleful influences of the French Revolution, and from the principles which it disseminated, was owing to the practical sense and prudence of the people on the one hand, and to the firmness and wisdom of Washington on the other. It seems, indeed, impossible that the country could have escaped untold evils under the circumstances, had there not been the strictest neutrality enforced. Yet at that very time the Cabinet was full of dissention; the people were tainted to some degree with French principles; and in a divided Congress, amid the bitter strife of parties, and the extravagant misrepresentations of the press, many persons thought there was evinced a tendency to the establishment of a monarchy. General Knox on one occasion showed the President a specimen of the printed libels which were then circulated; and among them, a pasquinade called "the funeral of George Washington," in which he was represented on a guillotine. The President burst forth into one of those transports of passion which were beyond his control; inveighed against the personal abuse that had been heaped upon him, and defied any man on earth to produce a single act of his since he had been in the Government, that had not been done from the purest motives. He had never repented but once the having slipped the opportunity of resigning his office, and that was every moment since. In the agony of his heart he declared he would rather be in the grave than in his present situation; that he would rather be on his farm than be made emperor of the world; and yet, said he, indignantly, they are charging me with wanting to be a king!

Affairs with Great Britain were at that time in a complicated condition. Mr. Hammond was then the resident British Minister, and Thomas Pinckney was Minister Plenipotentiary of the United States at the Court of St. James. The British still held the frontier posts, and British officers had recently impressed seamen within the jurisdiction of the United States. The orders in council gave instruction to British cruisers to board all ships laden with corn-meal or flour, bound for any French port; and ships of war were directed to detain all vessels carrying goods produced in any colony that belonged to France. Neutral rights were thus invaded, and this injustice caused remonstrances to be made which were injurious in their effects. Congress assembled on December 3d, 1793, and the President explained the reasons for the course he had adopted with foreign powers. He offered suggestions by which the rights of American citizens should be protected; and recommended not only that the country should be placed in a position to protect its citizens, but also to enforce its just claims.

In order to prevent hostilities, John Jay had been sent as envoy extraordinary to the Court of St. James. It was hoped that no conflict between the two nations might occur, but it was agreed to put the country into an efficient state of defence, by the fortification of the harbors, and by holding eighty thousand militia in a state of readiness for service. Additional taxes were imposed, and additional galleys were purchased; while the duty on the importation of arms was removed. This session of Congress was protracted, and its discussions stormy; but the administration of Washington stood unflinchingly to its duty, and carried out the views that animated it. In the ensuing winter, M. Fouchet arrived as French Minister to the United States; and Mr. Morris being recalled, Mr. Monroe, an opponent to the Administration, was chosen to succeed him.

Soon after the adjournment of Congress, an insurrection broke forth in Western Pennsylvania, in consequence of a duty imposed on distilled liquors. The law was openly resisted, and the revenue inspectors threatened with personal violence if they attempted to discharge their duty. The discontent had proceeded so far that a proclamation was issued, warning all persons to avoid a combination with the disaffected, and calling on all magistrates to execute the laws, and bring offenders to justice. The marshal, in serving bills of indictment against several offenders, was seized and maltreated; and at length the evil had spread so far as to assume a most serious and threatening aspect. The President waited to ascertain whether the insurrection would be quelled without the use of arms; and then determined to exercise his authority and put it down by force. He issued a proclamation on the 7th of August, 1794, and made a requisition for militia on the Governors of New Jersey, Pennsylvania, Maryland, and Virginia. Twelve thousand men were ordered out, and the number was afterward increased to sixteen thousand. The Governors of Pennsylvania and New Jersey were appointed to command the militia of those States; and the command of the whole was given to Governor Lee of Virginia. Bedford was the appointed place of rendezvous, while that of the Virginia and Maryland militia was at Cumberland, where Will's Creek unites with the Potomac. The President accompanied the Secretary of War to both these places, and inspected the troops. He ordered each division to march across the Allegheny Mountains, and act against the insurgents as necessity might dictate. He saw from personal examination that everything was ready, gave his written directions to General Lee, and then returned to Philadelphia, where he arrived after four weeks' absence. The disaffected were eventually put down without the effusion of blood.

Before the end of the ensuing session General Hamilton, who had found the salary of his office inadequate to the support of his family, resigned, and was succeeded by Oliver Wolcott; General Knox was, at the same time, succeeded in the war department by Timothy Pickering. The treaty with Great Britain which Mr. Jay had negotiated, arrived in March, and the President summoned the Senate to consider its provisions. The President was of opinion that, when taken altogether, it was the best that could have been obtained under the circumstances. He had given it the most careful scrutiny, and found it in some respects defective; but, on the whole, he regarded it of the utmost utility to the nation. He determined to affix his signature to it, in case the Senate gave it their approval, which was necessary according to the provisions of the Constitution. The Senate convened in June; and after the discussions of a fortnight, they advised that the treaty be ratified, with the exception of a single article, which allowed trade to be carried on between the United States and the West Indies in vessels of seventy tons, conveying the produce of the United States or of the Islands; but forbidding the transportation in American vessels, either from the United States or the Islands, of molasses, sugar, coffee, cocoa, or cotton.

Washington determined to ratify the treaty by affixing thereto his signature; and to accompany it with a memorial against the article in question. Meanwhile a member of the Senate had given to the editor of a newspaper a copy of the treaty; and thus it clandestinely came before the public, met with the greatest criticism and condemnation, and threw the nation into the most furious excitement. Washington stood firm in his position, though assailed by the resolves of meetings, by aspersions on his character, and by the vilest abuse which was ever heaped upon the head of a patriot. He signed the treaty, and soon the provisional order was repealed; and the country was not only saved from war, but was blessed with unexampled prosperity.

The day after Washington affixed his name to this memorable treaty, Mr. Randolph resigned his post as Secretary of State, in consequence of an intercepted letter of M. Fouchet to the French Government, which excited suspicion in reference to his conduct. He had received the letter from the hand of Washington in the presence of other members of the Cabinet, and before them had been asked for an explanation. He became offended, and resigned his office on the same day.

Affairs with foreign nations afterward became more promising in their aspect. A treaty with Algiers led to the liberation of American prisoners; and another with Spain opened the navigation of the Mississippi. These things were subjects of congratulation to Congress, when the President addressed them on the opening of the session of 1796. The subject of the treaty with Great Britain again came up for discussion, and when presented to Congress as ratified by the monarch of that country, a determination became apparent to refuse the enactment of those laws by which only it could be carried into effect. The instructions given to Mr. Jay, and other documents, were asked by the House of Representatives, which the President thought he had no right to grant; and therefore he firmly declined to comply with the requisition. The members of the House were greatly disappointed and dissatisfied; party spirit ran high; the subject of the refusal was fiercely debated on both sides; but in the end the necessary laws were enacted for the fulfilment of the treaty.

The second term of the presidency of Washington now approached its termination; and it was clearly understood that he would not again accept the office. He made an announcement of this fact at an early day, in order that a successor might be appointed;

and on the 15th of September, six months before the expiration of his office, he delivered his Farewell Address to the people of the United States. The different States testified the value which they attached to it, by causing it to be printed and published with the laws enacted by their legislatures. Washington met the two Houses in December, 1796, for the last time; and among the important counsels which he gave them were measures for the increase of the navy, the encouragement of agriculture and manufactures, the institution of a national university, and the establishment of a military academy. He delivered a separate message in reference to the relations with France. His views may be seen by a brief extract from his speech: "The situation in which I now stand, for the last time, in the midst of the representatives of the people of the United States, naturally recalls the period when the administration of the present form of government commenced; and I cannot omit the occasion to congratulate you and my country on the success of the experiment, nor to repeat my fervent supplications to the Supreme Ruler of the universe, and Sovereign Arbiter of nations, that his providential care may still be extended to the United States."

The French Directory labored, at this period, under the erroneous impression that the people of the United States would not support their Government; and this was confirmed by the reception which the British treaty had received. They therefore behaved with insolence, and rejected the overtures made to them; they still committed depredations on American commerce by means of French cruisers; and having first insulted the American plenipotentiary, then ordered him to leave the territories of the Republic. War therefore was the only alternative, and Congress authorized the President to raise an army of ten thousand men. Washington, who had retired to the grateful shades of Mount Vernon, was nominated to take the chief command; but he accepted the trust only in case of an *actual invasion.* He set about organizing the army, in order to be prepared for every event; and in doing so was much embarrassed in regard to the appointment of officers. The second in command was to be the inspector-general, according to the appointment tendered to Washington, who had given the President to understand that he must be allowed to choose his subordinates. Alexander Hamilton was accordingly appointed to that office; while Charles Cotesworth Pinckney and Henry Knox were major-generals. This arrangement offended Knox, who thought his services deserved the first place. The details of the new army engaged much of the time and attention of Washington; and his exertions and correspondence, which were immense, clearly evinced that growing years had not diminished his zeal or impaired his faculties. He spent a month in Philadelphia with his generals, engaged in the organization of the army: in the meanwhile the French, seeing the hostile attitude assumed by the United States, with Washington prepared to lead their forces, moderated their demands; and Bonaparte being placed at the head of the Republic, peace was eventually proclaimed on equitable terms.

Washington would have greatly rejoiced at the attainment of this result; but before the welcome news arrived he was no more. His health had remained excellent and unimpaired after his retirement, allowance being made for the infirmities incident to his advanced age. He was then in his sixty-seventh year, and capable of enduring great fatigue. Indeed his daily labors, both physically or mentally, were performed with undiminished ease and vigor; and he might be regarded as one who bade fair to live to extreme old age. On the 12th of December, 1799, he spent several hours on horseback, riding over his farms, and directing his superintendent. The day was inclement; he was exposed to the rain and sleet, and became chilled and wet. He apprehended no danger; but the next day being snowy, he did not go abroad, except for a very short time. He soon experienced symptoms of a sore throat, yet he did not pay much heed to it; and in the evening, though hoarse, he sat with his family by the fireside, and read aloud from the newspapers which were brought in. He conversed cheerfully also, and retired to rest at his usual hour. He was seized with ague during the night, and spoke with a great deal of difficulty. On the next day one of his overseers bled him, but was so much agitated that the general told him "not to be afraid." The incision was made, and the patient remarked that "the orifice is not large enough." The blood, however, ran pretty freely; but Mrs. Washington directed the operator to stop it. There were about fourteen ounces taken; yet the general said, as well as he could, "more, more." External remedies were applied to the throat, but they gave him no relief. Dr. Craik, the family physician, and two others, arrived about nine o'clock. Every possible remedy was then used, but to no purpose. Mrs. Washington was desired to come to his chamber about four o'clock; and he gave her his key, with directions to go to his room and apply it to the desk, where she would find two wills, one of which had superseded the other. He was then in perfect possession of his faculties, conversed with his friends as well as the nature of the disease would permit, and anticipated his end with the fortitude of a Christian hero. He suffered intense pain with the utmost patience and fortitude; and he sank by degrees until about eleven o'clock on the ensuing night, when he peacefully expired.

CHAPTER XXX.

PROFOUND IMPRESSION PRODUCED BY WASHINGTON'S DEATH—ESTIMATE OF HIS CHARACTER—HIS INTELLECTUAL QUALITIES—HIS MILITARY TALENTS—HIS ADMINISTRATIVE ABILITIES—HIS CHARACTER WHEN REGARDED AS A WHOLE—PROCEEDINGS IN CONGRESS IN HONOR OF HIS MEMORY—REMARKS OF MR. MARSHALL—RESOLUTIONS—ADDRESS OF THE SENATE—REPLY OF THE PRESIDENT OF THE UNITED STATES—FUNERAL SERVICES AT MOUNT VERNON.

THUS ended the memorable career of George Washington. The report of his sudden death threw a pall of sadness and unparalleled gloom over the whole nation. A grief so intense that no language could render fit utterance to it, pervaded the hearts of myriads; and never before or since has the departure of any public man, in this Confederacy, produced so profound and so lasting an impression. When the mournful intelligence was communicated to Congress, they unanimously passed such resolutions as were suitable to the occasion, and adopted all other appropriate signs of appreciation and respect in honor of the illustrious dead, who had assumed the first and highest place in the affections of his countrymen.

The personal qualities of this illustrious man have so often been delineated, that it seems almost a superfluous task to attempt a description of them. His best and most accurate portrait is to be derived from the examination of the actions which he performed, and of the results which he accomplished. The intellectual character of Washington was peculiar. Though he became the triumphant hero of a long and arduous war, his military talents were not of the highest order. In this respect he was inferior to many men who, in the career of arms, have achieved far less renown than he. He possessed little power of strategy, little of that promptness and intuitive sagacity which enables a commander to adapt himself to the sudden and unexpected emergencies which occur in the crises of great engagements. In this respect, if his plan of battle was once deranged by unforeseen accidents, he was unable to readjust the machinery of his army, or to confront and confound the operations of the foe by new and instantaneous combinations adapted to the emergency. In this respect Marlborough, Saxe, Prince Eugene, Frederick the Great, Napoleon, were all infinitely his superiors.

The chief *military* ability of Washington consisted in the prudence and skill with which he adjusted the details of an assault on an enemy who was posted in a firm position; and the energy and perseverance with which he persisted in the subsequent attack. Thus he was triumphant over the British at Boston and Yorktown, and achieved brilliant successes there, because he was enabled to prepare his plans of attack, and to adhere to them, without the possibility of having them disarranged by sudden and unforeseen movements of the enemy. His personal bravery was unquestionable; and he faced danger and death with the most perfect fortitude and indifference, when honor and duty required him so to do. His most prominent characteristic as a military commander, was his prudence; and it is probable that this solid quality was more available, under the existing circumstances, in weakening the foe by long delays, by harassing evasions, by cautious postponements of decisive actions, than by those more brilliant and showy talents which would have risked the fate of vast and important interests upon the issue of a few rash and imprudent conflicts.

A prominent element in the greatness of Washington consisted in the fact that, with respectable military talents, he combined far higher and greater abilities for the administration of government. He was placed at the head of this Confederacy at the most difficult and perilous period of its past career; when a thousand hostile and rival interests among the States, and between the separate States and the Federal Government, and between the Federal Government and the continental troops, and between several political factions in the Government, rendered it impossible so to steer as fully to meet the views and satisfy the demands of all parties. Yet that result was attained by Washington in a remarkable degree; and when, after an administration of eight eventful years, he retired from the Presidency, he left the Republic in a compact and united condition; the community at large flourishing and prosperous; and their reputation among foreign nations as a young and vigorous empire, unspotted, greatly respected, and destined to achieve with the lapse of time, a high and glorious position among the oldest communities on the globe. The triumphs of Washington as a civil and executive officer were far more honorable than even those attained by him on the battle-field.

Taken as a whole, therefore, his character was one of the most remarkable and estimable that ever existed among men. His predominating political attribute was Patriotism. His leading intellectual faculty was Sagacity. His chief social characteristics were Prudence and Self-control. His prominent moral qualities were Honesty and Conscientiousness. And all the several parts of his nature were combined together and proportioned in so admirable and equitable a measure, that he constituted a grand and harmonious *Whole*, such as is rarely exhibited in the chequered annals of this world's history. Many great and illustrious men have equalled George Washington in some one or other single quality; but scarcely any man of ancient or modern times possessed a mental and moral constitution of such admirable proportions, or of such beautiful, complete, and uniform development. Nature formed him truly great; but the peculiar circumstances in which he was placed—first of war and then of peace—conspired to render him, as possessing such faculties, greater still; until his position became at length firmly fixed among the few mortals whose majestic forms loom up sublimely through all times and ages, as specimens of spotless, peerless, and almost perfect Humanity.

When the intelligence of Washington's death was formally announced to Congress, Mr. John Marshall arose and delivered the following brief but appropriate remarks:*

"The melancholy event which was yesterday announced, without doubt has been rendered but too certain. Our Washington is no more! The hero, the sage, and the patriot of America — the man on whom, in times of danger, every eye was turned and all hopes were placed, lives now only in his own great actions, and in the hearts of an affectionate and afflicted people.

"If, sir, it had not been usual openly to testify respect for the memory of those whom heaven had selected as its intruments for dispensing good to man; yet, such has been the uncommon worth, and such the extraordinary incidents which have marked the life of him whose loss we all deplore, that the whole American nation, impelled by the same feelings, would call with one voice for a public manifestation of that sorrow which is so deep and so universal.

"More than any other individual, and as much as to one individual was possible, has he contributed to found this our wide-spreading empire, and to give to the western world its independence and its freedom. Having effected the great object for which he was placed at the head of our armies, we have seen him convert the sword into the ploughshare, and voluntarily sink the soldier in the citizen.

"When the debility of our federal system had be-

* The ensuing details respecting the proceedings in Congress in reference to the death of Washington, and the obsequies at Mount Vernon, are derived from the Ulster County Gazette, N. Y., of *January 4th*, 1800.

come manifest, and the bonds which connected the parts of this vast continent were dissolving, we have seen him the chief of those patriots who formed for us a Constitution which, by preserving the Union, will, I trust, substantiate and perpetuate those blessings our Revolution had promised to bestow.

"In obedience to the general voice of his country, calling on him to preside over a great people, we have seen him once more quit the retirement he loved, and in a season more stormy and tempestuous than war itself, with calm and wise determination pursue the true interests of the nation, and contribute, more than any other could contribute, to the establishment of that system of policy which will, I trust, yet preserve our peace, our honor, and our independence. Having been twice unanimously chosen the Chief Magistrate of a free people, we see him, at a time when his re-election with the universal suffrage could not have been doubted, affording the world a rare instance of moderation, by withdrawing from his high station to the peaceful walks of private life.

"However public confidence may change and the public affections fluctuate with respect to others, yet with respect to him they have, in war and in peace, in public and in private life, been as steady as his own firm mind, and as constant as his own exalted virtues.

"Let us, then, Mr. Speaker, pay the last tribute of respect and affection to our departed friend. Let the grand council of the nation display those sentiments which the nation feels.

"For this purpose, I hold in my hand some reso

lutions, which I will take the liberty to offer to the House:

"'Resolved, That this House will wait on the President of the United States, in condolence of this mournful event.

"'Resolved, That the Speaker's chair be shrouded with black, and that the Members and Officers of the House wear black during the session.

"'Resolved, That a committee, in conjunction with one from the Senate, be appointed to consider on the most suitable manner of paying honor to the memory of the man, first in war, first in peace, and first in the hearts of his countrymen.

"'Resolved, That this House, when it adjourns, do adjourn to Monday.'

"These resolutions were unanimously agreed to. Sixteen members were appointed on the third resolution.

"Generals Marshall and Smith were then appointed to wait on the President, to know at what time it would be convenient to receive the House.

"Generals Marshall and Smith having waited on the President with the first resolution, reported, that the President would be ready to receive them at 1 o'clock this day. The house accordingly waited on him.

"The Speaker then addressed the President in the following words:

"SIR:—The House of Representatives, penetrated with a sense of the irreparable loss sustained by the nation, by the death of that great and good man, the illustrious and beloved Washington, wait on you, sir, to express their condolence on this melancholy and distressing event."

"To which the President made the following reply:

"*Gentlemen of the House of Representatives:*

"I receive with great respect and affection the condolence of the House of Representatives on the melancholy and afflicting event in the death of the most illustrious and beloved personage which this country ever produced. I sympathize with you — with the nation, and with good men through the world, in this irreparable loss sustained by us all.

JOHN ADAMS."

"A message was received from the Senate, informing the House that they had agreed to the appointment of a joint committee, to consider a suitable manner of paying honor to the memory of the man, first in war, first in peace, and first in the hearts of his country, and that they had appointed even members to join a committee for that purpose.

"*To the President of the United States:*

"The Senate of the United States respectfully take leave, sir, to express to you their deep regret for the loss their country has sustained in the death of General George Washington. This event, so distressing to all our fellow-citizens, must be peculiarly heavy to you, who have long been associated with him in deeds of patriotism. Permit us, sir, to mingle our tears with yours: on this occasion it is manly to weep. To lose such a man at such a crisis, is no common calamity to the world: our country mourns her Father. The Almighty Disposer of human events has taken from us our greatest Benefactor and ornament. It becomes us to submit with reverence to him, who 'maketh darkness his Pavilion.'

"With patriotic pride, we review the life of our Washington, and compare him with those of other countries who have been pre-eminent in fame. Ancient and modern names are diminished before him. Greatness and guilt have too often been allied, but his fame is whiter than it is brilliant. The destroyers of nations stood abashed at the majesty of his virtue. It reproved the intemperate of their ambition, and darkened the splendor of victory. The scenes closed, and we are no longer anxious lest misfortune should sully his glory; he has travelled on to the end of his journey, and carried with him an increasing weight of honor; he has deposited it safely, where misfortune cannot tarnish it—where malice cannot blast it. Favored of Heaven, he departed without exhibiting the weakness of humanity; magnanimous in death, the darkness of the grave could not obscure his brightness.

"Such was the man whom we deplore. Thanks to God, his glory is consummated. Washington yet lives on earth in his spotless example—his spirit is in Heaven.

"Let his countrymen consecrate the memory of the heroic General, the patriotic Statesman, and the virtuous Sage; let them teach their children never to forget that the fruits of his labors, and his example, are their inheritance."

To this address the President returned the following reply:

"*Gentlemen of the Senate:*

"I receive with the most respectful and affectionate sentiments, in this impressive address, the obliging expressions of your regret, for the loss our Country has sustained in the death of her most esteemed, beloved, and admired Citizen.

"In the multitude of my thoughts and recollections, on this melancholy event, you will permit me only to say, that I have seen him in the days of Adversity, in some of the scenes of his deepest and most trying perplexities; I have also attended him in his highest elevation and most prosperous felicity; with uniform admiration of his wisdom, moderation, and constancy.

"Among all our original associates, in the memorable League of the Continent in 1774, which first expressed the sovereign will of a Free Nation in AMERICA, he was the only one remaining in the General Government. Although, with a constitution more enfeebled than his, at an age when he thought it necessary to prepare for retirement, I feel myself alone, bereaved of my last brother; yet I derive strong consolation from the unanimous disposition, which appears in all ages and classes, to mingle their sorrows with mine, on this common calamity to the world.

"The life of our Washington cannot suffer by a comparison with those of other countries, who have been most celebrated and exalted by Fame. The attributes and decorations of Royalty could only have served to eclipse the Majesty of those virtues, which made him, from being a modest citizen, a more resplendent luminary. Misfortune, had he lived, could hereafter have sullied his glory only with those superficial minds, who, believing that *character and actions are marked by success alone*, rarely deserves to enjoy it. *Malice* could never *blast his honor*, and *Envy* made him a singular exception to her universal rule. For himself he had lived enough, to life and to glory. For his fellow-citizens, if their prayers could have been answered, he would have been immortal. For me his departure is at a most unfortunate moment. Trusting, however, in the wise and righteous dominions of Providence over passions of men, and the result of their councils and actions, as well as over their Lives, nothing remains for me but HUMBLE RESIGNATION.

"His example is now complete, and it will teach wisdom and virtue to Magistrates, Citizens, and men, not only in the present age, but in future generations, as long as our History shall be read. If a Trajan found a Pliny, a Marcus Aurelius can never want Biographers, Eulogists, or Historians."

The ceremonies with which the "Father of his Country" was entombed at Mount Vernon, were simple and impressive. The following description of the solemn scene was written by an eye witness, dated at Georgetown, the 20th of December, 1800:

"On Wednesday last, the mortal part of Washington the Great—the Father of his Country and the Friend of man, was consigned to the tomb, with solemn honors and funeral pomp.

"A multitude of persons assembled, from many miles round, at Mount Vernon, the choice abode and last residence of the illustrious chief. There were the groves—the spacious avenues, the beautiful and sublime scenes, the noble mansion—but alas! the august inhabitant *was now no more*. That great soul was *gone*. His mortal part was there indeed; but ah! how affecting! how awful the spectacle of such worth and greatness, thus, to mortal eyes fallen!—Yes! fallen! fallen!

"In the long and lofty *Portico*, where oft the Hero walked in all his glory, *now* lay the shrouded corpse. The countenance still composed and serene, seemed to be impressed with the dignity of the spirit, which lately dwelt in that lifeless form. There those who paid the last sad honors to the benefactor of his country, took an impressive—a farewell view.

"On the ornament, at the head of the coffin, was inscribed SURGE AD JUDICIUM—about the middle of the coffin, GLORIA DEO—and on the silver plate,

GENERAL
GEORGE WASHINGTON,
DEPARTED THIS LIFE, ON THE 14TH DECEMBER,
1799, Æt. 68.

"Between three and four o'clock, the sound of artillery from a vessel in the river firing minute guns, awoke afresh our solemn sorrow—the corpse was moved—a band of music with mournful melody melted the soul into all the tenderness of woe.

"The procession was formed and moved on in the following order:

Cavalry, Infantry, Guard,	With arms reversed.

Music,
Clergy.

"The General's horse, with his saddle, holsters, and pistols.

Cols. Simms, Ramsay, Payne,	Pall Bearers.	CORPSE.	Pall Bearers.	Cols. Gilpin, Marsteller, Little.

Mourners,
Masonic Brethren,
Citizens.

"When the Procession had arrived at the bottom of the elevated lawn, on the banks of the Potomac, where the family vault is placed, the cavalry halted, the infantry marched towards the Mount and formed their lines—the Clergy, the Masonic Brothers, and the Citizens, descended to the Vault, and the funeral service of the Church was performed. The firing was repeated from the vessel in the river, and the sounds echoed from the woods and hills around.

"Three general discharges by the infantry, the cavalry, and eleven pieces of artillery, which lined the banks of the Potomac back of the Vault, paid the last tribute to the entombed Commander-in-Chief of the Armies of the United States, and to the departed Hero."

APPENDIX.[1]

I.

WASHINGTON'S FAREWELL ADDRESS.

FRIENDS, AND FELLOW-CITIZENS:

THE period for a new election of a Citizen, to administer the Executive Government of the United States, being not far distant, and the time actually arrived, when your thoughts must be employed in designating the person who is to be clothed with that important trust [[2]] it appears to me proper, especially as it may conduce to a more distinct expression of the public voice, that I should now apprise you of the resolution I have formed, to decline being considered among the number of those, out of whom a choice is to be made.

I beg you, at the same time, to do me the justice to be assured, that this resolution has not been taken, without a strict regard to all the considerations apper-

---

[1] The foot-notes which are here introduced, contain those alterations and interlineations which were found in the manuscript copy sent to the printer by Washington. The contents of this Appendix are reprinted from the valuable work issued by James Lenox, Esq., of New York, in 1850.

[2] for another term.

taining to the relation, which binds a dutiful citizen to his country — and that, in withdrawing the tender of service which silence in my situation might imply, I am influenced by no diminution of zeal for your future interest, no deficiency of grateful respect for your past kindness; but [am supported by][1] a full conviction that the step is compatible with both.

The acceptance of, and continuance hitherto in, the office to which your suffrages have twice called me, have been a uniform sacrifice of inclination to the opinion of duty, and to a deference for what appeared to be your desire. — I constantly hoped, that it would have been much earlier in my power, consistently with motives, which I was not at liberty to disregard, to return to that retirement, from which I had been reluctantly drawn. —— The strength of my inclination to do this, previous to the last election, had even led to the preparation of an address to declare it to you: but mature reflection on the then perplexed and critical posture of our affairs with foreign Nations, and the unanimous advice of persons entitled to my confidence, impelled me to abandon the idea. ——

I rejoice that the state of your concerns, external as well as internal, no longer renders the pursuit of inclination incompatible with the sentiment of duty, or propriety; and [am persuaded][2] whatever partiality [may be retained][3] for my services, [that][4] in the present circumstances of our country [you] will not disapprove my determination to retire.

The impressions, [with][5] which, I first [under-

---

[1] act under [2] that
[3] any portion of you may yet retain [4] even they [5] under

took][1] the arduous trust, were explained on the proper occasion.—In the discharge of this trust, I will only say, that I have, with good intentions, contributed [towards][2] the organization and administration of the government, the best exertions of which a very fallible judgment was capable—Not unconscious, in the outset, of the inferiority of my qualifications, experience in my own eyes, [perhaps] still more in the eyes of others, has [strengthened][3] the motives to diffidence of myself; and every day the increasing weight of years admonishes me more and more, that the shade of retirement is as necessary to me as it will be welcome.—Satisfied that if any circumstances have given peculiar value to my services, they were temporary, I have the consolation to believe, that while choice and prudence invite me to quit the political scene, patriotism does not forbid it. [[4]]

In looking forward to the moment, which is [intended] to terminate the career of my public life, my feelings do not permit me to suspend the deep acknowledgment [of][5] that debt of gratitude which I

---

[1] accepted [2] to [3] not lessened

[4] May I also have that of knowing in my retreat, that the involuntary errors, I have probably committed, have been the sources of no serious or lasting mischief to our country. I may then expect to realize, without alloy, the sweet enjoyment of partaking, in the midst of my fellow-citizens, the benign influence of good laws under a free government; the ever favorite object of my heart, and the happy reward, I trust, of our mutual cares dangers and labours.

In the margin opposite this paragraph is the following note in Washington's Autograph also erased, "obliterated to avoid the imputation of affected modesty."

[5] demanded by

owe to my beloved country,—for the many honors it has conferred upon me; still more for the stedfast confidence with which it has supported me; and for the opportunities I have thence enjoyed of manifesting my inviolable attachment, by services faithful and persevering, though [in usefulness unequal][1] to my zeal.—If benefits have resulted to our country from these services, let it always be remembered to your praise, and as an instructive example in our annals, that, [[2]] under circumstances in which the Passions agitated in every direction were liable to [mislead],[3] amidst appearances sometimes dubious,—vicissitudes of fortune often discouraging,—in situations in which not unfrequently want of success has countenanced the spirit of criticism [the constancy of your support] was the essential prop of the efforts and [a][4] guarantee of the plans by which they were effected.—Profoundly penetrated with this idea, I shall carry it with me to the grave, as a strong incitement to unceasing vows [[5]] that Heaven may continue to you the choicest tokens of its beneficence—that your union and brotherly affection may be perpetual—that the free constitution, which is the work of your hands, may be sacredly maintained—that its administration in every department may be stamped with wisdom and virtue—that, in fine, the happiness of the people of these States, under the auspices of liberty, may be made complete, by so careful a preservation and so prudent a use of this

---

[1] unequal in usefulness [2] the constancy of your support
[3] wander and fluctuate [4] the
[5] the only return I can henceforth make

blessing as will acquire to them the glory [[1]] of recommending it to the applause, the affection, and adoption of every nation which is yet a stranger to it.

Here, perhaps, I ought to stop.——But a solicitude for your welfare, which cannot end but with my life, and the apprehension of danger, natural to that solicitude, [urge me on an occasion like the present, to offer][2] to your solemn contemplation, and to recommend to your frequent review, some sentiments; which are the result of much reflection, of no inconsiderable observation, [[3]] and which appear to me all important to the permanency of your felicity as a People.—These will be offered to you with the more freedom as you can only see in them, the disinterested warnings of a parting friend, who can [possibly] have no personal motive to bias his counsels.——[Nor can I forget, as an encouragement to it your indulgent reception of my sentiments on a former and not dissimilar occasion.]

Interwoven as is the love of liberty with every ligament of your hearts, no recommendation of mine is necessary to fortify or confirm the attachment.——

The Unity of Government which constitutes you one people, is also now dear to you.——It is justly so;—for it is a main Pillar in the Edifice of your real independence; [the support] of your tranquillity at home; your peace abroad; of your safety; [[4]] of

---

[1] or satisfaction

[2] encouraged by the remembrance of your indulgent reception of my sentiments on an occasion not dissimilar to the present, urge me to offer

[3] and experience

[4] in every relation

your prosperity [[1]]; of that very Liberty which you so highly prize.—But as it is easy to foresee, that from [different][2] causes, and from different quarters, much pains will be taken, many artifices employed, to weaken in your minds the conviction of this truth;—as this is the point in your [political] fortress against which the batteries of internal and external enemies will be most constantly and actively (though often covertly and insidiously) directed, it is of infinite moment, that you should properly estimate the immense value of your national Union to your collective and individual happiness;—that you should cherish [[3]] a cordial, habitual, and immoveable attachment [to it, accustoming yourselves to think and speak of it as of the Palladium of your political safety and prosperity; watching for its preservation with jealous anxiety; discountenancing whatever may suggest even a suspicion that it can in any event be abandoned, and indignantly frowning upon the first dawning of every attempt to alienate any portion of our Country from the rest, or to enfeeble the sacred ties which now link together the various parts.][4]—

For this you have every inducement of sympathy and interest.—Citizens [by birth or choice of a com-

---

[1] in every shape [2] various [3] towards it

[4] that you should accustom yourselves to reverence it as the Palladium of your political safety and prosperity, adapting constantly your words and actions to that momentous idea; that you should watch for its preservation with jealous anxiety, discountenance whatever may suggest a suspicion that it can in any event be abandoned; and frown upon the first dawning of every attempt to alienate any portion of our country from the rest, or to enfeeble the sacred ties which now link together the several parts.

mon country],[1] that a country has a right to concentrate your affections. — The name of AMERICAN, which belongs to you, in your national capacity, must always exalt the just pride of Patriotism, more than any appellation [[2]] derived from local discriminations.—With slight shades of difference, you have the same Religion, Manners, Habits, and political Principles.—You have in a common cause fought and triumphed together. — The Independence and Liberty you possess are the work of joint councils, and joint efforts—of common dangers, sufferings and successes.

But these considerations, however powerfully they address themselves to your sensibility, are greatly outweighed by those which apply more immediately to your interest. — Here every portion of our country finds the most commanding motives for carefully guarding and preserving the union of the whole.

The *North* in an [unrestrained][3] intercourse with the *South,* protected by the equal Laws of a common government, finds in the productions of the latter [[4]] great additional resources of maritime and commercial enterprise — and precious materials of manufacturing industry. — The *South* in the same intercourse, benefiting by the agency of the *North,* sees its agriculture grow and its commerce expand. Turning partly into its own channels the seamen of the *North,* it finds its particular navigation envigorated; — and while it contributes, in different ways, to nourish and increase the general mass of the national navigation, it looks forward to the protection of a maritime

---

[1] of a common country by birth or choice [2] to be
[3] unfettered [4] many of the peculiar

strength to which itself is unequally adapted. — The *East*, in a like intercourse with the *West*, already finds, and in the progressive improvement of interior communications, by land and water, will more and more find, a valuable vent for the commodities which it brings from abroad, or manufactures at home.— The *West* derives from the *East* supplies requisite to its growth and comfort,—and what is perhaps of still greater consequence, it must of necessity owe the *secure* enjoyment of indispensable *outlets* for its own productions to the weight, influence, and the future maritime strength of the Atlantic side of the Union, directed by an indissoluble community of interest, as *one Nation.* — [Any other][1] tenure by which the *West* can hold this essential advantage, [whether derived][2] from its own separate strength, or from an apostate and unnatural connection with any foreign Power, must be intrinsically precarious. [[3]]

[[4]] While [then] every part of our Country thus [feels][5] an immediate and particular interest in Union, all the parts[6] [combined cannot fail to find] in the united mass of means and efforts [[7]] greater strength, greater resource, proportionably greater security from external danger, a less frequent interruption of their Peace by foreign Nations; and, [what is][8] of inestimable value! they must derive from Union an ex-

---

[1] The [2] either

[3] liable every moment to be disturbed by the fluctuating combinations of the primary interests of Europe, which must be expected to regulate the conduct of the Nations of which it is composed.

[4] And [5] finds [6] of it

[7] cannot fail to find [8] which is an advantage

emption from those broils and wars between themselves, which [so frequently][1] afflict neighbouring countries, not tied together by the same government; which their own rivalships alone would be sufficient to produce; but which opposite foreign alliances, attachments and intrigues would stimulate and embitter. — Hence likewise they will avoid the necessity of those overgrown Military establishments, which under any form of Government are inauspicious to liberty, and which [are to be regarded][2] as particularly hostile to Republican Liberty: In this sense it is, that your Union ought to be considered as a main prop of your liberty, and that the love of the one ought to endear to you the preservation of the other.

These considerations speak a persuasive language to [every][3] reflecting and virtuous mind,—[and][4] exhibit the continuance of the UNION as a primary object of Patriotic desire. — Is there a doubt, whether a common government can embrace so large a sphere? — Let experience solve it.—To listen to mere speculation in such a case were criminal.—[We are authorised][5] to hope that a proper organization of the whole, with the auxiliary agency of governments for the respective subdivisions, will afford a happy issue to the experiment. 'Tis well worth a fair and full experiment. [[6]] With such powerful and obvious motives

---

[1] inevitably [2] there is reason to regard [3] any

[4] they [5] 'Tis natural

[6] It may not impossibly be found, that the spirit of party, the machinations of foreign powers, the corruption and ambition of individual citizens are more formidable adversaries to the Unity of our Empire than any inherent difficulties in the scheme. Against

to Union, [affecting][1] all parts of our country [[2]] while experience shall not have demonstrated its impracticability, there will always be [reason][3] to distrust the patriotism of those, who in any quarter may endeavor to weaken its bands. [[4]]—

In contemplating the causes which may disturb our Union, it occurs as matter of serious concern, that [any ground should have been furnished for characterizing parties by][5] *Geographical* discriminations—

---

these the mounds of national opinion, national sympathy and national jealousy ought to be raised.

[1] as [2] have [3] cause in the fact itself

[4] Besides the more serious causes already hinted as threatening our Union, there is one less dangerous, but sufficiently dangerous to make it prudent to be upon our guard against it. I allude to the petulence of party differences of opinion. It is not uncommon to hear the irritations which these excite vent themselves in declarations that the different parts of the United States are ill affected to each other, in menaces that the Union will be dissolved by this or that measure. Intimations like these are as indiscreet as they are intemperate. Though frequently made with levity and without any really evil intention, they have a tendency to produce the consequence which they indicate. They teach the minds of men to consider the Union as precarious;—as an object to which they ought not to attach their hopes and fortunes;—and thus chill the sentiment in its favour. By alarming the pride of those to whom they are addressed, they set ingenuity at work to depreciate the value of the thing, and to discover reasons of indifference towards it. This is not wise.—It will be much wiser to habituate ourselves to reverence the Union as the palladium of our national happiness; to accommodate constantly our words and actions to that idea, and to discountenance whatever may suggest a suspicion that it can in any event be abandoned. (In the margin opposite this *paragraph* are the words, "Not important enough.")

[5] our parties for some time past have been too much characterised by

Northern and *Southern* — *Atlantic* and *Western*; [whence designing men may endeavour to excite a belief that there is a real difference of local interests and views.][1] One of the expedients of Party to acquire influence, within particular districts, is to misrepresent the opinions and aims of other districts.— You cannot shield yourselves too much against the jealousies and heart burnings which spring from those misrepresentations; — They tend to render alien to each other those who ought to be bound together by fraternal affection.—The inhabitants of our Western country have lately had a useful lesson on this [head.][2] — They have seen, in the negotiation by the Executive, and in the unanimous ratification by the Senate, of the Treaty with Spain, and in the universal satisfaction at that event, throughout the United States, a decisive proof how unfounded were the suspicions propagated among them of a policy in the General Government and in the Atlantic States unfriendly to their interests in regard to the MISSISSIPPI. — They

---

[1] These discriminations,—— the mere contrivance of the spirit of Party, (always dexterous to seize every handle by which the passions can be wielded, and too skilful not to turn to account the sympathy of neighborhood), have furnished an argument against the Union as evidence of a real difference of local interests and views; and serve to hazard it by organizing larger districts of country, under the leaders of contending factions; whose rivalships, prejudices and schemes of ambition, rather than the true interests of the Country, will direct the use of their influence. If it be possible to correct this poison in the habit of our body politic, it is worthy the endeavours of the moderate and the good to effect it.

[2] subject

have been witnesses to the formation of two Treaties, that with G. Britain, and that with Spain, which secure to them every thing they could desire, in respect to our Foreign Relations, towards confirming their prosperity.—Will it not be their wisdom to rely for the preservation of these advantages on the UNION by which they were procured?—Will they not henceforth be deaf to those advisers, if such there are, who would sever them from their Brethren, and connect them with Aliens?—

To the efficacy and permanency of your Union, a Government for the whole is indispensable.—No alliances however strict between the parts can be an adequate substitute.—They must inevitably experience the infractions and interruptions which all alliances in all times have experienced.—Sensible of this momentous truth, you have improved upon your first essay, by the adoption of a Constitution of Government, better calculated than your former for an intimate Union, and for the efficacious management of your common concerns.—This government, the offspring of our own choice uninfluenced and unawed, adopted upon full investigation and mature deliberation, completely free in its principles, in the distribution of its powers, uniting security with energy, and containing within itself a provision for its own amendment, has a just claim to your confidence and your support.—Respect for its authority, compliance with its Laws, acquiescence in its measures, are duties enjoined by the fundamental maxims of true Liberty.—The basis of our political systems is the right of the people to make and to alter their Constitutions of Government.—But the Constitution which at any time exists, 'till changed by an explicit and authentic act of the whole People, is sacredly obligatory upon all.—The very idea of the power and the right of the People to establish Government, presupposes the duty of every individual to obey the established Government.

All obstructions to the execution of the Laws, all combinations and associations, under whatever plausible character, with [the real] design to direct, controul, counteract, or awe the regular deliberation and action of the constituted authorities, are destructive of this fundamental principle and of fatal tendency.—They serve to organize faction, to give it an artificial and extraordinary force—to put, [1] in the place of the delegated will of the Nation, the will of a party;—often a small but artful and enterprizing minority of the community;—and, according to the alternate triumphs of different parties, to make the public administration the mirror of the ill-concerted and incongruous projects of faction, rather than the organ of consistent and wholesome plans digested by common councils and modified by mutual interests.—However combinations or associations of the above description may now and then answer popular ends, [2] they are likely, in the course of time and things, to become potent engines, by which cunning, ambitious and unprincipled men will be enabled to subvert the Power of the People and to usurp for themselves the reins

---

[1] it [2] and purposes

of Government; destroying afterwards the very engines which have lifted them to unjust dominion.—

Toward the preservation of your Government and the permanency of your present happy state, it is requisite, not only that you steadily discountenance irregular oppositions to its acknowledged authority, but also that you resist with care [[1]] spirit of innovation upon its principles however specious the pretexts.—One method of assault may be to effect, in the forms of the Constitution, alterations which will impair the energy of the system, [and thus to][2] undermine what cannot be directly overthrown.—In all the changes to which you may be invited, remember that time and habit are at least as necessary to fix the true character of Governments, as of other human institutions — that experience is the surest standard, by which to test the real tendency of the existing Constitution of a Country — that facility in changes upon the credit of mere hypothesis and opinion exposes to perpetual change, from the endless variety of hypothesis and opinion : — and remember, especially, that for the efficient management of your common interests, in a country so extensive as ours, a Government of as much vigour as is consistent with the perfect security of Liberty is indispensable — Liberty itself will find in such a Government, with powers properly distributed and adjusted, its surest Guardian.—[It is indeed little else than a name, where the Government is too feeble to withstand the enterprises of faction, to confine each member of the Society within the limits

---

[1] a [2] to

prescribed by the laws, and to maintain all in the secure and tranquil enjoyment of the rights of person and property.][1]

I have already intimated to you the danger of Parties in the State, with particular reference to the founding of them on Geographical discriminations.—Let me now take a more comprehensive view, and warn you in the most solemn manner against the baneful effects of the Spirit of Party, generally.

This Spirit, unfortunately, is inseparable from [our][2] nature, having its root in the strongest passions of the [human] mind.—It exists under different shapes in all Governments, more or less stifled, controuled or repressed; but in those of the popular form it is seen in its greatest rankness, and is truly their worst enemy.—[[3]]

---

[1] Owing to you as I do a frank and free disclosure of my heart, I shall not conceal from you the belief I entertain, that your Government as at present constituted is far more likely to prove too feeble than too powerful.

[2] human

[3] In Republics of narrow extent, it is not difficult for those who at any time hold the reins of Power, and command the ordinary public favor, to overturn the established [constitution]* in favor of their own aggrandizement.—The same thing may likewise be too often accomplished in such Republics, by partial combinations of men, who though not in office, from birth, riches or other sources of distinction, have extraordinary influence and numerous [adherents.]†—By debauching the Military force, by surprising some commanding citadel, or by some other sudden and unforeseen movement the fate of the Republic is decided.—But in Republics of large extent, usurpation can scarcely make its way through these avenues.—The powers and opportunities of resist-

* order † retainers

The alternate domination of one faction over another, sharpened by the spirit of revenge natural to party dissension, which in different ages and countries has perpetrated the most horrid enormities, is itself a frightful despotism.—But this leads at length to a more formal and permanent despotism.—The disorders and miseries, which result, gradually incline the minds of men to seek security and repose in the absolute power of an Individual: and sooner or later the chief of some prevailing faction, more able or more fortunate than his competitors, turns this disposition to the purposes of his own elevation, on the ruins of Public Liberty.

Without looking forward to an extremity of this kind, (which nevertheless ought not to be entirely out of sight), the common and continual mischiefs of the spirit of Party are sufficient to make it the interest and the duty of a wise People to discourage and restrain it.—

It serves always to distract the Public Councils and enfeeble the Public administration.—It agitates the community with ill founded jealousies and false alarms, kindles the animosity of one part against another, foments occasionally riot and insurrection.—It opens the door to foreign influence and corruption, which find a facilitated access [to the Government itself through the channels of party passions. Thus, the

---

ance of a wide extended and numerous nation, defy the successful efforts of the ordinary Military force, or of any collections which wealth and patronage may call to their aid.—In such Republics, it is safe to assert, that the conflicts of popular factions are the chief, if not the only inlets, of usurpation and Tyranny.

policy and the will of one country, are subjected to the policy and will of another.][1]

There is an opinion that parties in free countries are useful checks upon the Administration of the Government, and serve to keep alive the Spirit of Liberty.—This within certain limits is probably true — and in Governments of a Monarchical cast, Patriotism may look with indulgence, if not with favour, upon the spirit of party.—But in those of the popular character, in Governments purely elective, it is a spirit not to be encouraged.—From their natural tendency, it is certain there will always be enough of that spirit for every salutary purpose,—and there being constant danger of excess, the effort ought to be, by force of public opinion, to mitigate and assuage it.—A fire not to be quenched; it demands a uniform vigilance to prevent its bursting into a flame, lest, [instead of warming, it should][2] consume.—

It is important, likewise, that the habits of thinking in a free country should inspire caution in those entrusted with its administration, to confine themselves within their respective constitutional spheres; avoiding in the exercise of the powers of one department to encroach upon another.—The spirit of encroachment tends to consolidate the powers of all the departments in one, and thus to create, [[3]] whatever [the form of government, a real][4] despotism.—A just

[1] through the channels of party passions. It frequently subjects the policy of our own country to the policy of some foreign country, and even enslaves the will of our Government to the will of some foreign Government.

[2] it should not only warm, but [3] under [4] forms, a

estimate of that love of power, and [1] proneness to abuse it, which predominates in the human heart, is sufficient to satisfy us of the truth of this position.—The necessity of reciprocal checks in the exercise of political power, by dividing and distributing it into different depositories, and constituting each the Guardian of the Public Weal [against][2] invasions by the others, has been evinced by experiments ancient and modern; some of them in our country and under our own eyes.—To preserve them must be as necessary as to institute them.—If in the opinion of the People, the distribution or modification of the Constitutional powers be in any particular wrong, let it be corrected by an amendment in the way which the Constitution designates.—But let there be no change by usurpation; for though this, in one instance, may be the instrument of good, it is the [customary][3] weapon by which free governments are destroyed.—The precedent [4] must always greatly overbalance in permanent evil any partial or [transient][5] benefit which the use [6] can at any time yield.—

Of all the dispositions and habits which lead to political prosperity, Religion and morality are indispensable supports.—In vain would that man claim the tribute of Patriotism, who should labour to subvert these great Pillars of human happiness, these firmest props of the duties of Men and Citizens.—The mere Politician, equally with the pious man, ought to respect and to cherish them.—A volume

[1] the [2] from [3] usual and natural
[4] of its use [5] temporary [6] itself

could not trace all their connections with private and public felicity.—Let it simply be asked where is the security for property, for reputation, for life, if the sense of religious obligation *desert* the oaths, which are the instruments of investigation in Courts of Justice? And let us with caution indulge the supposition that morality can be maintained without religion.—Whatever may be conceded to the influence of refined education on minds of peculiar structure — reason and experience both forbid us to expect that national morality can prevail in exclusion of religious principle.—

'Tis substantially true, that virtue or morality is a necessary spring of popular government.—The rule indeed extends with more or less force to every species of Free Government.—Who that is a sincere friend to it, can look with indifference upon attempts to shake the foundation of the fabric? —

[Promote then as an object of primary importance, institutions for the general diffusion of knowledge.—In proportion as the structure of a government gives force to public opinion, it is essential that public opinion should be enlightened.]—[1]

---

[1] Cultivate industry and frugality, as auxiliaries to good morals and sources of private and public prosperity.—Is there not room to regret that our propensity to expense exceeds our means for it? Is there not more luxury among us and more diffusively, than suits the actual stage of our national progress? Whatever may be the apology for luxury in a country, mature in the Arts which are its ministers, and the cause of national opulence — can it promote the advantage of a young country, almost wholly agricultural, in the infancy of the arts, and certainly not in the maturity of wealth?

As a very important source of strength and security, cherish public credit.—One method of preserving it is to use it as [sparingly][1] as possible: — avoiding occasions of expense by cultivating peace, but remembering also that timely disbursements to prepare for danger frequently prevent much greater disbursements to repel it — avoiding likewise the accumulation of debt, not only by [shunning][2] occasions of expense, but by vigorous exertions in time of Peace to discharge the debts which unavoidable wars may have occasioned, not ungenerously throwing upon posterity the burthen which we ourselves ought to bear. The execution of these maxims belongs to your Representatives, but it is necessary that public opinion should [co-operate.][3]—To facilitate to them the performance of their duty, it is essential that you should practically bear in mind, that towards the payment of debts there must be Revenue — that to have Revenue there must be taxes — that no taxes can be devised which are not more or less inconvenient and unpleasant — that the intrinsic embarrassment inseparable from the selection of the proper objects (which is always a choice of difficulties) ought to be a decisive motive for a candid construction of the conduct of the Government in making it, and for a spirit of acquiescence in the measures for obtaining Revenue which the public exigencies may at any time dictate.—

Observe good faith and justice towards all Na-

(Over this paragraph in the original a piece of paper is wafered, on which the passage is written as printed in the text.)

[1] little **[2] avoiding** **[3] coincide**

tions. [1] Cultivate peace and harmony with all.—Religion and morality enjoin this conduct; and can it be that good policy does not equally enjoin it?—It will be worthy of a free, enlightened, and, at no distant period, a great nation, to give to mankind the magnanimous and too novel example of a People always guided by an exalted justice and benevolence.—Who can doubt that in the course of time and things, the fruits of such a plan would richly repay any temporary advantages which might be lost by a steady adherence to it? Can it be, that Providence has not connected the permanent felicity of a Nation with its virtue? The experiment, at least, is recommended by every sentiment which ennobles human nature.—Alas! is it rendered impossible by its vices?

In the execution of such a plan nothing is more essential than that [permanent, inveterate][2] antipathies against particular nations and passionate attachments for others should be excluded; and that in place of them just and amicable feelings towards all should be cultivated.—The Nation, which indulges towards another [an][3] habitual hatred or [an][4] habitual fondness, is in some degree a slave. It is a slave to its animosity or to its affection, either of which is sufficient to lead it astray from its duty and its interest.—Antipathy in one Nation against another [5]

---

1 and cultivate peace and harmony with all, for in public as well as in private transactions, I am persuaded that honesty will always be found to be the bust policy.

2 rooted 3 a 4 a

5 begets of course a similar sentiment in the other,

disposes each more readily to offer insult and injury, to lay hold of slight causes of umbrage, and to be haughty and intractable, when accidental or trifling occasions of dispute occur.—Hence frequent collisions, obstinate, envenomed and bloody contests.—The Nation prompted by ill-will and resentment sometimes impels to War the Government, contrary to [the best][1] calculations of policy. The Government sometimes participates in the [national] propensity, and adopts through passion what reason would reject;—at other times, it makes the animosity of the Nation subservient to projects of hostility instigated by pride, ambition, and other sinister and pernicious motives.—The peace often, sometimes perhaps the Liberty, of Nations has been the victim.—

So likewise a passionate attachment of one Nation for another produces a variety of evils.—Sympathy for the favourite nation, facilitating the illusion of an imaginary common interest in cases where no real common interest exists, and infusing into one [[2]] the enmities of the other, betrays the former into a participation in the quarrels and wars of the latter, without adequate inducement or justification: It leads also to concessions to the favourite Nation of privileges denied to others, which is apt doubly to injure the Nation making the concessions; [[3]] by unnecessarily parting with what ought to have been retained, [[4]] and by exciting jealousy, ill-will, and a disposition to retaliate, in the parties from whom equal privileges are withheld; and it gives to ambi-

[1] its own [2] another [3] 1stly [4] 2dly

tious, corrupted, or deluded citizens (who devote themselves to the favourite Nation) facility to betray, or sacrifice the interests of their own country, without odium, sometimes even with popularity:—gilding with the appearances of a virtuous sense of obligation, a commendable deference for public opinion, or a laudable zeal for public good, the base or foolish compliances of ambition, corruption or infatuation.—

As avenues to foreign influence in innumerable ways, such attachments are particularly alarming to the truly enlightened and independent Patriot.—How many opportunities do they afford to tamper with domestic factions, to practise the arts of seduction, to mislead public opinion, to influence or awe the public councils! Such an attachment of a small or weak, towards a great and powerful nation, dooms the former to be the satellite of the latter.

Against the insidious wiles of foreign influence, [I conjure you to] believe me, [fellow citizens],[1] the jealousy of a free people ought to be [*constantly*][2] awake, since history and experience prove that foreign influence is one of the most baneful foes of Republican Government.—But that jealousy to be useful must be impartial; else it becomes the instrument of the very influence to be avoided, instead of a defence against it.—Excessive partiality for one foreign nation and excessive dislike of another, cause those whom they actuate to see danger only on one side, and serve to veil and even second the arts of influence on the other.—Real Patriots, who may resist the intrigues

[1] my friends, [2] incessantly

of the favourite, are liable to become suspected and odious; while its tools and dupes usurp the applause and confidence of the people, to surrender their interests.—

The great rule of conduct for us, in regard to foreign nations is, [in extending our commercial relations], to have with them as little *Political* connection as possible.—So far as we have already formed engagements let them be fulfilled with [[1]] perfect good faith.—Here let us stop.—

Europe has a set of primary interests, which to us have none, or a very remote relation.—Hence she must be engaged in frequent controversies, the causes of which are essentially foreign to our concerns.—Hence therefore it must be unwise in us to implicate ourselves by [[2]] artificial [ties][3] in the ordinary vicissitudes of her politics, [or][4] the ordinary combinations and collisions of her friendships, or enmities.

Our detached and distant situation invites and enables us to pursue a different course.—If we remain one People, under an efficient government, the period is not far off, when we may defy material injury from external annoyance; when we may take such an attitude as will cause the neutrality we may at any time resolve [upon][5] to be scrupulously respected.—When [[6]] belligerent nations, under the impossibility of making acquisitions upon us, will [not] lightly hazard the giving us provocation [[7]]; when we may choose

---

[1] circumspection indeed, but with [2] an [3] connection
[4] in [5] to observe [6] neither of two
[7] to throw our weight into the opposite scale;

peace or war, as our interest guided by [[1]] justice shall counsel.—

Why forego the advantages of so peculiar a situation?—Why quit our own to stand upon foreign ground?—Why, by interweaving our destiny with that of any part of Europe, entangle our peace and prosperity in the toils of European ambition, rivalship, interest, humour or caprice?—

'Tis our true policy to steer clear of permanent alliances, [[2]] with any portion of the foreign world;—so far, I mean, as we are now at liberty to do it—for let me not be understood as capable of patronizing infidelity to [existing][3] engagements, ([I hold the maxim no less applicable to public than to private affairs][4] that honesty is [always] the best policy.)—[I repeat it therefore let those engagements][5] be observed in their genuine sense.—But in my opinion it is unnecessary and would be unwise to extend them.—

Taking care always to keep ourselves, by suitable establishments, on a respectably defensive posture, we may safely trust to [temporary][6] alliances for extraordinary emergencies.——

Harmony, liberal intercourse with all Nations, are recommended by policy, humanity and interest.—But even our commercial policy should hold an equal and impartial hand:—neither seeking nor granting exclusive favours or preferences;—consulting the natural course of things;—diffusing and diversifying by gentle means the streams of commerce, but forcing

---

[1] our [2] intimate connections [3] pre-existing
[4] for I hold it to be as true in public, as in private transactions.
[5] these must [6] occasional

nothing; — establishing with Powers so disposed — in order to give to trade a stable course, to define the rights of our Merchants, and to enable the Govern ment to support them — conventional rules of intercourse, the best that present circumstances and mutual opinion will permit; but temporary, and liable to be from time to time abandoned or varied, as experience and circumstances shall dictate; constantly keeping in view, that 'tis folly in one nation to look for disinterested favors [from][1] another,—that it must pay with a portion of its independence for whatever it may accept under that character — that by such acceptance, it may place itself in the condition of having given equivalents for nominal favours and yet of being reproached with ingratitude for not giving more.—There can be no greater error than to expect, or calculate upon real favours from Nation to Nation. —'Tis an illusion which experience must cure, which a just pride ought to discard.

In offering to you, my Countrymen, these counsels of an old and affectionate friend, I dare not hope they will make the strong and lasting impression, I could wish,—that they will controul the usual current of the passions, or prevent our Nation from running the course which has hitherto marked the destiny of Nations.—But if I may even flatter myself, that they may be productive of some partial benefit; some occasional good; that they may now and then recur to moderate the fury of party spirit, to warn against the mischiefs of foreign intrigue, to guard against the

---

[1] at

impostures of pretended patriotism, this hope will be a full recompense for the solicitude for your welfare, by which they have been dictated.—

How far in the discharge of my official duties, I have been guided by the principles which have been delineated, the public Records and other evidences of my conduct must witness to You, and to the World —To myself, the assurance of my own conscience is that I have at least believed myself to be guided by them.

In relation to the still subsisting War in Europe, my Proclamation of the 22d of April 1793 is the index to my plan.—Sanctioned by your approving voice and by that of Your Representatives in both Houses of Congress, the spirit of that measure has continually governed me: — uninfluenced by any attempts to deter or divert me from it.

After deliberate examination with the aid of the best lights I could obtain, [1] I was well satisfied that our country, under all the circumstances of the case, had a right to take, and was bound in duty and interest, to take a Neutral position.—Having taken it, I determined, as far as should depend upon me, to maintain it, with moderation, perseverance and firmness.—

[The considerations which respect the right to hold this conduct, [it is not necessary][2] on this occasion [to detail.] I will only observe, that according to my

([1] and from men disagreeing in their impressions of the origin, progress, and nature of that war,)

[2] some of them of a delicate nature would be improperly the subject of explanation

understanding of the matter, that right, so far from being denied by any of the Belligerent Powers, has been virtually admitted by all.—][1]

The duty of holding a neutral conduct may be inferred, without anything more, from the obligation which justice and humanity impose on every Nation, in cases in which it is free to act, to maintain inviolate the relations of Peace and Amity towards other Nations.—

The inducements of interest for observing that conduct, will best be referred to your own reflections and experience.——With me, a predominant motive has been to endeavour to gain time to our country to settle and mature its yet recent institutions, and to progress without interruption to that degree of strength and consistency, which is necessary to give it, humanly speaking, the command of its own fortunes.

---

[1] The considerations which respect the right to hold this conduct, some of them of a delicate nature, would be improperly the subject of explanation on this occasion. I will barely observe that according to my understanding of the matter, that right so far from being denied by any belligerent Power, has been virtually admitted by all.—

This paragraph is then erased from the word "conduct," and the following sentence interlined, "would be improperly the subject of particular discussion on this occasion. I will barely observe that to me they appear to be warranted by well-established principles of the Laws of Nations as applicable to the nature of our alliance with France in connection with the circumstances of the War, and the relative situation of the contending Parties.

A piece of paper is afterwards wafered over both, on which the paragraph as it stands in the text is written, and on the margin is the following note; "This is the first draft, and it is questionable which of the two is to be preferred."

Though in reviewing the incidents of my Administration, I am unconscious of intentional error—I am nevertheless too sensible of my defects not to think it probable that I [may] have committed many errors.—[Whatever they may be I][1] fervently beseech the Almighty to avert or mitigate [the evils to which they may tend.][2]—I shall also carry with me the hope that my country will never cease to view them with indulgence; and that after forty-five years of my life dedicated to its service, with an upright zeal, the faults of incompetent abilities will be consigned to oblivion, as myself must soon be to the mansions of rest. [[3]]

Relying on its kindness in this as in other things, and actuated by that fervent love towards it, which is so natural to a man, who views in it the native soil

---

[1] I deprecate the evils to which they may tend, and

[2] them

[3] May I without the charge of ostentation add, that neither ambition nor interest has been the impelling cause of my actions—that I have never designedly misused any power confided to me nor hesitated to use one, where I thought it could redound to your benefit? May I without the appearance of affectation say, that the fortune with which I came into office is not bettered otherwise than by the improvement in the value of property which the quick progress and uncommon prosperity of our country have produced? May I still further add without breach of delicacy, that I shall retire without cause for a blush, with no sentiments alien to the force of those vows for the happiness of his country so natural to a citizen who sees in it the native soil of his progenitors and himself for four generations?

On the margin opposite this paragraph is the following note: "This paragraph may have the appearance of self-distrust and mere vanity."

of himself and his progenitors for [several][1] generations; — I anticipate with pleasing expectation that retreat, in which I promise myself to realize, without alloy, the sweet enjoyment of partaking, in the midst of my fellow citizens, the benign influence of good Laws under a free Government,—the ever favourite object of my heart, and the happy reward, as I trust, of our mutual cares, labours and dangers. [[2]]

G^o^. WASHINGTON.

UNITED STATES, 19th September. } 1796.

---

[1] four

[2] The paragraph beginning with the words, "May I without the charge of ostentation add," having been struck out, the following note is written on the margin of that which is inserted in its place in the text: — "Continuation of the paragraph preceding the last ending with the word 'rest.'"

II.

STATEMENT OF MR. DAVID C. CLAYPOOLE.

Having been requested by some very respectable Gentlemen, to give an account of the circumstances attending the first Publication of the Valedictory Address of the late President Washington to the People of the United States.—I will now state them as accurately as my memory serves me.

A few days before the appearance of this highly interesting Document in print, I received a Message from the President by his Private Secretary, Col. Lear, signifying his desire to see me. I waited on him at the appointed time, and found him sitting alone in the Drawing Room. He received me very kindly, and after paying my respects to him, desired me to take a seat near him; then, addressing himself to me, said, that he had for some time contemplated withdrawing from Public Life, and had at length concluded to do so at the end of the [then] present term; that he had some Thoughts and Reflections on the occasion, which he deemed proper to communicate to the People of the United States, and which he wished to appear in the Daily Advertiser, of which I was Proprietor and Editor. He paused, and I took occasion to thank him for having selected that Paper as the channel of communication to the Public, especially as I viewed this choice as an evidence of his approbation of the principles and manner in which the work was conducted. He silently assented, and asked me when I could make the publication.——I answered that the time should be made perfectly convenient to himself, and the following Monday was fixed on;—he then said that his Secretary would deliver me the Copy on the next morning [Friday], and I withdrew.——After the Proof sheet had been carefully compared with the Copy and corrected by myself, I carried two different Revises to be examined by the President, who made but few alterations from the Original, except in the punctuation, in which he was very minute. The Publication of the address bearing the same date with the Paper, September 19th, 1796, being completed, I waited on the President with the Original, and in presenting it to him, expressed how much I should be gratified by being permitted to retain it; upon which in the most obliging manner, he handed it back to me, saying, that if I wished for it, I might keep it;—and I took my leave.

Any person of observation, who has read the handwriting of President Washington, would, on seeing a second specimen, at once recognize it. And, as I had formerly been honored by several written communications from him on public business, I may say that his writing was quite familiar to me, and I think I could at any time and without hesitation, identify it. The Manuscript Copy of the Address consists of 32 pages of Quarto Letterpaper, rather sparsely written, and with many alterations, as in some places whole Paragraphs erased and others substituted—in others several Lines struck out — in others sentences and words put out, and others put in their place. A critical examination of it will show that the whole with all the corrections from first to last was the work of one hand only; and I can confidently assert that no other pen ever touched the original now in my possession than that of the great man "who was first in the Hearts of his Countrymen."

III.

REPORT MADE BY WM. RAWLE, Esq., TO THE HISTORICAL SOCIETY OF PENNSYLVANIA.

December 16, 1825.

CONVERSATION WITH DAVID C. CLAYPOOLE.

Having been informed that Mr. Claypoole was in possession of the original MS. of the valedictory address of President Washington, I had written to him to inquire whether he was willing to deposit it with the Historical Society. In a polite letter, dated Dec. 5th, he declined parting with it. I wrote another letter, expressing a wish to hear from himself an account of the conversation he had with the President in respect to the printing the address,—and he this day called on me, and related that the President having sent his private secretary to him desiring to see him, he called at the appointed time, and found the President alone.

The latter then informed him that he wished him to print, in his daily paper, an address from himself to the people of the United States. Mr. Claypoole answered that he felt himself highly favored by the selection for that purpose, as he considered it as a mark that he approved of the mode of his conducting the paper. The President bowed, as assenting to it, and asked how soon it could be done. Mr.

Claypoole replied that it should be done at any time he would fix. He requested it might be as soon as possible, and expressed a wish to have the proofs sent to him.

The next morning the manuscript was sent down by the same person who brought the message, and it was immediately put to press — both the proofs and the revises were sent to him, and the publication appeared on the 19th September, 1796, about four days after the first interview.

After this Mr. Claypoole called on him with the manuscript to return it, but at the same time he told the President, in the most respectful manner, that he should consider it as an inestimable favor if he would allow him to keep it. The President answered, if it would be any satisfaction to him, he was welcome to it — and they then parted — Mr. Claypoole retaining this valuable autographical paper, and the possession of which he has never parted with.

After relating these facts, Mr. Claypoole produced to me the original, and I saw with reverence and delight a small quarto book, containing about thirty pages, all in the hand-writing of this great man. It bears throughout the marks of original composition; there are many erasures and interlineations — a transposition of paragraphs, and other indications of its coming immediately from the hands of an unassisted individual. I counted the number of lines in the whole work, which answered to 1086, and of lines erased there were 174.

Being perfectly acquainted with the hand-writing of President Washington, I am satisfied that every word in the text, whether written in regular course or interlined, is his, and his alone. The date, September 19, 1796, was the only part on which I had a doubt, and of that I can only say, that being well acquainted with the hand-writing of Alexander Hamilton, I do not believe it was written by him. It may have been written by the private Secretary. Mr. Claypoole, however, believes it to have been in the hand-writing of the President himself.

(Signed)

W. Rawle.

IV.

LETTER FROM CHIEF JUSTICE JAY TO RICHARD PETERS, Esq.

PUBLISHED IN THE MEMOIRS OF THE HISTORICAL SOCIETY OF PENNSYLVANIA.

BEDFORD, *March* 29*th*, 1811.

DEAR SIR:

I have received your letter of the 14th ult., and also the book on Plaister of Paris, which you was so obliging as to send me, and for which accept my thanks.

Your letter conveyed to me the first and only information I have received, that a copy of President Washington's Valedictory Address has been found among the papers of Gen. Hamilton, and in his handwriting; and that a certain gentleman had also a copy of it, in the same hand-writing.

This intelligence is unpleasant and unexpected. Had the address been one of those official papers which, in the course of affairs, the Secretary of the proper department might have prepared, and the President have signed, these facts would have been unimportant; but it was a personal act of choice, not of official duty; and it was so connected with other obvious considerations as that he only could with propriety write it. In my opinion President Washington must have been sensible of this propriety, and therefore strong evidence would be necessary to make me believe that he violated it. Whether he did or did not, is a question which naturally directs our attention to whatever affords presumptive evidence respecting it, and leads the mind into a long train of correspondent reflections. I will give you a summary of those which have occurred to me; not because I think them necessary to settle the point in question, for the sequel will show that they are not, but because the occasion invites me to take the pleasure of reviewing and bearing testimony to the merits of my departed friend.

Is it to be presumed from these facts that Gen. Hamilton was the *real*, and the President only the *reputed* author of that Address? Although they countenance such a presumption, yet I think its foundation will be found too slight and shallow to resist that strong and full stream of counter evidence which flows from the conduct and character of that great man; a character not blown up into transient splendour by the breath of adulation, but which, being composed of his great and memorable deeds, stands, and will for ever stand, a glorious monument of human excellence.

So prone, however, is "poor human nature" to dislike and depreciate the superiority of its cotemporaries, that when these facts come to be generally known, and generally known they will be, many with affected regret and hesitation will infer and hint that Washington had less greatness of talent, and less greatness of mind, than his friends and admirers ascribe to him. Nor will the number of those be few, who, from personal or party inducements, will artfully encourage and diligently endeavour to give currency to such imputations. On the other hand, there are men of candour and judgment, and time will increase their number, who, aiming only at truth, will cheerfully trace and follow its footsteps, and, on finding, fondly embrace it. Urged by this laudable motive, they will attentively examine the history of his life; and in it they will meet with such numerous proofs of his knowledge and experience of men and things in general, and of our national affairs in particular, as to silence all doubt of his ability to conceive and express every idea in that address. A careful perusal of that history will convince them that the principles of policy which it recommends as rules for the conduct of others, are precisely those by which he regulated his own.

There have been in the world but two systems or schools of policy, the one founded on the great principles of wisdom and rectitude, the other on cunning, and its various artifices. To the first of these belonged Washington, and all the other worthies of every other country who ascended to the Temple of Honour through the Temple of Virtue. The doctrines, maxims, and precepts of this school have been explained and inculcated by the ablest writers, ancient and modern. In all civilized countries they are known, though often neglected; and in free states have always been publicly commended and taught; they crossed the Atlantic with our forefathers, and in our days particularly, have not only engaged the time and attention of students, but have been constantly and eloquently displayed by able men in our senates and assemblies. What reason can there be that Washington did not understand those subjects? If it be asked what these subjects comprehend or relate to, the answer is this—they relate to the nature and duties of man, to his propensities and passions, his virtues and vices, his habits and prejudices, his real and relative wants and enjoyments, his capacities for social and national happiness, and the means by which, according to time, place, and other existing circumstances, it is in a greater or less degree to be procured, preserved, and increased. From a profound investigation of these subjects, enlightened by experience, result all that knowledge and those maxims and precepts of sound policy, which enable legislators and rulers to manage and govern public affairs wisely and justly.

By what other means than the practical use of this knowledge, could Washington have been able to lead and govern an army hastily collected from various parts, and who brought with them to the field all the license and all the habits which they had indulged at home? Could he, by the force of orders and proclamations, have constrained them to render to him that obedience, confidence, and warm attachment which he so soon acquired, and which, throughout all vicissitudes and distresses, continued constant and undiminished to the last? By what other means could he have been able to frustrate the designs of dark cabals, and the unceasing intrigues of envious competitors, and the arts of the opposing enemy? By what other means could he have been able, in so masterly a manner, to meet and manage all those perplexing embarrassments which the revolutionary substitution of a new government,—which the want of that power in Congress which they had not, and of that promptitude which no deliberative body can have,—which the frequent destitution and constant uncertainty of essential supplies,—which the incompetency of individuals on whom much depended, the perfidy of others, and the mismanagement of many, could not fail to engender? We know, and history will inform posterity, that, from the first of his military career, he had to meet, and encounter, and surmount a rapid succession of formidable difficulties, even down to the time when his country was enabled, by the success of their arms, to obtain the honorable peace which terminated the war. His high and appointed course being then finished, he disdained the intimations of lawless ambition to prolong it. He disbanded the army under circumstances which required no common degree of policy or virtue; and, with universal admiration and plaudits, descended, joyfully and serenely, into the shades of retirement. They who ascribe all this to the guidance and protection of Providence do well, but let them recollect that Providence seldom interposes in human affairs, but through the agency of human means.

When at a subsequent and alarming period, the nation found that their affairs had gone into confusion, and that clouds portending danger and distress were rising over them, in every quarter, they instituted under his auspices a more efficient government, and unanimously committed the administration of it to him. Would they have done this without the highest confidence in his political talents and wisdom? Certainly not — no novice in navigation was ever unanimously called upon to take the helm or command of a ship on the point of running aground among the breakers. This universal confidence would have proved universal mistake, had it not been justified by the event. The unanimous opinion entertained and declared by a whole people in favor of any fellow-citizen is rarely erroneous, especially in times of alarm and calamity.

To delineate the course, and enumerate the measures which he took to arrive at success, would be to write a volume. The firmness and policy with which he overcame the obstacles placed in his way by the derangement of national affairs, by the devices of domestic demagogues and of foreign agents, as well as by the deleterious influences of the French revolution, need not be particularized. Our records, and histories, and memories, render it unnecessary. It is sufficient to say, and it can be said with truth, that his administration raised the nation out of confusion into order, out of degradation and distress into reputation and prosperity; it found us withering — it left us flourishing.

Is it to be believed that after having thus led the nation out of a bewildered state, and guided them for many years from one degree of prosperity to another, he was not qualified, on retiring, to advise them how to proceed and go on? And what but this is the object and the burthen of his Valedictory Address? He was persuaded that, as the national welfare had been recovered and established, so it could only be preserved and prolonged by a continued and steady adherence to those principles of sound policy and impartial justice which had invariably directed his administration.

Although the knowledge of them had been spread and scattered among the people, here a little, and there a little, yet being desirous to mark even the last day of his public life by some act of public utility, he addressed and presented them to his fellow citizens in points of light so clear and strong as to make deep impressions on the public mind. These last parental admonitions of this Father of his Country were gratefully received and universally admired; but the experience of ages informs us, that it is less difficult to give good advice than to prevail on men to follow it.

Such, and so obvious is the force of the preceding considerations, as to render doubts of the President's ability to give the advice contained in the address too absurd to have many serious advocates. But it would not surprise me, if certain classical gentlemen, associating the facts you mention with the style and fashion of the address, should intimate that his ability to compass it substantially in his own mind does not prove that he was also capable of communicating his advice in a paper so well written. Let these gentlemen recollect the classical maxim which they learned at school:

"Scribendi recte, sapere est, et principium, et fons."

They may also be referred to another classical maxim, which teaches us that they who well understand their subject will be at no loss for words:

"Verbaque provisam rem non invita sequentur."

But his ability to write well need not be proved by the application of maxims; it is established by facts.

We are told to judge of a tree by its fruit; let us in like manner judge of his pen by its performances. Few men who had so little leisure have written so much. His *public* letters alone are voluminous, and public opinion has done justice to their merits. Many of them have been published, and they who read them will be convinced that at the period of the address he had not to learn how to write well. But it may be remarked that the address is more highly finished than the letters, and so it ought to be; that address was to be presented to the whole nation, and on no common occasion; it was intended for the present and future generation; it was to be read in this country and in foreign countries; and to be criticized not only by affectionate friends and impartial judges, but also by envious and malignant enemies. It was an address which, according as it should or should not correspond with his exalted character and fame, would either justify or impeach the prevailing opinion of his talents or wisdom. Who, therefore, can wonder that he should bestow more thoughts, and time, and pains on that address than a letter?

Although in the habit of depending ultimately on his own judgment, yet no man was more solicitous to obtain and collect light on every question and measure on which he had to decide. He knew that authors, like parents, are not among the first to discover imperfections in their offspring, and that consideration would naturally induce him to imitate the example of those ancient and modern writers (among whom were statesmen, generals, and even men of consular and royal dignity), who submitted their compositions to the judgment of their friends before they put the last hand to them. Those friends would make notes of whatever defects they observed in the draft, and of the correspondent amendments which they deemed proper. If they found that the arrangement would be improved, they would advise certain transpositions — if the connexion between any of the relative parts was obscure, they would make it more apparent — if a conclusion had better be left to implication than expressed, they would strike it out, and so vice versâ, if an additional remark or allusion would give force or light to a sentiment or proposition they would propose it — where a sentence was too long, they would divide it — they would correct redundancies, change words less apt for words more apt, &c. &c. To correct a composition in this way, is to do a friendly office, but to prepare a new one, and offer it to the author as a substitute for his own, would deserve a different appellation.

Among those to whose judgment and candour President Washington would commit such an interesting and delicate task, where is the man to be found who would have the hardihood to say to him in substance, though in terms ever so nice and courtly — "Sir, I have examined and considered your draft of an address — it will not do — it is really good for nothing, but, Sir, I have taken the trouble to write a proper one for you, and I now make a present of it. I advise you to adopt it, and to pass it on the world as your own; the cheat will never be discovered, for you may depend on my secrecy. Sir, I have inserted in it a paragraph that will give the public a good opinion of your modesty. I will read it to you; it is in these words:

"'In the discharge of this trust I will only say, that I have with good intentions contributed towards the organization and administration of the government, the best exertions of which *a very fallible judgment* was capable. Not unconscious in the outset of the *inferiority* of my qualifications, experience, in my own eyes, perhaps *still more* in the eyes of *others*, has strengthened the motives to diffidence of myself.'"

If it be possible to find a man among those whom he esteemed, capable of offering to him such a present, it is impossible to believe that President Washington was the man to whom such a present would have been acceptable. They who knew President Washington, and his various endowments, qualifications, and virtues, know that (aggregately considered) they formed a *tout ensemble* which has rarely been equalled, and perhaps never excelled.

Thus much for presumptive evidence, I will now turn your attention to some that is direct.

The history (if it may be so called) of the address is not unknown to me; but as I came to the knowledge of it under implied confidence, I doubted, when I first received your letter, whether I ought to disclose it. On more mature reflection I became convinced that if President Washington were now alive and informed of the facts in question, he would not only authorise, but also desire me to reduce it to writing; that, when necessary, it might be used to invalidate the imputations to which those facts give color.

This consideration terminated my doubts. I do not think that a disclosure is necessary at this moment, but I fear such a moment will arrive. Whether I shall then be alive, or in a capacity to give testimony, is so uncertain, that in order to avoid the risk of either, I shall now reduce it to writing, and commit it to your care and discretion. "De bene esse," as the lawyers say.

Some time before the address appeared, Colonel (afterwards General) Hamilton informed me that he had received a letter from President Washington, and with it the draft of a Farewell Address which the President had prepared, and on which he requested our opinion. He then proposed to fix on a day for an interview at my house on the subject. A day was accordingly appointed, and on that day Col. Hamilton attended. He observed to me in words to this effect, that after having read and examined the draft, it appeared to him to be susceptible of improvement. That he thought the easiest and best way was to leave the draft untouched, and in its fair state; and to write the whole over with such amendments, alterations and corrections, as he thought were advisable, and that he had done so; he then proposed to read it, and we proceeded deliberately to discuss and consider it, paragraph by paragraph, until the whole met with our mutual approbation. Some amendments were made during the interview, but none of much importance.

Although this business had not been hastily despatched, yet aware of the consequences of such a paper, I suggested the giving it a further critical examination; but he declined it, saying, he was pressed for time, and was anxious to return the draft to the President without delay.

It afterwards occurred to me that a certain proposition was expressed in terms too general and unqualified; and I hinted it in a letter to the President. As the business took the course above mentioned, a recurrence to the draft was unnecessary, and it was not read. There was this advantage in the course pursued; the President's draft remained (as delicacy required) fair and not obscured by interlineations, &c. By comparing it with the paper sent with it, he would immediately observe the particular emendations and corrections, that were proposed, and would find them standing in their intended places. Hence he was enabled to review, and to decide on the whole matter, with much greater clearness and facility, than if he had received them in separate and detached notes, and with detailed references to the pages and lines where they were advised to be introduced.

With great esteem and regard, I am, dear Sir, your obed't servant,

JOHN JAY.

RICHARD PETERS, ESQ.

V.

The following paper is taken from the "Writings of Washington," edited by Jared Sparks, Esq., now President of Harvard University. It forms Appendix No. 3 of the 12th volume of that work.

WASHINGTON'S FAREWELL ADDRESS.

The curiosity, which has been expressed respecting the authorship of the Farewell Address, would seem to require some notice of the subject in this work; although the question, as to the manner in which that address originated, is one of small moment, since its real importance consists in its being known to contain the sentiments of Washington, uttered on a solemn occasion, and designed for the benefit of his countrymen. Whether every idea embodied in it arose spontaneously from his own mind, or whether every word was first traced by his pen, or whether he acted as every wise man would naturally act under the same circumstances, and sought counsel from other sources claiming respect and confidence, or in what degree he pursued either or all of these methods, are points so unimportant, compared with the object and matter of the whole, as to be scarcely worth considering. Nor is it intended here to do anything more than to state a few facts, leaving the reader to draw his own inferences.

When Washington accepted the Presidency, to which he had been called by the unanimous voice of the people, it was not his intention to remain in the office more than one term. Towards the close of that term, he wrote the following letter to Mr. Madison, whom he had been in the habit of frequently consulting, and of whose ability, integrity, and practical wisdom, he entertained the highest opinion.

PRESIDENT WASHINGTON TO JAMES MADISON.

"MOUNT VERNON, 20 *May*, 1792.

"MY DEAR SIR:

"As there is a possibility, if not a probability, that I shall not see you on your return home; or, if I should see you, it may be on the road, and under circumstances, which may prevent my speaking to you on the subject we last conversed upon, I take the liberty of committing to paper the following thoughts and requests.

"I have not been unmindful of the sentiments expressed by you in the conversations just alluded to. On the contrary, I have again and again revolved them with thoughtful anxiety, but without being able to dispose my mind to a longer continuation in the office I have now the honor to hold. I therefore still look forward with the fondest and most ardent wishes to spend the remainder of my days, which I cannot expect to be long, in ease and tranquillity.

"Nothing but a conviction, that my declining the chair of government, if it should be the desire of the people to continue me in it, would involve the country in serious disputes respecting the chief magistrate, and the disagreeable consequences which might result therefrom in the floating and divided opinions, which seem to prevail at present, could in anywise induce me to relinquish the determination I have formed; and of this I do not see how any evidence can be obtained previous to the election. My vanity, I am sure, is not of the cast to allow me to view the subject in this light.

"Under these impressions, then, permit me to reiterate the request I made to you at our last meeting, namely, to think of the proper time and the best mode of announcing the intention, and that you would prepare the latter. In revolving this subject myself, my judgment has always been embarrassed. On the one hand, a previous declaration to retire, not only carries with it the appearance of vanity and self-importance, but it may be construed into a manœuvre to be invited to remain; and on the other hand, to say nothing implies consent, or at any rate would leave the matter in doubt; and to decline afterwards might be deemed as bad, and uncandid.

"I would fain carry my request to you farther than is asked above, although I am sensible that your compliance with it must add to your trouble. But, as the recess may afford you leisure, and I flatter myself you have dispositions to oblige me, I will, without apology, desire, if the measure in itself should strike you as proper, or likely to produce public good or private honor, that you would turn your thoughts to a Valedictory Address from me to the public, expressing in plain and modest terms, that, having been honored with the presidential chair, and to the best of my abilities contributed to the organization and administration of the government; that, having arrived at a period of life, when the private walks of it in the shades of retirement become necessary, and will be most pleasing to me; (and as the spirit of the government may render a rotation in the elective officers of it more congenial with the ideas [the people have] of liberty and safety) that I take my leave of them as a public man, and, in bidding them adieu, retaining no other concern than such as will arise from fervent wishes for the prosperity of my country, I take the liberty at my departure from civil [life], as I formerly did at my military exit, to invoke a continuation of the blessings of Providence upon it, and upon all those who are the supporters of its interests, and the promoters of harmony, order, and good government.

"That, to impress these things, it might among other topics be observed, that we are *all* the children of the same country, a country great and rich in itself, capable, and promising to be as prosperous and happy as any which the annals of history have ever brought to our view; that our interest, however diversified in local and smaller matters, is the same in all the great and essential concerns of the nation; that the extent of our country, the diversity of our climate and soil, and the various productions of the states consequent of both, are such as to make one part not only convenient, but perhaps indispensably necessary to the other part, and may render the whole, at no distant period, one of the most independent [nations] in the world; that the established government, being the work of our own hands, with the seeds of amendment engrafted in the constitution, may, by wisdom, good dispositions, and mutual allowances, aided by experience, bring it as near to perfection, as any human institution ever approximated, and therefore the only strife among us ought to be, who should be foremost in facilitating and finally accomplishing such great and desirable objects, by giving every possible support and cement to the Union; that, however necessary it may be to keep a watchful eye over public servants and public measures, yet there ought to be limits to it, for suspicions unfounded and jealousies too lively are irritating to honest feelings, and oftentimes are productive of more evil than good.

"To enumerate the various subjects, which might be introduced into such an address, would require thought, and to mention them to you would be unnecessary, as your own judgment will comprehend all that will be proper. Whether to touch specifically any of the exceptionable parts of the constitution may be doubted. All I shall add, therefore, at present, is to beg the favor of you to consider, first, the propriety of such an address; secondly, if approved, the several matters which ought to be contained in it; thirdly, the time it should appear, that is, whether at the declaration of my intention to withdraw from the service of the public, or to let it be the closing act of my administration, which will end with the next session of Congress; the probability being, that that body will continue sitting until March, when the House of Representatives will also dissolve.

"Though I do not wish to hurry you (the case not pressing) in the execution of either of the publications before mentioned, yet I should be glad to hear from you generally on both, and to receive them in time, if you should not come to Philadelphia before the session commences, in the form they are finally to take. I beg leave to draw your attention, also, to such things as you shall conceive fit subjects for communication on that occasion; and, noting them as they occur, that you would be so good as to furnish me with them in time to be prepared, and engrafted with others, for the opening of the session.

"With very sincere and affectionate regards, I am ever yours,

"GEORGE WASHINGTON."

A month after this letter was written, Mr. Madison answered it, and communicated at the same time a draft of a valedictory address, as above requested.

JAMES MADISON TO PRESIDENT WASHINGTON.

"ORANGE, 20 *June*, 1792.

"DEAR SIR:

"Having been left to myself for some days past, I have made use of the opportunity for bestowing on your letter of the 20th ultimo, handed me on the road, the attention which its important contents claimed. The questions, which it presents for consideration, are, first, at what time a notification of your purpose to retire will be most convenient; secondly, what mode will be most eligible; thirdly, whether a valedictory address will be proper and advisable; fourthly, if both, whether it would be more properly annexed to the notification, or postponed to your actual retirement.

"1. The answer to the first question involves two points, first, the expediency of delaying the notification; secondly, the propriety of making it before the choice of electors takes place, that the people may make their choice with an eye to the circumstances under which the trust is to be executed. On the first point, the reasons for as much delay as possible are too obvious to need recital. The second, depending on the times fixed in the several States, which must be within thirty-four days preceding the first Wednesday in December, requires that the notification should be in time to pervade every part of the Union by the beginning of November. Allowing six weeks for this purpose, the middle of September, or perhaps a little earlier, would seem a convenient date for the act.

"2. With regard to the mode, none better occurs than a simple publication in the newspapers. If it were proper to address it through the medium of the general legislature, there will be no opportunity. Nor does the change of situation seem to admit a recurrence to the State governments, which were the channels used for the former valedictory address.[1] A direct address to the people, who are your only constituents, can be made, I think, most properly through the independent channel of the press, through which they are as a constituent body usually addressed.

"3. On the third question, I think there can be no doubt, that such an address is rendered *proper* in itself, by the peculiarity and importance of the circumstances, which mark your situation; and *advisable*, by the salutary and operative lessons of which it may be made the vehicle. The precedent, at your military exit, might also subject an omission now to conjectures and interpretations, which it would not be well to leave room for.

"4. The remaining question is less easily decided. Advantages and objections lie on both sides of the alternative. The occasion, on which you are *necessarily* addressing the people, evidently introduces most easily and most delicately any *voluntary* observations that are meditated. In another view, a faro-

---

[1] General Washington's Address to the Governors of the States on disbanding the army.

well address, before the final moment of departure, is liable to the appearance of being premature and awkward. On the opposite side of the alternative, however, a postponement will beget a dryness, and an abridgment in the first address, little corresponding with the feelings, which the occasion would naturally produce, both in the author and the objects; and, though not liable to the above objection, would require a resumption of the subject apparently more forced, and on which, the impressions having been anticipated and familiarized, and the public mind diverted perhaps to other scenes, a second address would be received with less sensibility and effect, than if incorporated with the impressions incident to the original one. It is possible, too, that, previous to the close of the term, circumstances might intervene in relation to public affairs, or the succession to the presidency, which would be more embarrassing, if existing at the time of a valedictory appeal to the public, than if subsequent to that delicate measure.

"On the whole, my judgment leans to the propriety of blending together the notifying and valedictory addresses; and the more so, as the crisis, which will terminate your public career, may still afford an opportunity, if any intermediate contingency should call for a supplement to your farewell observations. But as more correct views of the subject may produce a different result in your mind, I have endeavored to fit the draft enclosed to either determination. You will readily observe, that, in executing it, I have aimed at that plainness and modesty of language, which you had in view, and which indeed are so peculiarly becoming the character and the occasion; and that I have had little more to do, as to the matter, than to follow the just and comprehensive outline, which you had sketched. I flatter myself, however, that, in every thing which has depended on me, much improvement will be made, before so interesting a paper shall have taken its last form.

"Having thus, Sir, complied with your wishes, by proceeding on a supposition that the idea of retiring from public life is to be carried into execution, I must now gratify my own by hoping, that a reconsideration of the measure, in all its circumstances and consequences, will have produced an acquiescence in one more sacrifice, severe as it may be, to the desires and interests of your country. I forbear to enter into the arguments, which in my view plead for it, because it would be only repeating what I have already taken the liberty of fully explaining. But I could not conclude such a letter as the present without a repetition of my anxious wishes and hopes, that our country may not, in this important conjuncture, be deprived of the inestimable advantage of having you at the head of its councils.

"With every sentiment of respect and affectionate attachment, I am, dear Sir, your most obedient friend and servant,

"James Madison."

MR. MADISON'S DRAFT.

"The period, which will close the appointment with which my fellow-citizens have honored me, being not very distant, and the time actually arrived at which their thoughts must be designating the citizen who is to administer the executive government of the United States during the ensuing term, it may be requisite to a more distinct expression of the public voice, that I should apprize such of my fellow-citizens as may retain their partiality towards me, that I am not to be numbered among those out of whom a choice is to be made.

"I beg them to be assured that the resolution, which dictates this intimation, has not been taken without the strictest regard to the relation, which as a dutiful citizen I bear to my country; and that, in withdrawing that tender of my service, which silence in my situation might imply, I am not influenced by the smallest deficiency of zeal for its future interests, or of grateful respect for its past kindness; but by the fullest persuasion that such a step is compatible with both.

"The impressions, under which I entered on the present arduous trust, were explained on the proper occasion. In discharge of this trust, I can only say, that I contributed towards the organization and administration of the government the best exertions of which a very fallible judgment was capable. For any errors, which may have flowed from this source,

I feel all the regret which an anxiety for the public good can excite; not without the double consolation, however, arising from a consciousness of their being involuntary, and an experience of the candour which will interpret them.

"If there were any circumstances, which could give value to my inferior qualifications for the trust, these circumstances must have been temporary. In this light was the undertaking viewed when I ventured upon it. Being moreover still farther advanced in the decline of life, I am every day more sensible, that the increasing weight of years renders the private walks of it, in the shade of retirement, as necessary as they will be acceptable to me.

"May I be allowed to add, that it will be among the highest as well as purest enjoyments that can sweeten the remnant of my days, to partake in a private station, in the midst of my fellow-citizens, of that benign influence of good laws under a free government, which has been the ultimate object of all our wishes, and in which I confide as the happy reward of our cares and labors? May I be allowed further to add, as a consideration far more important, that an early example of rotation in an office of so high and delicate a nature may equally accord with the republican spirit of our constitution, and the ideas of liberty and safety entertained by the people.

"[If a farewell address is to be added at the expiration of the term, the following paragraph may conclude the present.]

"Under these circumstances, a return to my private station, according to the purpose with which I quitted it, is the part which duty as well as inclination assigns me. In executing it, I shall carry with me every tender recollection, which gratitude to my fellow-citizens can awaken; and a sensibility to the permanent happiness of my country, which will render it the object of my increasing vows and most fer vent supplications.

"[Should no further address be intended, the preceding clause may be omitted and the present address proceed as follows.]

"In contemplating the moment at which the curtain is to drop for ever on the public scenes of my life, my sensations anticipate and do not permit me to suspend, the deep acknowledgments required by that debt of gratitude, which I owe to my beloved country for the many honors it has conferred upon me, for the distinguished confidence it has reposed in me, and for the opportunities I have thus enjoyed, of testifying my inviolable attachment by the most steadfast services, which my faculties could render.

"All the returns I have now to make will be in those vows, which I shall carry with me to my retirement and to my grave, that Heaven may continue to favor the people of the United States with the choicest tokens of its beneficence: that their union and brotherly affection may be perpetual; that the free constitution, which is the work of their own hands, may be sacredly maintained; that its administration in every department may be stamped with wisdom and with virtue; and that this character may be insured to it by that watchfulness over public servants and public measures, which on one hand will be necessary to prevent or correct a degeneracy, and that forbearance, on the other, from unfounded or indiscriminate jealousies, which would deprive the public of the best services, by depriving a conscious integrity of one of the noblest incitements to perform them; that, in fine, the happiness of the people of America, under the auspices of liberty, may be made complete, by so careful a preservation and so prudent a use of this blessing, as will acquire them the glorious satisfaction of recommending it to the affection, the praise, and the adoption of every nation, which is yet a stranger to it.

"And may we not dwell with well-grounded hopes on this flattering prospect, when we reflect on the many ties by which the people of America are bound together, and the many proofs they have given of an enlightened judgment and a magnanimous patriotism?

"We may all be considered as the children of one common country. We have all been embarked in one common cause. We have all had our share in common sufferings and common successes. The portion of the earth, allotted for the theatre of our fortunes, fulfils our most sanguine desires. All its essential interests are the same; while the diversities arising from climate, from soil, and from other local and lesser peculiarities, will naturally form a mutual relation of the parts, that may give to the whole a more entire independence, than has perhaps fallen to the lot of any other nation.

"To confirm these motives to an affectionate and

permanent union, and to secure the great objects of it, we have established a common government, which, being free in its principles, being founded in our own choice, being intended as the guardian of our common rights, and the patron of our common interests, and wisely containing within itself a provision for its own amendment, as experience may point out its errors, seems to promise everything that can be expected from such an institution; and, if supported by wise counsels, by virtuous conduct, and by mutual and friendly allowances, must approach as near to perfection as any human work can aspire, and nearer than any which the annals of mankind have recorded.

"With these wishes and hopes I shall make my exit from civil life; and I have taken the same liberty of expressing them, which I formerly used in offering the sentiments which were suggested by my exit from military life.

"If, in either instance, I have presumed more than I ought, on the indulgence of my fellow-citizens, they will be too generous to ascribe it to any other cause, than the extreme solicitude which I am bound to feel, and which I can never cease to feel, for their liberty, their prosperity, and their happiness."

The state of public affairs, and the loud call of his fellow-citizens from every part of the Union, prevailed on Washington to yield to a second choice, and remain in the presidency another term of four years. Hence no use was made of the above paper. He firmly resolved, however, in any event, to retire from public life at the end of this second period; and, as the time approached, he began to revolve in his mind an address to the people, which should commu nicate his determination, and convey to them such sentiments or advice, as the occasion might properly call forth, or as his long experience and services authorized him to give. There is proof, that the subject occupied his thoughts nearly a year before his term of office expired. In the mean time, the spirit of party, that bane of the private affections as well as of public concord, caused him to be estranged personally and politically in some degree from Mr. Madison, and to seek other counsellors.

Among these, none possessed a higher place in his confidence than Hamilton; of the talents, patriotism, honor, and honesty of none had he a more thorough conviction, and for none a more profound respect. A colossal pillar of his administration, Hamilton had stood by him in every hour of trial, equally firm and true in his friendship, and powerful in his support. To whom could Washington more safely apply for the fruits of a wise and disciplined mind? From whom could he hope for better counsel, or a more sacred regard to so confidential a trust?

The following note from Hamilton to Washington was probably the first written communication that passed between them on the subject.

"*New York, May 10th,* 1796.—Sir; When last in Philadelphia you mentioned to me your wish, that I should *re-dress* a certain paper, which you had prepared. As it is important, that a thing of this kind should be done with great care, and much at leisure, touched and retouched, I submit a wish, that, as soon as you have given it the *body* you mean it to have, it may be sent to me."

This note is dated more than four months before the Farewell Address was published, and it appears that a draft of some sort had already been "prepared" by Washington. It also appears, that Hamilton had been invited, and was well disposed, to lend his assistance in giving it completeness and finish.

What were the contents of the draft here alluded to, or whether it was the one afterwards sent to Hamilton, there are now no means of ascertaining. It is certain, however, that it was Washington's original idea to embody in the address the substance and the form of Mr. Madison's draft, and to make such additions as events and the change of circumstances seemed to require. A paper of this description has been preserved, in which is first inserted Mr. Madison's draft, and then a series of memoranda, or loose hints, evidently designed to be wrought into the address. These are here printed as transcribed from the original manuscript.

HINTS, OR HEADS OF TOPICS.

"Had the situation of our public affairs continued to wear the same aspect they assumed at the time the foregoing address was drawn, I should not have taken the liberty of troubling you, my fellow-citizens, with any new sentiment, or with a repetition more in detail of those, which are therein contained; but con siderable changes having taken place, both at home and abroad, I shall ask your indulgence while I express, with more lively sensibility, the following most ardent wishes of my heart.

"That party disputes among all the friends and lovers of their country may subside, or, as the wisdom of Providence has ordained that men on the same subjects shall not always think alike, that charity and benevolence, when they happen to differ, may so far shed their benign influence, as to banish those invectives, which proceed from illiberal prejudices and jealousy.

"That, as the All-wise Dispenser of human blessings has favored no nation of the earth with more abundant and substantial means of happiness than United America, we may not be so ungrateful to our Creator, so wanting to ourselves, and so regardless of posterity, as to dash the cup of beneficence, which is thus bountifully offered to our acceptance.

"That we may fulfil with the greatest exactitude *all* our engagements, foreign and domestic, to the *utmost* of our abilities, whensoever and in whatsoever manner they are pledged; for in public, as in private life, I am persuaded that honesty will for ever be found to be the best policy.

"That we may avoid connecting ourselves with the politics of any nation, farther than shall be found necessary to regulate our own trade, in order that commerce may be placed upon a stable footing, our merchants know their rights, and the government the ground on which those rights are to be supported.

"That every citizen would take pride in the name of an American, and act as if he felt the importance of the character, by considering, that we ourselves are now a distinct nation, the dignity of which will be absorbed, if not annihilated, if we enlist ourselves, farther than our obligations may require, under the banners of any other nation whatsoever. And, moreover, that we should guard against the intrigues of any and every foreign nation, who shall endeavor to intermingle, however covertly and indirectly, in the internal concerns of our country, or who shall attempt to prescribe rules for our policy with any other power, if there be no infraction of our engagements with themselves, as one of the greatest evils that can befall us as a people; for, whatever may be their professions, be assured, fellow-citizens, and the event will, as it always has, invariably prove, that nations as well as individuals act for their own benefit, and not for the benefit of others, unless both interests happen to be assimilated, and when that is the case there requires no contract to bind them together; that all their interferences are calculated to promote the former; and, in proportion as they succeed, will render us less independent. In a word, nothing is more certain, than that, if we receive favors, we must grant favors; and it is not easy to decide beforehand under such circumstances as we are, on which side the balance will ultimately preponderate; but easy indeed is it to foresee, that it may involve us in disputes, and finally in war, to fulfil political alliances. Whereas, if there be no engagements on our part, we shall be unembarrassed, and at liberty at all times to act from circumstances, and the dictates of justice, sound policy, and our essential interests.

"That we may be always prepared for war, but never unsheath the sword except in self-defence, so long as justice, and our essential rights, and national respectability, can be preserved without it; for without the gift of prophecy it may safely be pronounced, that, if this country can remain in peace twenty years longer (and I devoutly pray, that it may do so to the end of time), such, in all probability, will be its population, riches, and resources, when combined with its peculiarly happy and remote situation from the other quarters of the globe, as to bid defiance, in a just cause, to any earthly power whatsoever.

"That, whensoever and so long as we profess to be neutral, our public conduct, whatever our private affections may be, may accord therewith; without suffering partialities on one hand, or prejudices on the other, to control our actions. A contrary practice is not only incompatible with our declarations, but is pregnant with mischief, embarrassing to the administration, tending to divide us into parties, and ultimately productive of all those evils and horrors, which proceed from faction.

"That our Union may be as lasting as time; for, while we are encircled in one band, we shall possess the strength of a giant, and there will be none who can make us afraid. Divide, and we shall become weak, a prey to foreign intrigues and internal discord, and shall be as miserable and contemptible, as we are now enviable and happy.

"That the several departments of government may be preserved in their utmost constitutional purity, without any attempt of one to encroach on the rights or privileges of another; that the general and State governments may move in their proper orbits; and that the authorities of our own constitution may be respected by ourselves, as the most certain means of having them respected by foreigners.

"In expressing these sentiments it will readily be perceived, that I can have no other view now, whatever malevolence might have ascribed to it before, than such as results from a perfect conviction of the utility of the measure. If public servants, in the exercise of their official duties, are found incompetent, or pursuing wrong courses, discontinue them. If they are guilty of mal-practices in office, let them be more exemplarily punished. In both cases, the constitution and laws have made provision; but do not withdraw your confidence from them, the best incentive to a faithful discharge of their duty, without just cause; nor infer, because measures of a complicated nature, which time, opportunity, and close investigation alone can penetrate, for these reasons are not easily comprehended by those, who do not possess the means, that it necessarily follows they must be wrong. This would not only be doing injustice to your trustees, but be counteracting your own essential interests, rendering those trustees, if not contemptible in the eyes of the world, little better at least than ciphers in the administration of the government, and the constitution of your own choosing would reproach you for such conduct."

Whether these hints were sent to Hamilton, as here written, or to what extent they were previously en larged and arranged, cannot now be told. It will be seen, however, that they include nearly all the *elements* of the principal points of the address, as it was finally published. After the draft had been transmitted to Hamilton, he discouraged the idea of incorporating Mr. Madison's draft, in its distinct form, on account of the apparent incongruity of the thing, and because he thought some of its sentiments not suited to the objects proposed in this last address. He accordingly sketched two plans, or drafts, one on the basis of an incorporation, the other on that of an original form, submitting it to the judgment of Washington to decide which was the preferable method. He chose the latter. Several letters passed between them. Suggestions were made on both sides, some of which were approved and adopted, others disapproved and rejected. The drafts were sent back and forth from the one to the other. The work was nearly four months in hand; and was executed with a deliberation and solicitude, which prove the deep sense that each entertained of its importance, and of the advantages to be derived from it to the country.

THE END.

www.ingramcontent.com/pod-product-compliance
Lightning Source LLC
LaVergne TN
LVHW021146110826
845150LV00005B/1139

* 9 7 8 1 4 2 5 5 4 7 9 6 7 *